Buying a House in

FRANCE

André de Vries

Distributed in the USA by
The Globe Pequot Press, Guilford, Connecticut

Published by Vacation Work, 9 Park End Street, Oxford
www.vacationwork.co.uk

BUYING A HOUSE IN FRANCE
by André de Vries

First edition 2003
Reprinted 2003
Copyright © 2003

ISBN 1-85458-298-4

Publicity by Roger Musker

Cover design by Miller Craig & Cocking Design Partnership

Illustrations by Mike Siddens

Typeset by Brendan Cole

Printed and bound in Italy by Legoprint SpA, Trento

CONTENTS

VIVE LA FRANCE!

LOCATION, LOCATION...

THE PURCHASING PROCEDURE

WHAT HAPPENS NEXT

ACKNOWLEDGMENTS

During the writing of this book, many French and foreign residents of France have shared their experiences of life in France with me, and given me hospitality during my travels. As they say in France: *les copains d'abord.* I am particularly indebted to Mark Salik, *un véritable puits de science,* and Frédérique Dalhoum for their generous help, as well as Sandrine Trillaud, Hélène Audiot and Régis Rousseau.

Whilst researching, I had the good fortune to stay with (amongst others) Lt-Col. and Mrs Michael Chilcott in Bayeux, and Jane and John Edwards in Celles, Dordogne, who were informative and helpful beyond the call of duty. Others who gave me the benefit of their specialist knowledge include: David Evans on electrics, Gordon Eaton on health insurance, Lynda Durr on swimming pools and much else, Tony Trujillo on telecoms, Henry Dyson on SCIs, and Islay Currie of Currie French Property Services on building. Sam Crabb, of Sam Crabb Consultants, generously shared his extensive experience of the French property scene with me.

I am particularly grateful to my colleague Victoria Pybus, whose *Live & Work in France* provided a starting point for my own text in many instances. I was also blessed with some entertaining interviewees for the case studies, namely: Richard and Christina Coman, Richard Burton and James Ferguson. Finally, I should like to thank Claire de Vries and Ian Mitchell for obtaining French magazines and newspapers for me, and some expert advice on various aspects of building.

Special thanks to Mick Siddens for his illustrations of French houses.

FOREWORD

It would be no exaggeration to say that there has been a veritable stampede towards French property in the last few years. Estate agents and notaries in France are reporting that enquiries are up 75% in 2002 compared with 2001. The demand has left many of them struggling to cope.

The causes have much to do with the UK housing market. Many owners have found that their properties have shot up in value and are tempted to remortgage to buy a holiday home in France. Some can sell their UK property and split the proceeds between a smaller home in the UK and a second home in France. The fact is that property is and will remain cheap in France compared with the UK.

There is also a more fundamental reason for the move towards France, which is not based on financial considerations, but the widespread realisation that quality of life is generally better in France than in the UK. France has excellent public services, trains that run on time, and a more laid-back attitude towards work. Stress, high crime, pollution, and the general aggravations of life in an Americanised Britain are driving many to consider moving to a more civilised environment across the Channel. While it is not easy to find work in France, there are many who could carry on their profession there, and for others it is a matter of running a bed and breakfast, or using some ingenuity to offer services to other expatriates.

Another important factor is the ease with which one can travel to France. There is not only the Eurostar, already running for 10 years, but also a wealth of cheap flights to more and more provincial French destinations. The extension of the French motorway network has also played a large role, opening up many previously remote areas of France to foreign buyers.

The French property boom will continue, but finding the right property at the right price may mean considering areas that have been ignored by most up to now. With this in mind, we have included sections on up-and-coming areas and the kinds of properties that you might expect to find there.

André de Vries, Oxford
March 2003

Part I

VIVE LA FRANCE!

LIVING IN FRANCE

RESIDENCE & ENTRY

LIVING IN FRANCE

CHAPTER SUMMARY

- **Getting There.** France has never been easier to get to, and fares are at an all-time low.
- **History.** France has had a long and often stormy relationship with England.
- **Climate.** There are several climate zones, ranging from British-style weather to the balmy South of France.
- **Geography.** Most of France is thinly populated, giving Brits a delightful feeling of space.
- **Culture Shock.** The lifestyle is generally more relaxed than in the UK, and geared to having fun rather than working too hard.
- **The French.** Anglo-Saxons may struggle to fit in unless they make an effort to understand the French mentality.
- **Food and Drink.** There is no doubt that France has the world's greatest wines and food, drawing foreign visitors who want to sample the French *art de vivre*.
- **Schools.** The French education system is excellent, but may be difficult for British children to adjust to, unless they start very young.
- **Crime.** While there is generally less crime than in the UK, some areas, such as the Riviera, have a high level of street crime.
- **Language.** Learning the language is the key to settling down successfully, so start learning before you leave.
- **Festivals.** The French are keen on festivals, and the climate in the South helps to make them possible most of the year.

If you are reading this book you have probably visited France many times and you won't need much convincing that this is a place where you would like to live. France represents everything that the British think might be missing in their own country: good food and drink, fine weather, exuberant people, a relaxed lifestyle, and culture everywhere. The first and last of these you will certainly find here, the others are not necessarily always present. As the Belgian Prince de Ligne said in the 18th century: 'Every man has two fatherlands: his own and France.' This was at a time when France dominated the intellectual scene in Europe. Even if the 11 million Britons who visit France every year are perhaps not quite as Francophile as the Prince de Ligne, this is still a place that is holding out against Americanisation and thus it offers an indispensable perspective on the world for many of us.

HISTORY

Origins

Where have the French come from? In spite of the current policy of trying to keep immigrants out at all costs, the French are a very mixed bunch, more so than the British. The earliest historical peoples that one can say much about are the Celts, who came from much further east starting from 1000 BC. While they were related to the Celts in Britain and Ireland, their language was far closer to Latin than that spoken by their offshore cousins. For this reason they quickly gave up Gaulish and started speaking Latin when the Romans arrived; there are still some Gaulish words in modern French. The ancient Greeks also colonised the Mediterranean coast starting from 800 BC; some place names, such as Nice and Antibes are originally Greek. The next invaders were the Romans, who established the province of Gallia Narbonensis from 121 BC. In the following century, in 52 BC, Julius Caesar, by remarkable feats of arms, conquered the rest of Gaul.

For some 500 years, Gaul was an integral part of the Roman Empire. After the collapse of the Empire, the first stable dynasty to appear were the Merovingians, from 451 AD, German-speaking Franks who had come to the aid of the Romans in repelling Attila the Hun. The Frankish language was never written down, but modern French is full of Frankish words, and the Franks, of course, gave the country a new name. Three-hundred years later, in 751, the Carolingian dynasty took over, and one of their rulers, Charlemagne, set up a new Roman Empire in the West. His empire, much larger than modern France, was divided up between his three sons on his death in 843, leading to a slow but inevitable disintegration.

The English Connection

The Carolingian state was weakened by internal strife and could not withstand the assault of the Vikings, who occupied Rouen in 912. A new strongman emerged, in the shape of Hugues Capet in 987, thus starting the Capetian dynasty of kings, based around Paris and the Ile de France. The Vikings were pacified by ceding them the province of Normandy, and it was from here that William the Conqueror launched his successful invasion

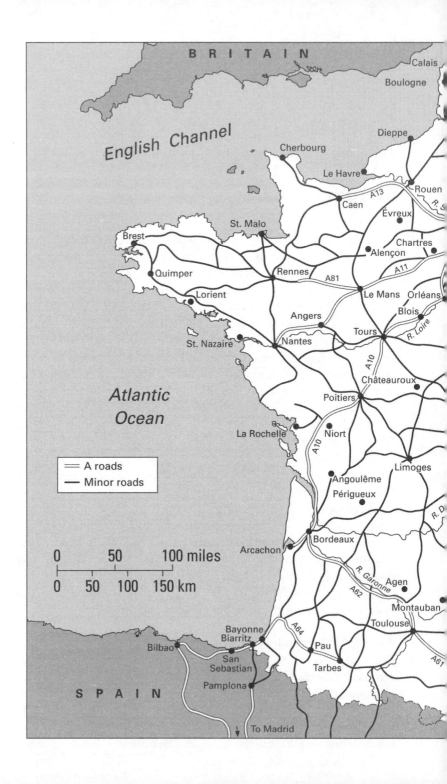

Major Towns and Cities of France

of England in 1066. At the same time the English Norman kings still held on to their French possessions. The situation was aggravated when the charismatic Eleanor of Aquitaine (1122-1204) decided to divorce the dull French King Louis VI and marry the more exciting English King Henry II, bringing all of her substantial French territories with her. Eleanor was a romantic figure, one of the few significant women in French history, and the mother of Richard the Lionheart and King John of England. After her death, the French king Philip Augustus soundly defeated the English at Bouvines in 1214 (never mentioned in English schoolbooks) and turfed the English out of most of France. Philip Augustus was without doubt the real founder of the French state. His is a name one should try to remember if you want to impress the French with your knowledge of history.

The Capetian dynasty gave way to the House of Valois from 1326, but this was disputed by the English Plantagenet kings thus starting the so-called Hundred Years War. After the great victories at Crécy (1346) and Poitiers (1356), the situation looked good for the English, and all of southwestern France was under their control. An even greater victory in 1415 at Agincourt led to King Henry V being recognised as the heir to the French throne, but he died before he could become king of both England and France. When French fortunes were at a low ebb, Joan of Arc appeared – inspired by visions of the Virgin Mary – and led the fightback, which saw the English losing almost all their French possessions by 1436.

Although the French were rid of the English, the French kings only controlled half of what is modern-day France. The powerful Duchy of Burgundy only became part of France in 1477, and Brittany in 1491. Through constant warfare and expansion, most of the modern French heartlands were brought under control by 1610, but the country was still smaller than it is today on the northern and eastern sides.

France steered its own erratic course through the Wars of Religion between Protestants and Catholics. After the infamous St Bartholomew's Day Massacre of 1572, when thousands of Protestants were slaughtered, a Protestant king – Henri IV – came to the throne in 1589 and the Edict of Nantes was issued, giving the Protestants the right to control certain towns. Louis XIV, however, decided that he wanted to win favour with Rome, and revoked the Edict in 1685, with the result that the Protestants had to go abroad or reconvert to Catholicism. The exodus of the Huguenots, as they were known, damaged the French economy, as many of them were skilled artisans, or intellectuals, and thus helped Britain and Holland to develop faster than France.

A great warmonger, Louis XIV, decided to expand in all directions, and acquired Flemish and German-speaking areas in the north and east, but he also united the rest of Europe against him, and had to retreat in the

Why choose a mortgage from HSBC for your new home in France?

If you're thinking about buying in France, talk to us about our unique homebuying service in association with CCF, a fellow member of the HSBC Group. CCF has bilingual French/English mortgage advisors in many of the major towns and cities in France, giving you direct access to invaluable local expertise.

And they'll also cut through the language barrier by putting you in contact with estate agents, notaries (French conveyancing lawyers) and UK based solicitors specialising in French property law.

The Guide to buying a home in France takes you through the buying process and includes a special offer for 'France' magazine, a map and guide to the regions of France, useful property search web links and information on Estate planning.

So for practical help from a global bank with local connections, visit **www.hsbc.co.uk** or call **0800 085 8887** or textphone **0800 028 0126.**

HSBC **◆X◆**
The world's local bank

face of superior British-led forces. It is interesting to note that in 1700 the population of France was 27 million, against 9 million for England and Wales, and 2 million in Holland. France was in one sense overwhelmingly powerful, but at the same time economically and politically backward. By the mid-18th century England was 30 years ahead of France technologically, and had a far more liberal political system, which was greatly admired by French intellectuals like Voltaire (hard to believe today). France was far behind northern Europe in terms of its public institutions and had not begun to develop a modern banking system, an essential prerequisite for international trade.

Revolution

The stubborn insistence of the French ruling classes in holding on to their medieval privileges meant that when the Revolution came, it outdid all the other revolutions in terms of violence. Since France had supported the United States in its revolution, the people saw that it was possible to overthrow the established order. The first period of idealism after the storming of the Bastille in 1789, gave way to the Terror, when thousands were guillotined, sometimes for quite trivial reasons. The anarchy required a new strong man, who arrived in the form of the Corsican Napoleon Bonaparte. Napoleon brought stability, but also pursued a policy of imperial expansion which gave France a short-lived period of glory that is often evoked today. While Napoleon restored some aspects of the *ancien régime* in the new Empire, such as reviving the orders of nobility, he followed anti-clerical policies, and the Catholic Church was severely weakened. Napoleon's final defeat in 1815 brought in a new period of monarchical rule, under Louis XVIII, a brother of Louis XVI. Louis still believed in the divine right of kings, and would not act as a constitutional monarch. The fear that the old order had come back led to more unrest and a more liberal constitution from 1830, under King Louis-Philippe.

France lagged behind the rest of northern Europe as far as industrial development was concerned. Political unrest was ongoing. The extreme inequality of French society led to the insurrection of 1848; the king was exiled to England and a Second Republic declared. It was only a few months before Napoleon's nephew, Louis-Napoleon, won the first election for President. With the myth of his uncle behind him, he mounted a coup d'état in 1851 and declared himself Emperor Napoleon III. The new emperor had the same desire for glory as his uncle, and large swathes of North Africa came under French rule during his tenure. Generally, he provided stable government, and gradual reform, helped by favourable economic conditions. His disastrous decision to declare war on Prussia in 1870, however, and subsequent capture, made the Third Republic inevitable. The monarchy

was finally dead and buried at the third attempt.

The end of the 19th century saw the prestige of French culture reach its
absolute zenith, with exceptional achievements in all the arts. There was
also a sea change in relations between France and Great Britain, when they
formed a close alliance – the Entente Cordiale – in 1904. The First World
War, coming soon after, changed France forever. The mass slaughter of
young men on the Western Front led to a drop in the population that is
still very evident today. The period between 1918 and 1940 was one of
constant political and economic crisis, with the extreme left and right
often fighting it out on the streets. In May 1940 France was invaded
again, and half the country occupied, while the other half remained
under the control of a puppet regime, with the First World War hero,
Marshal Pétain, as leader. Not everyone was wholeheartedly on the side of
the British; the sinking of the French fleet in North Africa in July 1940
by the British still rankles with some. The maverick Charles de Gaulle
carried on the fight for a free France from London, and was rewarded by
being allowed to enter Paris at the head of French forces in August 1944,
restoring French wounded pride.

De Gaulle and After

France reconstructed quickly after World War II, but was still plagued with political instability. The Fourth Republic was declared in 1945. The Communists were at the height of their power, thanks to their leading role in fighting the Germans, and won 28% of the vote in the general election of 1946. The problem of decolonisation eventually destroyed the Fourth Republic. The humiliating defeat in Vietnam in 1954 was followed by the start of the Algerian War of Independence. Algeria had the same status as mainland France, and a large European population. When the French government appeared to be ready to consider independence for Algeria in 1958, the European settlers and French army in Algeria declared their willingness to fight against their own country; with the prospect of a military coup in Paris, the state turned to General de Gaulle to save the situation. De Gaulle assumed the powers of a dictator for six months, and extricated the country from its Algerian nightmare. A Fifth Republic was declared, with a constitution that gave the president, who was now to be elected every seven years, far more power than before. The electoral system also ensured that the Communists would have far fewer seats in parliament.

Algeria finally got its independence in 1962, and France had to deal with a large influx of *pieds noirs,* European settlers, as well as pro-French Muslim troops, the *harkis.* Politics was dominated by the right wing, one factor that triggered off serious disturbances in May 1968, which could have led to the overthrow of the republic. De Gaulle survived, but was replaced by Georges Pompidou in 1969, who died in 1974 before he could complete his term in office. The next president, Valéry Giscard d'Estaing, was another conservative, ruling in tandem with a conservative administration. Against all expectations, the veteran socialist François Mitterrand won the presidency in 1981, and was re-elected in 1988. Mitterrand was able to rule in concert with a left-wing government from 1982. This was the year when the regions first set up in 1972 were given elected assemblies. In the face of severe economic difficulties, Mitterrand and the Socialists found themselves obliged to follow more market-oriented policies. In 1986, the right won elections, and the President had to work with a government led by the Gaullist Jacques Chirac, the first instance of 'cohabitation'. From 1988 the left were back in power, but they suffered a crushing defeat in the 1993 elections. Jacques Chirac won the presidency in 1995, following the death of Mitterrand. He immediately infuriated the rest of the world by conducting nuclear tests in the Pacific, probably to boost morale at home.

In spite of allegations of corruption Chirac won re-election in 2002. The Socialist candidate, Lionel Jospin, came in third behind the anti-immigrant extremist Jean-Marie Le Pen who gained 18.8% of the vote in the second round of voting. Chirac is generally regarded as affable and relaxed, if not particularly competent. In 2002 the right again formed the government under new Prime Minister Jean-Pierre Raffarin, whose selection came as a total surprise to everyone. One can expect a right-wing legislative programme, with more privatisation, and a watering down of the 35-hour week. From 2002 the President will only remain in office for five years, making it possible for parliamentary elections to coincide with presidential ones, and perhaps avoiding the inconvenience of cohabitation.

In the new millennium, France is still struggling to deal with fundamental economic problems. Although it has a constant trade surplus, this is founded on its self-sufficiency in agricultural products. Unemployment has not budged below 8% since the 1970s, to a large extent because the French franc has not been devalued since that time. The rigidity of the labour laws and the lack of a market-driven economy are intractable obstacles to an improvement in the employment situation.

POLITICAL STRUCTURE

The first French republic was founded in 1792 after the Revolution. After the Empire and several monarchs, the republican system has remained in place since 1870. In common with the United States France has a written constitution and an executive President who is not only the head of state but also the head of the government. The President has the right to dissolve the lower house of parliament, the *Assemblée Nationale*, but not the *Sénat* or *Haute Assemblée*. If the President dies in office, or has to resign, then the Speaker of the Senate takes over temporarily as President. The upper house reviews legislation but cannot prevent its passage. One-third of the 321 seats are up for re-election every three years, the electors being the local councillors (*conseillers généraux*).

The *Assemblée* serves for a term of five years, which from now on coincides with the presidential elections. The 577 members or *députés* are chosen by a double-ballot system, where there is a run-off between the two candidates who receive the largest number of votes in the first round. The same system applies to presidential elections. Depending on which political grouping has the most seats, a government of 42 ministers is formed; ministers give up their seats in the Assembly to a preselected deputy, or *adjoint*. The Prime Minister may not be from the same political party as the President, in which case, the President tends to exercise more power. Legislation is drafted by the President's office, and then debated in parliament.

Women are very under-represented in French politics; there has only been one woman Prime Minister – Édith Cresson – between 1991 and 1992, and she was deemed a failure. Women did not even receive the vote in France until 1945. The original Napoleonic constitution classed them with children and lunatics.

Administration

Régions. The introduction of a new layer of government between Paris and the departments was initiated in 1972. From 1982 each *région* was given an elected assembly and an executive. This is not really devolution as we would see it in the UK. The regions have powers in the area of culture, education and business. The main purpose was to reduce the power of the departments, and to restore some feeling of regional identity, which had been deliberately negated by the organisation into departments after 1789.

Départements. France is logically, and conveniently, divided into 100 *départements* or departments, four of which are overseas. The rest make up what is called La Métropole, or La France Métropolitaine. Each department has a two-digit number which is, again very logically, used for postcodes and licence plates. Napoleon placed a prefect or *préfet* in charge of each department, in a deliberate imitation of the Roman Empire, an unelected official directly appointed by the President. Since 1982, the prefect has been replaced by the President of the General Council. The General Council is elected for a period of six years by local councillors. The chairman is elected for three years by the General Council.

Arrondissements and **Cantons.** The *départements* are divided up into *arrondissements* and these are again divided up into *cantons*. These units have some significance in organising voting and public services, but no directly elected representatives.

Communes. The level of government that everyone comes into contact with is the commune, of which there were about 36,700 at the last count, most of them with fewer than 1000 inhabitants. The voters elect a municipal council for six years, while the chief executive officer is the *maire* or mayor, who is not only an official of the municipality, but also a government agent, and a member of the *police judiciaire.* The *maire* is obliged to keep the civil register, and often performs marriages. He or she also establishes the electoral roll and publicises laws. Anyone holding a *carte de séjour* can vote in the municipal and mayoral elections. The French government's policy is to encourage, or force, *communes*, to work together in groups, within the limits of their official competencies, in order to run the country in a more rational and democratic manner.

Pays. Since 1995, following the Loi Pasqua, different regions or communes can band together to form a *pays* (literally 'country'), to promote their economic interests and strengthen cultural ties. By 1996 there were already 200 *pays* in France, a throwback to the pre-Revolutionary *ancien régime.* The more republican French are concerned about the weakening of the departments, and fear a return to the pre-1789 organisation of the country.

Political parties

No one political party can form a government on its own in France; the only possibility is 'cohabitation' or coalition. The main parties on the left are the Parti Socialiste (PS), and the very much reduced Parti Communiste Français (CPF). On the right there are the Rassemblement pour la République (RPR), a Gaullist party organised by Jacques Chirac, and the non-Gaullist Union pour la Démocratie Française (UDF), originally started by Giscard d'Estaing. The RPR and UDF generally work together, but are sometimes in conflict. There is a plan to unite them into one party from 2003. On the fringes are the Front Nationale (FN), an extreme right-wing party under Jean-Marie Le Pen, and Les Verts (the Greens).

GEOGRAPHICAL INFORMATION

Physical Features

France is popularly called 'l'Hexagone' on account of its (roughly) six-sided shape. It is the largest country in the EU with a surface area of 544,500 square kilometres. It is also one of the most thinly populated, with a mere 109 inhabitants per square kilometre. Most of the land is habitable, being less than 200 metres above sea level. The three main mountain ranges are the French Alps, including Europe's highest mountain, Mont Blanc, the Pyrenees, running along the border with Spain, and the less mountainous Massif Central, in south-central France. The English Channel – which is called La Manche here – is just 22 miles wide at its narrowest point. France has land borders with Belgium, Luxembourg, Germany, Switzerland, Italy, Andorra and Spain.

The main rivers are the Loire, the Rhône, the Seine and the Garonne. In total there are 8500 kms of navigable rivers and waterways.

Population

Current estimates suggest that there are 62 million people living in France, which includes a possible 3 million illegal immigrants. There is a steady movement from the countryside to the towns; around 75% of the people are urban dwellers. Paris is Europe's largest conurbation with 11.1 million people. Other urban areas are:

Lyon	1,600,000
Marseille	1,400,000
Lille	1,100,000
Toulouse	920,000

Bordeaux   890,000
Nice   556,000
Rouen   450,000

In 2000 7.5% of the population were of foreign origin, numbering 3.5 million, including 2 million from the EU. Algerians and Moroccans make up 1.2 million.

Other Territories

Along with metropolitan France, there are a number of remnants of the French Empire, which are loosely labelled the DOM-TOM. DOM stands for Départements d'Outre-Mer, and includes French Guyana, Martinique, Guadeloupe, Mayotte and Réunion. The Territoires d'Outre-Mer (TOM) include French Polynesia, New Caledonia, the Antarctic territories, Wallis and Futuna Islands, and St Pierre et Miquelon off the coast of Canada. The DOM are full departments of France, with some degree of autonomy, while the TOM are directly administered from Paris.

The Principality of Monaco is neither a department of France, nor a truly independent country. The head of state is a hereditary Prince, but France controls many aspects of the government. The small mountain principality of Andorra in the Pyrenees recognises the French President and a Spanish bishop as heads of state, but is more or less independent.

Climatic Zones

France has substantial variations of climate, given its great size. The north-west, bordering the Atlantic has a similar climate to southwest England, if somewhat warmer. The dividing line between north and south as far as climate goes is the Loire valley.

Continental Zone. The north and east of France have a continental climate, characterised by predictably warm summers and cold winters, with fairly high rainfall, similar to southern England. Auvergne and Burgundy come under this zone.

Mediterranean Zone. The south and southeast experience a Mediterranean climate, with regularly hot summer and mild winters, and unpredictable low rainfall. The south is subject to strong winds like the *mistral*, and sudden storms.

Mountainous Zone. The mountain regions of the Pyrenees, Alps and Massif Central generally have heavy snowfall in winter, and cool, sunny summers with frequent rain.

AVERAGE MONTHLY TEMPERATURES (CENTIGRADE) AND RAINFALL (MM)

	Jan	Feb	Mar	Apr	May	Jun	Jul	Aug	Sep	Oct	Nov	Dec
Bordeaux												
Max	9	11	14	16	19	23	26	26	23	18	13	10
Min	2	3	4	6	10	13	15	15	12	9	5	3
rainfall	76	64	66	66	71	66	53	58	71	86	89	86
Cherbourg												
Max	8	8	10	12	15	18	19	20	19	15	12	10
Min	4	4	5	7	9	13	15	14	13	10	8	5
rainfall	110	75	61	50	37	36	52	73	77	100	125	118
Dijon												
Max	5	6	12	16	20	23	26	25	22	16	9	6
Min	-2	-1	2	5	9	12	14	13	11	6	2	0
rainfall	48	41	48	51	58	69	64	64	53	74	71	58
La Rochelle												
Max	9	10	13	16	19	23	24	25	23	18	12	8
Min	3	3	4	7	9	13	14	14	12	9	6	3
rainfall	63	59	64	57	54	50	44	49	52	90	97	93
Lille												
max	6	6	9	12	17	19	22	23	19	14	9	7
min	1	1	3	4	8	11	13	13	11	7	4	2
rainfall	48	41	43	43	51	56	61	58	56	64	61	58
Marseille												
Max	11	12	14	17	21	26	29	28	25	20	14	12
Min	3	3	6	8	12	16	19	18	16	11	7	3
rainfall	48	41	46	46	46	25	15	25	64	94	76	58
Paris												
Max	6	7	11	14	18	21	24	24	21	15	9	7
Min	1	1	3	6	9	12	14	14	11	8	4	2
rainfall	53	48	37	43	54	52	55	61	53	50	51	50
Tours												
Max	6	8	12	16	19	23	24	24	21	16	10	7
Min	1	1	3	6	9	12	14	13	11	7	4	2
rainfall	60	55	48	46	60	48	48	60	58	60	62	65

THE FRENCH MENTALITY

Foreigners choose to go and live and France because they like the lifestyle, not necessarily because they like the French. There is a crucial difference between a foreigner who goes to live in the UK or the USA and who over time is accepted as a Brit or an American because they have adopted British or American habits and so successfully blend in with the locals, and an Anglo-Saxon who goes to live in France and somehow never seems to be quite accepted by the French as one of them. Someone who has no Latin ancestry is never likely to metamorphose themselves into a Frenchman or Frenchwoman. The gulf between the Germanic and Latin cultures is simply too great for this ever to happen, and why should it? There are areas of France where a more Germanic mentality tends to prevail. The people of northwest France, in the formerly Flemish-speaking areas of Pas-de-Calais have a lot in common with their placid, good-natured cousins over the border in Belgium. The area of Alsace-Lorraine, where German is still in everyday use, is in many ways more German than French. In the southwest of the country, the Basques have an entirely different mentality.

France is a country with a strong tendency towards uniformity, so it is not exactly difficult to make generalisations about it. The social mores are very similar everywhere, but there is no doubt that people are generally friendlier and less formal in the south than in the north and centre. Taken as a whole, French social customs are old-fashioned by Anglo-Saxons standards, and there is a whole system of etiquette and formal behaviour that one will need to learn about if one wants to mix with any of the social classes and not constantly offend people. It is well worth investing in a manual of French etiquette, the best being *French or Foe?* and *Savoir Flair* by the American Polly Platt (www.pollyplatt.com). Unless you learn about the customs of the French your stay could be unnecessarily difficult.

Making Friends

The first thing to remember is that the French draw a very clear distinction between people they know and strangers. Walk into a bar in rural France, and people often look at you as though you had landed from Mars. No one will say a word to you, thus confirming your worst prejudices about the locals. Until you have made some kind of personal contact, i.e. found something that you have in common, not much conversation will take place. It is quite possible to start chatting with people on trains and buses, but there has to be some good reason. People are generally suspicious of strangers, and would rather not get involved with them too quickly. Smiling at everybody regardless is a big mistake. Smiling is reserved for appropriate occasions, otherwise it is seen as insincere and hypocritical. Talking loudly is also to be avoided. Conversations should be carried on discreetly; you will notice that the French generally keep their voices down in public places.

Being accepted into French social circles is difficult, admittedly, and if you are it is an honour. The French generally have networks of friends dating back to their early schooldays, so it is hard for a foreigner to get a look-in. By all accounts, Paris is the most difficult place of all to make friends; it can be a very lonely place for outsiders. Foreigners will tend to stick together; if your workplace is informal you may become friendly with your colleagues outside working hours. Joining a sports club, or ramblers' group is a good way to meet people, but in general the French are not great ones for organised social activities.

France is an intensely competitive society; from the time children go to school they are conditioned to compete and they are criticised mercilessly by their teachers and parents if they fail to do their best. Every foreigner in France soon notices that, while the French are always making fun of foreigners, they become very upset if anyone criticises them or their country. There is always a lighthearted banter going on between the French – everyone appreciates witty repartee – but when foreigners try the same thing it sounds as though they are making personal criticisms, and the well-known French touchiness manifests. The French are undoubtedly volatile and often appear inconsistent to northern Europeans and Americans. The French want excitement and drama in their day-to-day life, but none of it is taken too seriously.

Brits and Americans may feel their self-esteem rapidly sinking in the face of so many one-sided jokes at their expense, so it is vital not to take things personally. The French respect people who are self-confident and proud of their country; they dislike the kind of self-disparagement practised by the British. Conversation is an art form here. There are things that you must not talk about with people you don't know well, in particular French politics, or anything concerning one's private life. The fact that there are virtually no taboos about what close friends can talk about should not mislead foreigners into thinking that they can reveal everything to casual acquaintances.

A key issue in whether you can get on in French society is the degree to which you master the French language. The importance of mastering the language cannot be overemphasised; it is virtually the key to being able to fit in here. If you can read French literature in the original, you will never be at a loss for a topic of conversation, and you will gain a great deal of respect. Being up on French *chansons* will win you a lot of brownie points. The French have boundless respect for education and learning: one's status in life is determined by how much you have of it. On the other hand, they dislike pomposity. It is a major social gaffe to talk for too long about any subject or too much about oneself. In a typical conversation, people interrupt each other or talk at the same time; the main thing is to be entertaining.

Meeting and Greeting

Knowing how to greet people is a must. At the very least you should shake people's hands when you meet them. It is very important to use people's titles *Monsieur, Madame* (or *Mademoiselle* for girls under 16) but not with their surname. If they have a professional title, then you should use it: *Monsieur/Madame le Professeur/le Docteur* and so on. In the workplace you will not be on first-name terms with superiors unless you are working for a foreign-based company. The boss will always remain *Monsieur le Directeur.*

Kissing is a subject to be familiar with. It is customary to give women two pecks – *deux bises* – on the cheek on leaving a party, or once one is on friendly terms. For a man to give a woman three pecks – *trois bises* – implies something more than just being casual friends; to do so may give offence. For family and close friends it is expected, but you should take your lead from other people. One kiss on the cheek is also over-familiar. Rather confusingly, some women give four pecks to their good friends. In the South of France, three pecks is more acceptable between casual friends. When work colleagues meet for the first time in the morning, it is normal to kiss twice; foreigners should follow the lead of the locals.

Hand-shaking is another big ritual which you need to get right. The first time you meet in the morning in your office you should shake hands with male colleagues (if you are male), and when you leave in the evening. The person who is socially superior or doing you a favour takes the initiative in shaking hands; you should not extend your hand to your boss before he or she does so. There is no need to shake hands with tradesmen or cleaners, but you should shake hands with notaries, architects and other professional people.

The French and Authority

One of the typical features of the French is their ambivalent attitude towards authority. While the British make jokes about sex, the French make jokes about authority. In the 18th century authority rested with an aristocratic class who had absolute power. These days it is civil servants who exercise absolute power. Once you are admitted to a post of civil servant, you are virtually irremovable, and you can make life and death decisions about citizens' lives. Everyone envies civil servants. France is probably the world's most bureaucratic country: you can hardly do anything in this country without filling a form in. But at the same time, if you happen to know the right people, almost anything becomes possible. Everything depends on personal relationships: state functionaries can make a phone call and fix things for you should they so wish. It is very much at their whim, just as it was under Louis XIV. France rates as one of Europe's more corrupt countries: on a par with Portugal but not as bad as Greece and Italy.

The strictness of French upbringing and the all-pervasive interference of the state in every aspect of life has, not surprisingly, led to a backlash, a desire to defy authority and completely ignore all rules. The worst manifestation of this anarchic tendency is the way the French drive without any consideration for other motorists, turning the streets into a war-zone. You are at far greater risk of being killed in a car accident here than in the UK.

It would be a mistake to think that everyone just does as they please here. If you are going to break the rules, then you have to know how to do it, otherwise you will just get into trouble. Because this is basically a socialistic society, there are a lot of rules which exist to protect weaker members of society. Other regulations, however, appear to be completely irrational or arbitrary, and designed to make life difficult, such as the rule that you have to submit certified copies of your degrees and qualifications every time you apply for a job, or the fact that anyone who graduates from secondary school can go to university.

If you come to live in France from another country, then it is just as well to understand how things are done here, and not to get too upset when it doesn't match your expectations. After all, you came here to experience a different culture...

Quality of Life

By any objective standards, France should be a paradise to live in. The citizens are well looked after; according to UNESCO, France has the second highest quality of life after Canada (a country with a strong French influence). France has a permanent trade surplus – it is self-sufficient in food – and a style of life that led the German poet Schiller to coin the term 'to live like God in France'. Pleasure definitely comes before work here. The government started to institute a compulsory 35-hour working week back in 1997, much to the irritation of big business. The French do not actually work 35 hours a week, they simply get more holidays a year in lieu. There are still many who work far more hours. The underside of the French dream is all too evident if you walk around the big cities. With permanent high unemployment, there is a huge underclass of dispossessed poor who will never live the life that they would want.

The fact that many French are chronically dissatisfied with their lifestyle is amazing to foreigners who would love to have a second home here. The roots of the malaise seem to lie in the excessive conformism of French society. If you don't earn a good salary and have a respectable job, if you can't afford to spend the whole of August in your holiday home, then you have failed to live up to the French model. In a sense there are two countries here: the idealised France and the reality. What appears at first sight to be a society devoted to hedonism and working as little as possible, turns out to be intensely competitive and snobbish about material possessions. One possible consequence of the pressure to conform can be seen in the fact that the French use twice as many anti-depressants and tranquillisers as the British; the French are the second biggest consumers of pharmaceuticals in the world after Japan, another high-pressure society. It is estimated that one-third of French teenage girls are on medication for psychological problems.

While 75% of the French live in towns and cities, their roots are very much in rural France. Most of the towns are small by British or American standards; there are three huge cities: Paris, Lyon and Marseille, while the rest of the country appears quite empty. You can drive for half an hour without seeing a soul or a single house. The depopulation of the countryside started in World War I, and is something of immense concern because it threatens to undermine the basis of what it is to be French. The key to French identity lies in the short distance that separates the people from their peasant origins. Their basic values have not changed that much. This is still a peasant culture, with an overlay of sophistication.

Party Animals

Whenever French people get together it's party time. Any social meeting is a big occasion here. The emphasis is on sharing and not standing on ceremony. The French generally prefer to buy some expensive ingredients to cook at home, rather than going out to an expensive restaurant. It is a fact that the French spend less of their income on going to restaurants than the British, because they know how to cook. Buying food and drink to prepare at home is often the biggest item in the family budget.

When you are invited for a meal at someone's home, which will hopefully happen sooner rather than later, you are not necessarily expected to take a gift. In informal situations you can give something. Banquets and wedding feasts can go on for hours and involve ten courses; Brits may be shocked at such unashamed gluttony. It is considered bad form to leave a party before the end; even if it is five o'clock in the morning and you are collapsing, it is best to try to keep going as long as possible. A phone call to thank your host or a thank you note for a good time will be appreciated.

GETTING THERE

Travelling to France from the UK has never been cheaper or easier than it is now, with the opening of the Channel Tunnel and the revolution in low-priced air travel of recent years. Despite these developments many Britons still prefer to take the ferry, to cut down on the distance they have to drive at the other end.

Trains

Since 1993 there has been a direct rail link between London and Paris, run by Eurostar. The journey time is set to fall from three to two-and-a-half hours or less when the high-speed rail link between London and Folkestone comes into operation during 2004. You can also leave the train at Lille, near the Belgian border, and change to a TGV (French high-speed train) which will bypass Paris entirely and take you to Lyon, Marseille, the ski-fields, and other destinations. There is also a direct train from London to Avignon once a week. For the Eurostar, call 08705-186 186 in the UK or see www.eurostar.com. You can book a French railpass or any other rail ticket in France, by calling Rail Europe on 08705-848 848 (www.raileurope.co.uk), or you can go in person to the French tourist office at 178 Piccadilly, London W1V 0AL. Main railway stations around the UK can also sell rail passes and Eurostar tickets.

By Car

Although you cannot actually drive through the Channel Tunnel, you can put your car onto a train, and drive off the other end. If you want to take a car through the tunnel, you need the Eurotunnel/Le Shuttle service, which starts from Cheriton, Folkestone (0870 535 3535; www.eurotunnel.com). You can buy your ticket at Folkestone. The journey is short (35 minutes) and spartan.

If you dislike the idea of driving far on the right in France, it is easy enough to put your car on a train in Calais and collect it again at your destination, while you head for your sleeper carriage. The cost is fairly steep, but worth it. This is an overnight service; the destinations are Brive, Avignon, Toulouse, Nice and Narbonne. There are no drinks or refreshments available on the train; breakfast is served at the destination. There is a limit to the vehicle's height. The full details are on www.frenchmotorail.com; ☎ 0870 241 5415.

Route planning within France is easy if you have access to the internet. Several sites give you detailed routes from any street in the UK to any street in France: see www.mappy.com; www.michelin-travel.com; www.theaa.com; www.rac.co.uk. These sites will estimate the time and cost of your journey. For a further refinement, you can download maps of larger French towns, and photos of houses, from 'Ma Ville' on www.wanadoo.fr.

French Driving

House-hunting in France is easiest done with a car. You will need to look around places on your own as well as in the company of an estate agent; public transport is simply not adequate for getting around the countryside. The roads are generally good, especially the motorways or *autoroutes,* which are financed by tolls. The annual road tax has been abolished.

It can be a pleasure driving off the beaten track where there is little traffic. The downside is the driving of the French who want to prove their non-conformism by ignoring the highway code. One simply has to accept drivers not signalling, or driving far too close to you. The worst drivers are in the south of the country.

French roads are classified according to three letters:

A – *Autoroute* (equivalent to M grade roads in UK). These are almost all toll roads – *autoroutes à péage*. The cost of using them is about €5 per 100km. You will be given a computer card when you join the motorway and you pay on exit. A quicker way of paying is to go to a *télépéage* with your French RIB (bank account number), where you can have a transponder fitted to your windscreen that allows you to pay by direct debit. You should not drive to the *télépéage* if you have no French bank account, and you do not wish to pay by direct debit. One potential hazard of the computerised cards is that your journey will be timed, and if you have averaged over the speed limit you will receive a hefty fine. See www.autoroutes.fr for more information.

N – *Route Nationale* (A road in UK). These were the main roads before the motorways. They are single or dual carriageway and pass through towns, which makes journeys slower. They often run alongside motorways and are generally best avoided if possible.

D – *Route Départementale* (B-grade road in UK).

Speed Limits. The speed limit on all *autoroutes* is 130kph (80mph); this is reduced to 110kph (65mph) in bad weather. The limit is 110kph on non-toll *autoroutes*. The speed limit on dual carriageways is 110kph and 90kph (55mph) on single carriageways, both reduced by 10kph in wet weather. A new speed limit of 50kph has been introduced for foggy conditions, where visibility is reduced to 50 metres. *Rappel* means the restriction is continued.

The limit in towns varies between 45kph (30mph) and 60kph (38mph).

The *priorité à droite* rule. There is a rule that you must give way to traffic joining from the right from another road (but not driveway), however minor. Drivers coming from the right will pull out regardless, and they expect you to do the same. On the whole this rule does not apply on major roads. There are signs such as a red diamond bordered with white, or *passage protégé* to show that you have priority. The sign *cédez le passage* means 'give way'.

Driving Licences. EU citizens including those from the UK can continue to drive on their own country's licences as long as their licence remains valid in their home country. They may also choose to apply for a French licence. US citizens may use their own licences, or a certified translation of an international driving licence for 90 days. If they apply for a *carte de séjour* they may drive for one year on a US licence with a certified translation (but not an international licence). After a year you will either have to take a French driving test, or if your state has an agreement with France, you may exchange your licence for a French one at a *préfecture de police*. Ask for the *service permis de conduire*. For information on importing a car into France, see chapter 10, *Making the Move*.

By Sea.

Many thought that the ferries would go out of business when the Channel Tunnel opened but this has not happened, mainly because the ferry companies have banded together to fight their common competitor. The introduction of high-speed catamarans, which can make the crossing from Dover to Calais in 45 minutes, has preserved their competitive edge. The ferries stress the cruise aspect of the journeys they offer and offer restaurants and entertainment to try make things more interesting.

Note that it is sometimes easier to take a ferry to Belgium if you are going to northern France.

Brittany Ferries: ☎ 0990-360 360; www.brittany-ferries.co.uk. Portsmouth to St Malo/Caen; Poole to Cherbourg; Plymouth to Roscoff.

Condor Ferries: ☎ 01305-761 551; fax 01305-760776; www.condorferries.co.uk. Poole to St. Malo via the Channel Islands. May to September only.

Norfolkline: ☎ 0870-870 1020; www.norfolkline.com. Dover to Dunkerque.

P&O European Ferries: ☎ 0870-6000 600; www.poportsmouth.com. Portsmouth to Cherbourg/Le Havre.

P&O Stena Line: ☎ 0870-6000 600; www.posl.com. Dover to Calais. Dover to Ostend (Belgium).

Hoverspeed: ☎ 08705 240 241; fax 01304-865 203; www.hoverspeed.com. Folkestone to Boulogne; Dover to Calais; Newhaven to Dieppe. High-speed SeaCat only operates between April and September. Also conventional ferry between Newhaven and Dieppe.

P&O North Sea Ferries: ☎ 0870-129 6002; fax 01482-706438; www.ponsf.com. Hull to Zeebrugge (Belgium).

Sea France: ☎ 08705 711 711; www.seafrance.com. Dover to Calais.

Two ferry companies, Brittany Ferries and P&O Portsmouth, run frequent traveller schemes for property owners in France, offering 33% and 36% discounts respectively. This can be extended to people renting your property. Eurotunnel has a similar scheme. You can also get lower fares by going through Ferry Savers: ☎0870 444 88 99; www.ferrysavers.com.

By Air

The real revolution in travel to France has come about with Ryanair flying to small airports all over France from the UK, and also now from Ireland and

AIRLINES SERVING FRANCE FROM THE UK

	Air France	bmiBaby	British Airways	British European	British Midland	Easyjet	MyTravel-Lite	Ryanair
Bergerac								
Biarritz								○
Bordeaux								
Brest								
Caen								
Carcassonne								○
Chambéry								
Clermont-Ferrand	○			○				
Dijon								
Dinard								○
Grenoble								
La Rochelle								
Le Havre	○							
Limoges								
Lyon	○		○	○		○		
Marseille			○					
Montpellier			○					○
Nantes	○		○	○				
Nice		○				○		
Nîmes								○
Paris Beauvais							○	○
Paris CDG	○	○			○	○		
Paris Orly				○		○		
Pau								○
Perpignan								○
Poitiers								
Reims								○
Rennes	○							
St Étienne								○
Strasbourg	○			○				○
Toulon								
Toulouse		○		○	○			
Tours								

Belgium. Other low-cost airlines such as Buzz and Easyjet then got in on the act. Destinations can change, and new ones are being added. It is important to bear in mind that routes can be axed and fares can rise, if the proximity of an airport has a bearing on where you buy your property. You need to check the websites regularly to see what is on offer. Prices also change from day to day: as planes fill up the price goes up, so you need to try to book as early as possible. Ryanair sometimes offers free flights, but you have to add on something for taxes. Other airlines, such as BA and Air France, are still quite expensive, but you get a free meal. The quickest way to see what fares are on offer is to look on the websites www.ebookers.com or www.lastminute.com.

The main airport serving Paris is Roissy-Charles de Gaulle (CDG) to the north of the city; to the south of the city there is Paris-Orly. Both have good rail connections to the city. The main advantage of Charles de Gaulle airport is the TGV station, from where you can get direct trains to Marseille, Rennes in Brittany, the skiing resorts in the Alps, and Brussels, but you can just as easily take the Eurostar to Lille and pick up the train there. The location of the third Paris airport is a subject of intense debate; it is going to be north of Charles de Gaulle.

Ryanair bought the airline Buzz in January 2003 and as this book goes to press they have cancelled all its flights for a month, and permanently cancelled 12 routes thereafter, while its future is reviewed. It is possible that the airline may cease to exist as a separate entity; for the latest see www.buzzaway.com.

Air France fly from Birmingham, London City and Manchester: ☎ 0845-0845 111 (UK); 08 20 82 08 20 (F); www.airfrance.co.uk.

bmi British Midland fly from Edinburgh, Leeds, London Heathrow, Manchester, Teesside: ☎ 0870-60 70 555; www.flybmi.com

bmibaby.com fly from Cardiff and East Midlands: ☎ 0870-264 2229; www.bmibaby.com.

British Airways fly from Aberdeen, Birmingham. Edinburgh, London Heathrow/Gatwick/City, Manchester and Newcastle: ☎ 0845-773 3377; www.britishairways.com.

British European fly from Belfast, Birmingham, Bristol, Edinburgh, Glasgow, Guernsey, Isle of Man, Jersey, London Heathrow, London Gatwick, London City and Manchester: ☎ 0870-567 6676; www.flybe.com.

Easyjet: ☎ 0870 600 0000; www.easyjet.com.

MyTravelLite fly from Birmingham: ☎ 08701-564564; www.mytravellite.com.

Ryanair fly from Dublin, Cork and London Stansted: ☎ 0870-333 1244; www.ryanair.com.

Note that some flights are only seasonal and that schedules frequently change.

COMMUNICATIONS

Television

If you come from the UK, you will quickly be struck by the poor quality of French television. Many of the offerings are American series dubbed into French spoken at breakneck speed, so you will never catch a word. There are interesting political discussions, where everyone talks at once, but nothing like the kind of aggressive interviewing one sees in the UK.

The main terrestrial channel is the formerly state-owned TF1. FR2 and FR3 are still owned by the state. The fourth channel is Canal Plus, a private subscription channel. Channel 5 shows La Cinq – a state-run cultural channel – in the daytime, and the Franco-German Arte after 7 pm. The latter is by far the most highbrow terrestrial channel, broadcasting high-quality films and documentaries in the evening, with no news bulletins. Channel 6 is a light entertainment channel.

Access to English Television. If you want to have access to the BBC and other English-language stations, then you could have cable, but satellite is a far more satisfactory option. Cable TV is only available in certain areas. The cable channel Noos offers BBC World and BBC Prime, along with CNN as part of its 'bouquet' of channels. TPS and CanalSat are satellite subscription stations which offer English-language channels; the hire of the decoder and dish are included in a monthly charge of around €40.

To get the maximum number of English-language channels you need to subscribe to Sky in the UK. As long as you have a UK address, Sky will supply a decoder which may or may not continue to work in France. Depending on what you pay, you can get a range of UK terrestrial and news channels. The BBC supplies its channels free of charge to Sky in a bid to persuade subscribers to switch to digital TV. All the British channels are relayed by the Astra 2 satellite; French stations use other satellites. You need a parabola dish – 50cm is adequate for all of France – installed somewhere on the outside of your house. If you live in a *co-propriété* you will need the permission of the other residents.

The other option is to get the decoder and a smart card which the BBC will supply to anyone with a UK licence: if you don't have a licence any more you need to coax someone who does to hand theirs over to you. You can then get a large range of English-language channels, except for the Sky subscription channels, free of charge; there is no need to buy a UK TV licence, but you do, of course, have to have a French TV licence, a *redevance*, payable to the local Trésor Public (there is talk of abolishing this tax). If you are over 70 you are exempt from the *redevance*.

Some Brits have reported that they are still able to pick up non-subscription Free To Air channels after their Sky subscription has expired. Another great advantage of having satellite TV is that it enables you to pick up British radio stations, without the expense of accessing them over the internet.

If you are starting from scratch with satellite TV, the whole installation can cost €800 or £500. There are adverts for installation and equipment in English-language magazines such as *The News*, published from the Dordogne but sold all over France.

Telephoning

For the moment the telephony scene in France is straightforward: France Télécom is the only company that can install your phone and all calls go through them. You can benefit from cheaper rates by signing up to Onetel and 9 Télécom. A comparison of their prices can be found on the website www.comparatel.com. There are plans to privatise France Télécom and this may not be an entirely positive development, especially if you live in a country area. Up until now there has been no difference in price betwen having a new phone line installed in a city or in the remotest parts of the hinterland. Sooner or later, France Télécom may decide it cannot spend thousands of euros on connecting rural customers to the nearest exchange.

British handsets need an adaptor to work in France; the British variety have three wires, while the French ones have only two. The keys on French telephones are much the same as on British ones. The only point to note is that the hash symbol is called *dièse* – the same as a 'sharp' in music – needed for cheap-rate telephone cards. Both business and private phone numbers are on the internet. The Yellow Pages are on www.pagesjaunes.fr and private subscribers on www.annuaire.com. There is also Minitel, which is expensive but can be used free in post offices. There is always Directory Enquiries: dial 12.

Telephone boxes mostly work with cards; those that work with coins are inside cafés or other private buildings, so it is essential to always have a card with you. The France Télécom is not good value for money; the post office sells a better card – Kertel – particularly good for phoning abroad. Ask a French speaker to explain how to get the cheapest rate for foreign calls. You can also use French telephone boxes with a UK card such as BT Globalcard, which is expensive but useful in an emergency.

Mobile Phones

The topic of mobile phones is one that raises a lot of hackles in France. It has been the practice to lock customers into unfair contracts and this is still going on. Unless you are prepared to stay with one company for a certain time, you will not be able to keep the same phone number or list of numbers if you buy another phone. If you spend any amount of time in France you will want to rent or buy a mobile phone there, but before you sign a contract it is worth considering the small print. You can try to have the SIM card in your phone replaced with a French one, so you can carry on using the same phone. If your phone is 'SIM-locked', i.e. the card cannot be changed, then you need a French mobile. Unless you are officially resident in France, French mobile phone companies will only let you use a phone with a pre-paid card, on production of your passport. The well-known deals are Orange La Mobicarte, SFR La Carte, and Bouygues Carte Nomad.

To buy a phone you need a proof of identity and a proof of address. You also have to produce an RIB – a bank account number – which is in any case unavoidable if you pay by direct debit. You will also be asked to produce a cheque written out to you that has gone through your account, or a French credit card.

An alternative to renting a phone in France is to rent from a US or UK-based company such as Planetfone.com. The phone is delivered to you wherever you are, and you are then ready to start using it without having to go into a French phone store. While there is no cost saving you are spared the hassle of having to choose between all the different French rental contracts. Other sites to check out for this option include: www.callphone.com, www.rent-a-cellphone.com, and www.acetelecom.com.

As France is relatively thinly populated in comparison to the UK, mobile phone coverage is not guaranteed, and there are areas in the countryside where you will not have any reception. Out of the three main phone companies, Orange and SFR are supposed to have better coverage than Bouygues Télécom in country areas. They generally claim to cover 98% of the population and 87% of the land area. The three main operators are now planning to co-operate in putting up phone masts. While some local mayors have tried to prevent masts from being put up, the French government does not place any restrictions on erecting phone masts.

The mobile phone market is competitive and rapidly changing. For a clear overview of the different deals on offer, look at the website www.comparatel.com. From this it is evident that there is not that much to choose between the three main operators, although Bouygues comes out slightly better if you are a light user. For the three main companies see: www.orange.fr, www.sfr.fr and www.bouyguestelecom.fr.

Internet and e-mail

It would be fair to say that France is some years behind the UK in terms of internet use and availability. This is to some extent because of the pioneering system known as Minitel started in 1985, which provides a service similar to the internet. Minitel is a keyboard and screen that sits alongside your telephone; although it is expensive to use it is still popular. You can access Minitel from the UK, by logging on to www.minitel.fr. If you are travelling around in France it can be difficult to find cybercafés outside the big towns. The French government has had the bright idea of installing internet terminals in a thousand post offices. Unfortunately, these terminals have had their cookies disabled, meaning you can't send e-mails or use interactive sites like the SNCF timetables. You can create an e-mail account with the post office – see www.laposte.net – which is best done at home, as you can't do it in the post office itself. The terminals (if you can get them to work) take pre-paid cards. Some tourist offices have also seen a money-making opportunity with internet terminals, and will try to charge outrageous prices for prepaid cards. Otherwise you may find internet terminals in the backs of cafés and other unlikely locations. It is wise to have a webmail address, such as Hotmail, or Yahoo, as well as your regular UK internet service provider in case the latter doesn't work properly in France.

The French are still trying to decide on a word for 'e-mail'. The Académie Française favours *courriel*, an abbreviation of *courrier électronique*, but almost no one has taken this up. Most people prefer the ugly-sounding *mél* or *mèl;* a lot of companies use the word *e-mail*, but it is not likely to become the standard written form of the word here.

Once you have settled in to your new home in France, you can look at the different internet service providers' offerings, which are more limited than what you would find in the UK. If you are a light user, you may do well with Wanadoo.fr or Club-internet.fr. Wanadoo (owned by France Télécom), Club-internet, Tiscali, Free and Freesurf also offer 'free' packages where you only pay for the telephone call. If you are connected to cable, you can get good deals with Noos. You will only be able to have ADSL (high-speed connections) in certain areas; remote country areas are never likely to have ADSL. Even if your modem speed is 56kbps it may effectively be only 10kbps or less. For more information about different ISP charges look at the website www.comparatel.com or some back issues of the French consumer magazine *Le Particulier*.

Computers

There is no reason why your UK or US computer (the latter with an adapter) should not work in France; the only downside is that your keyboard will be different from the French one, and it will be somewhat less convenient for typing French. The French keyboard, called AZERTY, has the peripheral characters in different places from the English QWERTY; the main bother is that the numbers have to be accessed with the shift key, while their place has been taken by accented French characters. The spacing on the screen will also appear different from in the UK. There is a simple remedy for this, which is to go to System Tools and change the keyboard language from French back to English (UK) or (US). You can also plug a UK keyboard into a computer bought in France; the computer should be turned off when you change the keyboard, unless you use a USB port. You will also need a different cable for your modem.

French has its own internet and computer terminology which is worth knowing:

adresse électronique	e-mail address
annexe	attachment
arobase	@ (at) symbol
clavier	keyboard
cursif	italic
écran	screen
kilo-octet/Ko	kilobyte
mémoire vive	RAM memory
mot de passe	password
moteur de recherche	search engine
navigateur	browser
octet	byte
police	font
site web/internet	website
télécharger	download

FOOD AND DRINK

Eating and drinking mean a great deal more than just keeping body and soul together: the French have taken the arts of wining and dining to heights that can only amaze lesser mortals, to the extent that they have become a spiritual activity. The whole thing goes too far, perhaps, but there is an undeniable sense of shock when one returns to the UK, a country where people only eat to live.

In restaurants and cafés one expects, and generally receives, a quality of food that is mostly unobtainable in the UK. The average French household, rather strangely, spends less on going out to eat than does a British family, but a great deal more on buying food to prepare at home. In contrast with the UK, there are still plenty of small supermarkets (*supermarchés*) and greengrocers (*primeurs*). There is also the trend towards hypermarkets (*hypermarchés*) selling every possible kind of product under one roof. Local supermarkets are generally smaller than in the UK; in small towns there is usually only a general grocer's or *superette* in the town centre. City-dwellers like to go to local markets for fresh produce and meat.

One of the positive sides of small country supermarkets is that the produce is often locally sourced. The downside is that fruit is sold ready to eat, and may not keep for very long. The meat in France is also hung for longer, to be more tasty, and sold without the fat and gristle that comes with British meat. French meat appears expensive by weight, but the quality is far better.

Perhaps through poverty, the French have been inventive about finding food to eat. Everyone knows about frog's legs. Spare a thought for the frogs: their legs are chopped off while they are still alive. Items like pig's trotters and tripe are still very much on the menu. It's just as well to know what you are eating. All kinds of small birds are blasted out of the sky on their migratory routes, for the sake of their meat, especially larks or *alouettes*. Larks that have been captured and fattened up are *mauviettes*. Even blackbirds are not safe here. For one of his last meals, the late President Mitterrand is said to have dined on *ortolans,* a protected species of bunting, the last word in extravagance and decadence.

The Etiquette of Eating Out

The etiquette of eating in a high-class restaurant in France is not that different from what you would expect anywhere else. It is considered good manners to eat off the back of the fork, and to keep your hands on the table when you are not eating. You should make sure that your fellow diners' glasses are kept topped up. If you are eating out with French friends, they will know which wines go with different courses, otherwise the wine-waiter – *le sommelier* – can advise you. It is best to be clear about who is going to pick up the tab beforehand. Unless you are in informal company, one person should pay for everyone. Going Swiss – *faire suisse* – as they say, is OK if it is decided in advance. The French like everything to be clear.

Discussing business matters during a meal is acceptable, as long as it is done after the cheese course. Before this time you should stick to other topics. By the time the fruit course comes round everyone should be in a good mood, and you may be able to clinch a good deal.

There are certain odd rituals in French cafés and *chambres d'hôte* that are worth noting. You may be expected to hold on to the same knife and fork for your hors d'œuvre or entrée as for the main course; in other words: *gardez vos couverts.* If you have bread with your meal, or for breakfast, you are not given a plate to put it on. Leaving crumbs and a few stains on the table is a sign that you had a good meal; the tablecloth is washed daily anyway.

If you order meat in a restaurant it is vital to ask for it to be well cooked:

bien cuit. Even then it will be undercooked by British standards. The French like their meat bloody – *saignant* – and need to be persuaded that you can cook meat all the way through. There are no such problems with fish.

In cafés and bars, you are not expected to pay for your drinks or food until you are ready to leave. The bar staff will give you a ticket for each item, or you ask for the bill (*l'addition* – colloquially *la note/l'ardoise*) at the end. They may ignore you if you ask how much you owe after your first drink. It is alright to ask for tapwater, but be careful about asking for 'soda': you are likely to get Coca-Cola. If you want fizzy water, ask for *une eau gazeuse.* For flat mineral water, ask for *eau non-gazeuse* or *eau plate.*

Smokers are generally considerate towards non-smokers in bars. There are no particular regulations about providing non-smoking areas. Finally, if you have to, ask for *les toilettes* and not *la toilette,* which means a washstand.

EDUCATION

France has the reputation of having one of the world's best education systems: it is certainly one of the most effective for stuffing facts into pupil's heads, but not that good for encouraging independent thinking or personal development. The main emphasis is on intellectual achievement, in particular in French grammar, science and mathematics. The downside is the harshness of the school regime. It is at school that the French learn how to compete; the general absence of sports (apart from gymnastics) is another difference from the British system. It is generally received wisdom that you should never put English-speaking children over the age of seven into the French school system: the language deficit, combined with the rigorous nature of French education, could make their lives unbearable. The other alternative is to put them into a school where part of the French national curriculum is taught in English, so that they can then take a French international baccalaureate. A few schools even mix French and British curriculums. There are international schools, but these are expensive and only in the big cities.

Education is compulsory between ages 6 and 16. Until recently there was a virtually uniform system over the whole country; most schools are state schools (*les écoles publiques*). There are also private schools (*les écoles privées*), which are partly subsidised by the state or by the church, mostly religious-based. If you want to send your child to a private school, the state or municipality may offer financial assistance, depending on your means. You should in the first instance go to the *service des écoles* at your local *mairie,* who will give you a list of the schools in your area.

Structure of Education. French children go into nursery schools as early as possible. Since 1989 every child from the age of 3 has been entitled to a place in a nursery school (*école maternelle*). There is also the infants' school (*jardin d'enfants*) for 2-3 year-olds (which is not free).

From the age of 6 all children go into the primary system – *école primaire* or *élémentaire* – which comprises grades 11 to 7. From age 11 to 15 children go into the *collège d'enseignement secondaire* (CES), the same as a British comprehensive. Depending on their aptitudes, students go on to a *lycée* or a specialised *lycée technique,* where they prepare for one of a number of possible leaving qualifications. The more academic stream will take the General or Technical Baccalaureate, which qualifies them automatically to go on to university.

For more information on the education system, ask the French Embassy to send you their leaflet *Primary and Secondary Education in France* (see www.ambafrance.org.uk and www.ambafrance.org.us) or look at the government website: www.education.gouv.fr. Most of the English-medium schools in France belong to the ELSA organisation (see below) and are listed on their website.

The French higher education system is very different from that in the UK or US. Universities are the second tier in the system; everyone aspires to go the Grandes Écoles, elite institutions that train the brightest and best to become civil servants and high government officials. There are specialised colleges for engineers, scientists, businessmen and administrators; graduating from one of them guarantees high social status and a job for life. In the case of the universities, there is a chaotic struggle at the beginning of the academic year to get onto courses, and many change subjects or drop out. Because of the lack of grants, most students continue to live at home while they go to university. On average they stay with their parents until they are 22.

International Schools. For those who can afford them, an international school, or a school offering the same curriculum as in your country, may be the best or even the only solution. Most of these schools offer the International Baccalaureate which is accepted for university entrance in many countries. Some offer a mixture of instruction in English and French. Some have nursery sections. Tuition fees go up to £16,000 a year or more; French private schools are much cheaper. There are liaison organisations in the UK and US who can advise you on where to find an international school in your area. The following is a short list of schools; for more details see *Live & Work in France* (published by Vacation Work; www.vacationwork.co.uk).

International Schools in Paris
American School of Paris: 41 rue Pasteur, 92210 St Cloud; ☎ 01 41 12 82 45; www.asparis.org.
British School of Paris: 38 quai de l'Ecluse, 78290 Croissy-sur-Seine; ☎ 01

34 80 45 90; www.rmplc.co.uk/eduweb/sites/paris.

Collège International de Fontainebleau: 48 rue Guérin, 77300 Fontainebleau; ☎ 01 64 22 11 77; www.anglophonesectionfontainebleau.com.

The International School of Paris: 6 rue Beethoven, 75016 Paris; ☎ 01 42 24 09 54; www.isparis.edu.

Schools outside Paris

Bordeaux International School: 53 rue de Laseppe, 33000 Bordeaux; ☎ 05 57 87 02 11; www.bordeaux-school.com.

Cité Scolaire Internationale: 2 place de Montréal, 69361 Lyon Cedex 07; ☎ 04 78 69 60 06; www2.ac-lyon.fr/etab/lycees.

CIV International School of Sophia Antipolis (Nice): B.P. 097, 06902 Sophia Antipolis Cedex; ☎ 04 92 96 52 24; www.civissa.org.

Collège-Lycée Cévenol International: 43400 Le Chambon-sur-Lignon; ☎ 04 71 59 72 52; www.members.aol.com/lecevenol.

Collège et Lycée de Sèvres: Sections Internationales de Sèvres, rue Lecocq, Sèvres 92310; ☎ 01 46 23 96 35; http://perso.wanadoo.fr/association/sis/en.

Ecole Internationale Michelin: 5 rue Bansac, 63037 Clermont-Ferrand Cedex; ☎ 04 73 98 09 73; e-mail ec.intern.cf@wanadoo.fr.

International School of Toulouse: 2 allée de l'Herbaudière, route de Pibrac, 31770 Colomiers; ☎ 05 62 74 26 74; www.intst.net.

Mougins School: 615 ave Dr Maurice Donat, Font de l'Orme, B.P. 401, 06251 Mougins; ☎ 04 93 90 15 47; www.mougins-school.com.

Part-English Medium Schools

Collège International de Meaux: 12 rue de la Visitation, 77100 Meaux; ☎ 01 64 36 35 30; e-mail agesi77@wanadoo.fr.

Ecole-Collège-Lycée Massillon: 2 bis, quai des Célestins, 75180 Paris Cedex 04; ☎ 01 53 01 91 60; http://www.perso.wanadoo.fr/elsa.france/massillon.

Eurécole: 5 rue de Lübeck, 75116 Paris; ☎ 01 40 70 12 81; e-mail direction@eurecole.com.

Institut de la Tour: 86 rue de la Tour, 75116 Paris; ☎ 01 45 04 73 35; www.institutdelatour.com.

Institut Notre-Dame: 3 rue de Témara BP 4259, 78104 St Germain-en-Laye; ☎ 01 30 87 17 87; www.scolanet.org.

Institution Notre-Dame la Riche: 30 rue Delpérier, 37058 Tours; ☎ 02 47 36 32 00; e-mail ndlr@wanadoo.fr.

L'Ermitage: 46 ave Eglé, 78600 Maisons-Laffitte; 01 39 62 04 02; e-mail Ermitage@Ermitage.fr.

Les Amis de l'Enseignement International de Reims: 168 rue des Capucins,

51100 Reims; ☎ 03 26 82 30 59; e-mail neil.joyce@wanadoo.fr.
Lycée Isle de France: 15 Ave Charles Tillon, 35083 Rennes; ☎ 02 99 54 44
  43; http://pharouest.ac-rennes.fr/e0352009u.
Vive l'Enfance International Montessori School: 29 rue de Noisy, 78870
  Bailly; ☎ 01 34 62 51; www.vive-l-enfance.fr.

Information Sources

Centre National de Documentation sur l'Enseignement Privé: 20 rue
  Fabert, 75007 Paris; ☎ 01 47 05 32 68.
Council of British Independent Schools in the European Community
  (COBISEC): Lucy's, Lucy's Hill, Hythe, Kent CT21 5ES; tel/fax 01303
  260857; e-mail cobisec@cs.com; www.cobisec.org.
English Language Schools Association France (ELSA): 86 rue de la Tour,
  75116 Paris; ☎ 01 45 04 48 52; e-mail elsa.france@wanadoo.fr; http:
  //perso.wanadoo.fr/elsa.france.
European Council of International Schools: 21 Lavant Street, Peters-
  field, Hants GU32 3EL; ☎ 01730-268244; fax 01730-267914; e-mail
  ecis@ecis.org; www.ecis.org.
ECIS North America: 105 Tuxford Terrace, Basking Ridge, New
  Jersey 07920, USA; ☎ 908-903 0552; fax 908-580 9381; e-mail
  malyecisna@aol.com; www.ecis.org.
Ministère de l'Éducation Nationale et de la Culture: 110 rue de Grenelle,
  75357 Paris Cedex 07; 01 49 50 10 10; www.education.gouv.fr.

HEALTH

It has been acknowledged by the World Health Organisation that France
has the best, or at least the most cost-effective health care system in the
world. This has come about as the result of the French government spending liberally to bring an unsatisfactory system up to scratch. In spite of
this, there are still shortages of doctors and everyone fears that the situation
is going to deteriorate in the future. France spends 9.8% of its GDP on
health, as opposed to 7% in the UK, and 16% in the US. French employees
pay a specific 8% of their wages for healthcare insurance, but health care is
still not free. You pay as you go and reclaim most of the cost afterwards. You
will be treated in case of emergencies without undergoing a 'wallet biopsy';
the bills come afterwards.

British Non-Residents

If you are just going on holiday to France, or planning to stay for less than
three months, don't forget to have your E111 form stamped at the post
office. The leaflet T6, available from post offices, contains both an application form for the E111 (for the post office's records), and the E111 itself,

a standard form for the whole European Union. There are plans to replace the paper E111 with an electronic smart card during 2004.

Not having the E111 can be disastrous financially if you fall ill in France. If you do need treatment, show the E111 to the doctor or clinic, who must be *conventionné*, i.e. part of the French state system. You will then be able to reclaim up to 75% of the costs of treatment. The E111 is not a blank cheque to use the French healthcare system. It runs out after three months, by which time you should be paying into the French social security system. If you make several trips a year to France, you can keep the same E111. It is advisable to take out health insurance anyway for trips abroad: a stay in a French hospital can cost up to £2,000 a day in the case of major surgery.

If you forget to apply for the E111 before you leave, the International Services section of the Inland Revenue will send it to you: International Services, Longbenton, Newcastle upon Tyne NE98 1ZZ (☎ 0845-915 4811 *or= +44 191 225 4811 from abroad; fax 0845 915 7800 *or= +44 191 225 7800 from abroad). Allow one month for International Services to process your application. Details are also available on the Inland Revenue website: www.inlandrevenue.gov.uk/nic/intserv/osc.htm.

Once you are a permanent resident in France, you are no longer entitled to use the National Health Service free of charge in the UK, but in practice, the French authorities allow Brits to go on relying on the NHS and the E111 for about 18 months after their arrival; this is one case where theory and practice do not match. Pensioners may continue to use the NHS in the UK longer than those who are working in France; contact the Department of Work and Pensions for further details (www.dwp.gov.uk). If you work in France, but pay National Insurance contributions in the UK, it is also possible to go on using the NHS; contact International Services at the DWP and ask for forms E106 or E128. If you are retiring to France and are entitled to a UK state pension, ask for form E121.

French Healthcare System

Paying into the social security system in France entitles you and your dependants to medical treatment, and other expenses, free of charge up to a statutory limit for each type of treatment. The contributions are collected by a departmental organisation called CPAM, which then distributes the money to different *caisses*, or sickness funds, depending on your profession. Once you pay in you will receive the all-important *Carte Vitale*, a green smart card that stores all your administrative details on a microchip. The *Carte* does not hold any medical details, nor is it a payment card. You can read the information on it by inserting it into a *borne vitale* at any surgery or hospital.

Social security generally pays 75-90% of the cost of treatment, and 35-70% of the cost of medicines. The full cost will be paid for serious illnesses or in specific hospital practices. Hospitals and general practices can charge as much as they want for their services, but in every area groups of doctors agree to charge fees within the limits set by social security. Doctors who follow these agreements are known as *conventionné*. Rates for treatment are publicised on Minitel.

Private Health Insurance

To cover the shortfall in the cost of treatment, it is advisable to have additional private health insurance. Most French have additional insurance, but many foreign residents do not. Different professions have special plans – known as *complémentaires* or *mutuelles* – or your employer may pay for this. Well-known British-based health insurers include BUPA and Expacare. You need to verify that the insurer has an existing link with French social security and that they offer adequate cover. Once you are resident in France you have to have a social security number; private health cover taken out in another country does not exempt you from paying social security contributions. The Brittany-based insurer, Agence Eaton, has bilingual staff and deals with all kinds of insurance.

When choosing additional health insurance, it is important to check whether the insurer already has a direct link with the social security office in France, which will speed up reimbursement of your costs. Costly dental treatment is mainly paid by the patient; a good *complémentaire* will refund more than the state scheme. The situation is similar with opticians. Opticians will always accept payment by a *complémentaire*.

If you pass retirement age in France, you will only pay a small contribution from your pension for sickness cover, but you will still have to pay the difference between the cost of treatment and the amount refunded, unless you have a chronic illness.

Health Insurers

Agence Eaton: Continent Assurances, 28 rue du Lt.-Col. Maury, BP
  285, 56008 Vannes Cedex; ☎ 02 97 47 31 97; fax 02 97 47 98 94;
  www.french-insurance.com.
British United Provident Association (BUPA): Russell House, Russell
  Mews, Brighton BN1 2NR; ☎ 01273-208181; www.bupa-int.com.
Expacare Insurance Services: Columbia Centre, Market Street, Bracknell,
  Berkshire RG12 1JG; ☎ 01344-381650; fax 01344-381690; e-mail
  info@expacare.net; www.expacare.net.
Goodhealth Primary International Ltd: Springfield House, Springfield Rd,
  Horsham, West Sussex RH12 2RG; ☎ 04 94 40 66 70 (France).

Doctors and Dentists

Once you know you are going to remain in France, do find a local doctor
and dentist. Although it is not essential to be registered with a doctor
first, it is easier if you know in advance who to go to. Ask them if they are
conventionné and what their charges are. Doctors are highly educated and
most will be able to speak some English; other expatriates can tell you who
is the most appropriate. The local *commissariat de police* can tell you where
to find a doctor out of office hours.

Up until 2002, after your course of treatment was finished the
doctor gave you a receipt – *feuille de soins* – which you then sent to
the local Caisse Primaire d'Assurance Maladie to get your refund. The
pharmacist would attach a price tag (*vignette*) to your prescription
(*ordonnance*) for you to send to your health insurer. A new electronic
system has been brought in which speeds up the process of reimbursing
your payments. The paperwork follows later. Your details are registered
on your electronic smart card – the *Carte Vitale* – which is read when
you enter a hospital or surgery; your refund should be automatically
credited to your bank account within five working days. In some areas
the electronic system is not yet in use.

Chemists. Pharmacists (*pharmaciens*) are highly trained and can give basic
healthcare advice. The French consume excessive amounts of pills and
remedies and there is much wringing of hands about this, but somehow it
is always other people who are using too many pills. Just look in any French
medicine cupboard. The main problem lies in the fact that the amount
of pills prescribed is often more than what is required for the course of
treatment.

As a basic principle, medicines for life-threatening conditions are free,
even where the condition is chronic, which is good news for the retired.
For run-of-the-mill problems the refund rate may be as low as 35%; some

items will not be refunded at all. There are schemes in operation allowing you to obtain prescription medicines out of hours. There will be a hole in the wall where you can insert your *Carte Vitale*.

SHOPPING

If you come from northern Europe or North America one of the first things you will notice in France is the way shopkeepers deal with customers. The customer is not king here; you may feel that the shopkeeper is doing you a favour by letting you into their private domain. Servile behaviour does not come naturally to the French. In department stores the situation is even worse, because the workers know that they would have to physically assault a customer before anyone would sack them. Being asked to open up your bag for inspection at the checkout in supermarkets can also be very disconcerting for Brits. Opening hours are another bugbear. Smaller shops can only open on five days a week, so many opt to close on Monday and stay open on Saturday, which gives rural towns a strangely dead atmosphere on a Monday. This also includes estate agents.

The best advice is to appeal to the shop assistant's more helpful side: simply saying 'Pourriez vous m'aider, madame/monsieur' will work wonders, rather than 'Avez-vous un . . .'. The French love to help anyone in trouble, especially if you address them respectfully. It is not necessary to thank shop assistants too effusively. It is normal to wish them a 'nice day' (*bonne journée*).

The retail scene in France is very different from the UK. While there are supermarkets (*supermarchés*) – smaller than in the UK – and hypermarkets (*hypermarchés*), there are few shopping malls. Most French would like to keep a personal relationship with their local shopkeepers, with the idea that they will get a better, or at least friendlier, service.

Relative Prices. Comparisons of retail prices in different countries are notoriously unreliable: the data that exist are between London and Paris, neither of which is at all typical. Most Britons find that the cost of living in France is about 15-20% lower than in the UK, outside of the very expensive areas of Paris and the Côte d'Azur. Groceries in London and Paris cost about the same, with notable exceptions such as alcohol and French specialities like olive oil. Petrol is more or less the same price in both countries. The cheapness of France is largely attributable to the current strength of sterling: when the pound was only worth 7.5 francs back in 1995, France was very expensive indeed. All the signs are that sterling will go down against the euro as Britain ponders whether to enter Euroland. The only goods that are particularly expensive in France are books and newspapers. Foreign imported goods have always been more expensive than French ones, although the difference is tending to diminish.

The French equivalent of VAT – the *Taxe sur la Valeur Ajoutée* (TVA) is charged on most goods and services at 19.6%, while some items – including food, travel, hotels, books, non-reimbursable medicines and utilities – are only subject to 5.5%. There is a 2.1% super-reduced rate on magazines, reimbursable medicines, and TV licences.

Electrical Goods. If you are moving over to France you will have to consider whether to bring electrical equipment with you or not. The general opinion is that French electrical goods are not that cheap and are of worse quality than British ones. Old plugs can literally disintegrate so you need to be very careful if you are using old equipment. The drawback with British electrical equipment is that it will be difficult to repair or find spare parts for, so it seems best to go with the French goods even if they do not last as long.

Furniture is best bought in France; there are amazing bargains to be found if you are willing to travel around and look in at the *brocanteurs* (second-hand merchants). Even brand-new furniture is cheaper than in England, so there may not be much point in bringing it over from home. In any case, English furniture may look out of place in your southern French retreat.

Bargain Hunting. If you are looking for a bargain, the best place is a factory shop (*magasin d'usine*), where you can buy well-known brands at a large discount. *The Factory Shop Guide to Northern France*, by Gillian Cutress and Rolf Stricker, is a useful guide, but out of print at the time of writing. The French equivalent, *Guide des Magasins d'Usine,* by Marie-Paule Dousset, is a useful alternative. In Paris, Anne and Alain Riou's *Paris Pas Cher* (published annually) has become a sort of shopper's bible, and includes 500 restaurants and every other conceivable type of retailing, graded with Eiffel Tower symbols.

MEDIA

Newspapers

The newspaper scene in France bears no comparison to that in the UK. The national newspapers have a small circulation; regional newspapers are often more popular. At the weekend you will have to make do with one paper for Saturday and Sunday, or Sunday and Monday. The only Sunday newspaper comparable to those in England is *Le Figaro*. The highbrow *Le Monde* is pretty dry, and does not even have photographs in the news section, mainly consisting of long and well-written essays on current topics of interest. *Libération* is a more colourful leftwing offering, and then there is *L'Humanité* founded by Jean-Paul Sartre. The daily *Le Figaro* represents conservative opinion. The business daily *Les Échos* is considered right-wing. Regional newspapers concentrate on local news and sport; they are useful for property adverts.

The French produce good magazines: apart from the original celebrity glossy *Paris-Match* there are excellent general interest mags like *Express, Nouvel Observateur* and *Le Point.*

For expats, trying to get hold of your British newspaper on the day of publication is a frustrating exercise. While there is no problem in Paris or northwest France, elsewhere the distribution network is often not up to delivering a British newspaper on the same day. Even more annoying than having to read a paper that is one day old, is the fact that supplements are removed to save on weight. The US *International Herald Tribune* is available all over France on the day of publication.

There are now some decent English magazines for expats in France, the best being the monthly *The News* which has useful analyses of French happenings. The following is a list:

French Times: Quarterly published from Dordogne; www.french-times.com.
FUSAC. Leading free weekly in Paris; stands for France-USA Contacts; www.fusac.fr.
The Irish Eyes. Free monthly in Paris; www.irisheyes.fr.
New Riviera-Côte d'Azur. Glossy up-market magazine published every three months; e-mail newriviera@smc-france.fr.
The News: Monthly. www.the-news.fr; essential reading for expat residents.
Paris Voice: Free monthly. www.parisvoice.com.
Riviera Reporter: Monthly. www.riviera-reporter.com.
Riviera Times: Monthly. www.mediterra.com.

CRIME

Taken as a whole, there is less crime in France than in the UK, but what there is is heavily concentrated in certain areas such as Paris and the Riviera. There is a widespread feeling that *'l'insécurité'* is rising, based on the idea that crime is increasing along with immigration and asylum seekers. The result was to make the neo-fascist Front National France's second party ahead of the socialists at the presidential elections in 2002. The new centre-right government has got the message and appointed a tough new interior minister, Nicolas Sarkozy, to show that it is serious about cracking down on crime.

Crime rates vary considerably around France. There are villages where there is hardly any crime at all, and other places where it is dangerous to go out at night. Paris has the worst rate, with 147 crimes per 1000 inhabitants in 2001, but these are heavily concentrated in the depressed areas such as St-Denis. Nice and the Côte d'Azur are not that far behind; muggings are a serious problem. Strasbourg, Mulhouse, Lyon, Bordeaux, Marseille and La Rochelle have very high crime rates. The presence of large numbers of tourists generates a lot of crime in the summer. The Riviera has a heavy concentration of private security staff to protect the rich, but this does not help the average person on the street. Crime rates are publicised by the magazine *Le Point* in its annual survey of French towns: see www.lepoint.fr.

For more information on anti-crime measures, caretakers and insurance see under chapter 4, *Finance,* and chapter 9 *Services.*

THE FRENCH LANGUAGE

The French are exceedingly proud and possessive about their language, which is the primary vehicle for spreading French culture around the world. The 20th century saw French lose its predominant position as the international language of diplomacy. The younger generation of French have given up some of their feelings of snobbery about their language; they are happy to use British and American expressions, which are creeping into the media more and more, while the Académie Française regularly issues edicts banning these linguistic intruders.

The prospective Anglo-Saxon resident should not imagine that this is a language that is about to throw in the towel in the face of English language imperialism. Many British visitors are irritated or puzzled to find that when they address the locals in their own language they will often reply in English, flatly refusing to carry on a conversation in French with you. They are just trying to be helpful: they reason that the conversation will be clearer if they speak in English, because clarity in expressing oneself is of primary importance here.

On the whole, the average Brit or American tends to overestimate their own French-speaking abilities. The fact that English is full of French loanwords which came in from 1066 onwards, leads them to believe that they can instantly understand French without studying it. Most of the commonly used French words used in English don't actually mean the same in French as they do in English and there are whole dictionaries devoted to explaining these 'false friends'. The same holds true for French. One is reminded of a current tourist brochure that describes southwest France as 'a land of evasions'.

The French are realistic about their ability to speak foreign languages.

They regard precision of language as paramount, and feel uncertain about what they are really saying when they speak in another language. Needless to say, if you speak French well, and can talk knowledgeably about French literature, you will earn respect as someone who is 'cultivé'. It cannot be emphasised too much how important learning French is: people who have given up and gone back to the UK often cite not speaking the language as one of the main reasons for their disenchantment.

Where to Learn French

Learning a foreign language should be fun. If it isn't, then you might as well not bother. Unfortunately, the trend in British schools for many years has been to teach French without teaching grammar – a prerequisite for learning any language. Brits and Americans also need to pay attention to their pronunciation. It is vitally important to realise that French has no diphthongs (pairs of vowels, of which there are many in English); it also makes little distinction between long and short vowels. Taking care to pronounce French vowels correctly makes all the difference between mangling the language and sounding reasonably authentic.

The French state expends vast sums on trying to promote French abroad; if you are lucky, there may be an Alliance Française near you offering evening classes (they also exist in the USA). Your local College of Further Education, or Community Education Centre will certainly offer courses in French; the price can be as low as £120 per year. It is a good idea to aim for an examination, such as an A Level, so that you have some objective measure of your actual competence. If you are in France, it is worth asking at the local *mairie* to see if there are any low-priced courses available.

These days there are numerous courses available on cassette, video, CD-Rom and internet, which can be useful in supporting one's learning programme, even if they can't take the place of a native speaker. Courses that make absurd claims, such as 'You'll be speaking fluently in ten days,' may not be bad courses, but you do need to know how to make the best possible use of them. If you have some notion of language learning methods, the cheapest and most effective way of learning is to advertise for a language exchange partner: you offer English in exchange for French. Simply listening to a French person speaking, and getting them to explain what you don't understand, can work wonders. In some places in France there are discussion groups where French and English-speakers get together to speak first in one and then the other language (see Parler-Parlor below). If you do have to pay for language tuition, try to tape the lesson on a mini-disc or cassette so that you can go over it later.

With written French, one is confronted with an absurdly complicated system of accents, which was originally devised by the Académie Française in the 18th century to prevent people from changing the pronunciation of words. The great Enlightenment writers like Voltaire got by perfectly well with one accent, but they are now here to stay. Unlike with Italian or Spanish, the accents may not be ignored; they serve a useful purpose in telling you how the word should be pronounced, and distinguishing one word from another.

A good dictionary is a must: Collins Robert is by far the best. It is best to buy a new dictionary, because the language is changing so fast. You can more or less dispense with printed dictionaries if you have the internet: the website www.yourdictionary.com has several excellent online dictionaries which cover all sorts of specialised topics. The best one is the Canadian www.granddictionnaire.com.

Useful Addresses

Alliance Française: 101 bvd Raspail, 75270 Paris; ☎ 01 42 84 90 00; e-mail info@alliancefr.org; www.alliance.fr.org.

Alliance Française de Londres: French Courses, 6 Porter St, London W1U 6DD; ☎ 020-7224 1865; e-mail fbaf@clara.co.uk; www.alliancefranc aise.org.uk.

The French Institute: Studies in France, 17 Queensberry Place, London SW7 2DT; 020-7073 1350; www.institut.ambafrance.org.uk.

Linguaphone: 111 Upper Richmond Rd, London SW15 2TJ; ☎ 020-8333 4898; www.linguaphone.co.uk, www.linguaphone.com/usa.

Parler Parlor: e-mail info@parlerparlor.com; www.parlerparlor.com.

Language Manners

As has already been said, the French take their language very seriously. They will quickly put you in your place if you try to make out that your French is better than it really is. In order not to sound like an uncouth yob, there are certain ground rules to observe. In the first place, you should address anyone you don't know as *Monsieur* or *Madame*, even if you are talking to the local drunk in the park. *Mademoiselle* is quite OK for someone under 16, but otherwise stick to *Madame*. On initial acquaintance, you should always start with *vous* rather than *tu* (meaning 'you') unless everyone around is using *tu*. Immigrants may address everyone as *tu* (the verb is *tutoyer*), but it is best not to copy them. With people of your own age and social grouping, the transition to *tu* should happen quite quickly. If everyone around you is addressing each other as *tu* it will seem odd if you don't do the same. With people of the opposite sex you should be more careful, in case you appear over-familiar. If you look very young, older people may address you as *tu* and you will reply using *vous*.

The use of the more respectful *vous* – the verb is *vouvoyer* – is also rather loaded. With strangers you must use *vous*. If you continue to use *vous* with social acquaintances then you are keeping your distance. If you address your wife and children as *vous*, then people may think you have had a serious domestic rift, or perhaps you are just a mad foreigner. Once you start using *tu* you cannot go back to *vous*, although it is quite possible that in the course of an evening people will address you as *tu* and then go back to *vous* the following day.

French Letters

Although the expression raises a smile – the French have got their revenge by calling a condom a *capote anglaise* – writing letters in French is no laughing matter. A foreigner who wants to write a formal letter in French is best advised to use a model letter such as can be found in *330 Modèles de Lettres et de Contrats* (publ. Prat, 2002). It pays to be careful when writing formal letters; the most crucial part is to get the salutation and the close right. You should never begin a letter *Cher Monsieur* or *Chère Madame*, unless you are on friendly terms with the addressee. The salutation with officials and business people is *Monsieur* or *Madame*. If they have a title it is best to use it. One of the oddities of titles is that some of them remain masculine even when used for women: thus *Madame le Professeur, Madame le Notaire, Madame le Docteur*. On the other hand, you can say *la secrétaire* as well as *le secrétaire*. Some titles have feminine forms: *Madame la Directrice*.

It is also crucial to get the ending right. There are literally dozens of permutations of endings which can run to a whole tortuous sentence. The safest one is: 'Recevez, Monsieur (or Madame), l'assurance de mes salutations distinguées.' Some people avoid using formulas which substitute 'sentiments' for 'salutations' with people of the opposite sex. A more informal ending is 'Cordialement', but you can't use this the first time you write to someone.

SUMMARY OF HOUSING

Until recently, it was reasonably accurate to say that the French are less concerned about spending money on their homes than the northern Europeans. This is no longer true, and the French spend a greater percentage of their household income on housing than the British. There has been a strong shift from renting to owning in recent year, although the French have not yet caught up with the British. Some 62% of dwellings are owner-occupied. Of the 38% that are rented, 16% are social housing, as opposed to 21% in the UK. The state promotes housebuilding with all kinds of subsidised loans and incentives to buy-to-let, but coupled with strict rental controls.

On the face of it, France has plentiful housing, and is building new housing at a far faster rate than the UK although the two countries have approximately the same population: 320,000 new units per year as opposed to 170,000 in the UK. There are 2 million empty or abandoned housing units: some 6.9% of the housing stock. The high costs associated with buying and selling property discourage people from moving too often. All of the foregoing factors mean that property prices are not likely to rise that fast. The last two years have seen unusually high rises; 9% in 2001 and 5% in 2002. This is related to low interest rates and regional factors, and is not likely to last. Property is still very cheap by British standards. There is a general movement of the population away from the northeast and centre towards the west coast and the Riviera. It is the migration of the population, and the trend for more people to live alone that has created housing shortages, rather than a lack of houses.

The emptying out of the countryside – or *'désertification'* as it is called – is tending to be reversed, as more workers choose to live out of town and commute long distances to work. There is also a new type of countryside dweller, the telecottager, which along with an influx of artisans and the tourism business will see some areas revitalised. The less popular parts of the countryside, basically central France, will continue to lose their native population. Every year some 100-150 villages are abandoned, and there are probably not enough outsiders to take their place. France is a land of second homes: there are some 2.6 million of them. Of these about 450,000 or more belong to Britons, 140,000 to the Dutch, and similar numbers to Germans, Belgians and Swiss.

PUBLIC HOLIDAYS AND LOCAL FESTIVALS

France does not have an inordinate number of public holidays; they all commemorate something, rather than being just bank holidays.

PUBLIC HOLIDAYS	
1 January	New Year's Day
Easter Monday (*Pâques*)	as UK
1 May	Labour Day (*Fête du Travail*)
8 May	Victory in Europe Day
May	Ascension Day
May/June	Whitsun (*Pentecôte*)
14 July	Bastille Day
15 August	Assumption
1 November	All Saints Day
11 November	Remembrance Day
25 December	Christmas Day

Festivals

France has an extraordinary number of festivals each year. Many of them are put on to promote tourism in remote areas. The French love any excuse for a party and they know how to put on a good show. Festivals are important for anyone who is thinking of running *gîtes* or *chambres d'hôte* as a way of pulling in the punters. There are thousands of concerts, plays, happenings and festivals advertised on the internet on sites such as: www.culture.fr, www.francefestivals.com, www.festivalsaoste.com, www.viafrance.com – and on tourist office websites. The following is only a small selection of what is available. The phone numbers are sometimes only in use during the month before the festival.

FESTIVALS IN FRANCE			
Month	**Festival**	**Telephone**	**Website**
January	Ice Sculpture Competition. Valloire, Savoie.	04 79 59 03 96	www.valloire.net
	St Blaise's Festival of local produce, grapes and folklore, Alpes-Maritimes. Continues into February.	04 93 12 34 56	www.alpes-azur.com/vsa
	Foire Grasse, Limoges, Haute Vienne. Foie gras, truffles, goose, duck products. Also February.	03 55 34 46 87	www.tourismelimoges.com
	Journée de la Truffe-Truffles Day, Uzès, Gard.	04 66 22 68 88	www.ville-uzes.fr
February	International Festival of Short Films in Clermont-Ferrand.	04 93 12 34 50	www.clermont-filmfest.com
	Carnaval, Nice.	04 93 92 82 82	www.carnavaldenice.net
	Fête du Citron-Lemon Festival, Menton, Alpes-Maritimes.	04 92 41 76 76	www.feteducitron.com
March	International Carnival, Mulhouse, Alsace.	03 89 35 48 48	www.ot.ville-mulhouse.fr
	Grenoble Jazz Festival.	04 76 51 00 04	www.jazzgrenoble.com
April	Laughing Spring Festival of Humour, Toulouse.	05 62 21 23 24	www.printemps-du-rire.com
	Musicora Classical Music Festival, Paris.	01 49 53 27 00	www.lesalondelamusique.com
May	Cannes Film Festival.	01 53 59 61 00	www.festival-cannes.fr
	St Émilion Open Door Days, Gironde.	05 57 55 50 55	www.saint-emilion-tourisme.com

	Chocolate Days, Bayonne, Pyrénées Atlantiques.	05 59 46 01 46	www.bayonne-toursime.com
	Wine And Food Festival, Plombières, Vosges.	03 29 66 01 30	www.plombieres-les-bains.com
June	Summer in Bourges Music Festival, Bourges, Cher.	02 48 24 93 32	www.ville-bourges.fr
	International Garden Festival, Chaumont-sur-Loire, Loir-et-Cher.	02 54 20 99 22	www.chaumont-jardins.com
	Jazz en Franche-Comté.	03 81 83 39 09	www.besancon.com
	Bordeaux Fête Le Vin-Wine Festival.		www.bordeaux-fete-le-vin.com
	Fête de la Tarasque, Tarascon, Provence. Folklore, concerts, bullfighting.	04 90 91 03 52	www.visitprovence.com
	Vinexpo, Bordeaux. Wine and spirits exhibition.	05 56 56 00 22	www.vinexpo.fr
July	Festival de Cornouaille-Celtic Festival, Quimper, Brittany.	02 98 55 53 53	www.festival-cornouaille.com
	La Félibrée-Occitan Festival, Dordogne.	05 53 07 12 12	www.felibree.fr.st
	Fête de l'Agneau-Lamb Festival, Sisteron, Alpes-de-Haute-Provence.	04 92 61 36 50	www.provenceweb.fr
	Festival International de Folklore, Gap, Alpes-de-Haute-Provence.	04 92 52 33 73	http://paysgavot.free.fr/festival
	Fête des Géants-Festival of Giants, Douai, Nord.	03 20 14 57 57	crt-nordpasdecalais.fr
	Les Tombées de la Nuit, Rennes, Brittany. Theatre, music, dance.	02 99 67 11 11	www.ville-rennes.fr/tdn
	Festival Européen du Pain-European Bread Festival, Brantôme, Périgord.	05 53 05 80 52	www.ville-brantome.com
	Bataille de Castillon, Périgord. Spectacular re-enactment of 1453 battle. Also August.	05 57 40 14 53	www.batailledecastillon.com
	Festival d'Avignon, Provence. Also August.	04 90 14 14 14	www.festival-avignon.com
August	Inter-Celtic Festival, Lorient, Brittany.	02 97 21 24 29	www.festival-interceltique.fr
	Mimos International Mime Festival, Périgueux, Dordogne.	05 53 53 18 71	www.ville-perigueux.fr/mimos
	Tournois de Joutes-Water Jousting, Sète, Hérault.	04 67 74 71 71	www.ville-sete.fr/tourisme

	Fête de la Lavande-Lavender Festival, Digne, Hautes Alpes.	04 92 36 62 62	www.ot-dignelesbains.fr
	Feria-Catalan Fiesta, Collioure, Pyrénées Orientales.	04 68 82 15 47	www.collioure.com
	Jazz à Montauban, Tarn-et-Garonne.	05 63 20 46 72	www.jazzmontauban.com
September	Fêtes Médiévales, Arles-sur-Tech, Pyrénées-Orientales.	04 68 39 12 22	www.arles-sur-tech.fr
	International Music Festival, Besançon, France-Comté.	03 81 25 05 80	www.besancon.com
	European Sand-Yachting Championships, La Barre-de-Monts, Vendée.	02 51 68 51 83	www.ville-labarredemonts.fr
	World Puppet Festival, Charleville-Mézières, Ardennes.	03 24 59 94 94	www.marionnettes.com
October	Octobre en Normandie; throughout major cities of Normandy. Starts September.	02 32 10 87 07	www.octobre-en-normandie.com
	Fête des Vendanges-Grape Picking Festival, St Émilion, Gironde.	05 57 55 28 28	www.saint-emilion-tourisme.com
November	Jazz dans les Feuilles, Côtes d'Armor, Brittany.	02 96 78 89 24	www.jazzdanslesfeuilles.com
	Journées Mycologiques-Mushroom Festival, Entrevaux, Alpes-Maritimes.	04 93 05 46 73	www.entrevaux.info
	Fête de l'Olivier, Manosque, Haute Provence.	04 92 78 68 80	www.provenceweb.fr
	Salon International du Livre Gourmand, Périgueux, Dordogne. Cookery book fair.	05 53 53 10 63	www.ville-perigueux.fr/SILG
December	Fête aux Santons, Marseille, and Provence. Nativity crib figures.	04 91 13 89 00	www.marseille-tourisme.com

CONVERSION CHART

LENGTH (NB 12inches = 1 foot, 10 mm = 1 cm, 100 cm = 1 metre)

inches	1	2	3	4	5	6	9	12
cm	2.5	5	7.5	10	12.5	15.2	23	30

cm	1	2	3	5	10	20	25	50	75	100
inches	0.4	0.8	1.2	2	4	8	10	20	30	39

WEIGHT (NB 14lb = 1 stone, 2240 lb = 1 ton, 1,000 kg = 1 metric tonne)

lb	1	2	3	5	10	14	44	100	2246
kg	0.45	0.9	1.4	2.3	4.5	6.4	20	45	1016

kg	1	2	3	5	10	25	50	100	1000
lb	2.2	4.4	6.6	11	22	55	110	220	2204

DISTANCE

mile	1	5	10	20	30	40	50	75	100	150
km	1.6	8	16	32	48	64	80	120	161	241

km	1	5	10	20	30	40	50	100	150	200
mile	0.6	3.1	6.2	12	19	25	31	62	93	124

VOLUME

1 litre = 0.2 UK gallons   1 UK gallon = 4.5 litres

1 litre = 0.26 US gallons   1 US gallon = 3.8 litres

CLOTHES

UK	8	10	12	14	16	18	20
Europe	36	38	40	42	44	46	48
USA	6	8	10	12	14	18	

SHOES

UK	3	4	5	6	7	8	9	10	11
Europe	36	37	38	39	40	41/42	43	44	45
USA	2.5	3.3	4.5	5.5	6.5	7.5	8.5	9.5	10.5

RESIDENCE AND ENTRY

CHAPTER SUMMARY

- ○ Although France is in the EU, EU nationals still require a residence permit to stay for more than three months.
- ○ No one has the right to remain indefinitely in France unless they can show that they have sufficient funds to support themselves.
- ○ Applications for a residence permit have to be accompanied by at least eight personal documents, but it is no longer necessary to make official translations in advance.
- ○ You will need to show proof of where you are staying.
- ○ You need to know the names, dates and places of birth of your parents and grandparents for many official documents in France.
- ○ The residence permit has to be renewed periodically.
- ○ US citizens have to apply in advance for a long-stay visa, and complete eight copies of the same form.
- ○ EU citizens do not require a work permit.
- ○ If you want to start a business in France, you will have to register with the chamber of commerce, and follow a compulsory training course.
- ○ **French Nationality.** Children born in France to foreign parents can claim French citizenship at the age of 18.

France officially discourages immigration – there may be anything up to 3 million illegal immigrants in the country – but allows some categories of people in, including UK nationals. While France is part of the European Union, there are still formalities to be gone through if a citizen of another EU country wants to settle down here. British citizens are entitled to live and work in France, as long as they obtain the *carte de séjour*, or residence permit. For non-EU citizens the situation is a lot more complicated: in principle, anyone from outside the EU who wants to remain in France other than as a tourist has to arrange their residence permit before going to France.

OBTAINING A RESIDENCE PERMIT

EU Nationals

Nationals of other EU countries (Austria, Belgium, Denmark, Eire, Finland, Germany, Greece, Italy, Luxembourg, the Netherlands, Portugal, Spain, Sweden and the United Kingdom) have the right to settle permanently in France, under certain conditions. Swiss citizens have similar rights. In the case of the UK, your passport must state that you are a 'British Citizen', meaning you have the right of abode in the UK. If you have another type of British passport, contact a French consulate in your home country to find out whether you can move to France.

Travelling to France is easy enough for British citizens. The French immigration authorities may not even look at your passport. There are French immigration police at the Eurostar terminal in Waterloo looking for undesirables trying to get to France, but British passport holders should have nothing to worry about. Once in France, you have the right to remain for three months to look for a job, without registering with the police or any other authorities. There will be no stamp in your passport, so it is not that easy for anyone to know how long you have been in France.

If you plan to look for a job, or want to stay more than three months, you should apply for a *carte de séjour* (residence permit), before the three months are up. In the first instance, go along to the nearest *préfecture de police* (police station), or *mairie* (town hall or municipal office) to apply. It can take several months to obtain. In the meantime you will be given a receipt (*récépissé*) which will enable you to legally take up a job. Britons who own property in France, and want to stay there for longer than three months at a time are officially also required to have a *carte de séjour:* if you come and go several times a year, you can manage without it.

Documents. A number of documents are required to apply for a *carte de séjour:* a valid passport, four passport photographs, a birth certificate, and a marriage certificate, if you have one. If you are a single parent with dependent children, you will need proof that your children can leave the UK. The authorities may require you to have your birth and marriage certificate officially translated and legalised, although this seems to be happening less and less. Certainly if you get married in France you will need a legalised translation of your birth certificate. Even original British documents are not necessarily considered legally valid, and translations have to be legalised. If you use a translator in France, they must be sworn in, or *assermenté*, all of which adds to the cost, of course. Any old translator from the yellow pages will not do. Finding a translator who is *assermenté* is difficult in the UK so you are best advised to find a translator through a British consulate in

France. Documents can be legalised by a French vice-consul, i.e. stamped and signed, in the UK. In France, documents are legalised by a notaire. If you are in southwestern France (e.g. Dordogne or Lot) your nearest consulate is in Bordeaux. It is advisable to have several copies made of documents and have them all legalised at the same time, in case you need them in the future. At some point you are also likely to be asked for copies of your parents' and grandparents' birth certificates: these can easily be obtained from the Family Records Centre in London (☎0870-243 7788; e-mail certificate.services@ons.gov.uk; www.familyrecords.gov.uk).

British Consulates in France

British Consulate: 18bis rue d'Anjou, 75008 Paris; ☎ 01 44 51 31 00; fax 01 44 51 31 27; e-mail consulare-mailpavis2@fco.gov.uk. Covers: Aube, Calvados, Cher, Côtes-Du-Nord, Eure, Eure-et-Loir, Finistère, Ille-et-Vilaine, Indre, Indre-et-Loire, Loir-et-Cher, Loire, Loire-Atlantique, Loiret, Maine-et-Loire, Manche, Marne, Haute-Marne, Mayenne, Meurthe-et-Moselle, Meuse, Morbihan, Moselle, Nièvre, Oise, Orne, Bas-Rhin, Haut-Rhin, Sarthe, Paris (Seine), Seine-Maritime, Seine-et-Marne, Yvelines, Vendée, Vosges, Yonne, Essonne, Hauts-de-Seine, Seine-St Denis, Val de Marne, Val d'Oise and DOM-TOM. Opening hours: Monday/Wednesday/Thursday/Friday, 9.30am-12.30pm and 2.30-5pm. On Tuesdays the consulate is open from 9.30am to 4.30pm without a break. Emergency number: 01 44 51 31 00.

British Consulate: 353 bvd du Président Wilson, 33073 Bordeaux; ☎ 05 57 22 21 10; fax 05 56 08 33 12; e-mail postmaster.bordeaux@fco.gov.uk. Covers: Ariège, Aveyron, Charente, Charente-Maritime, Corrèze, Creuse, Dordogne, Haute-Garonne, Gers, Gironde, Landes, Lot, Lot-et-Garonne, Pyrenées-Atlantiques, Hautes-Pyrénées, Deux-Sèvres, Tarn, Tarn-et-Garonne, Vienne and Haute-Vienne. Emergency number: 06 85 06 38 32. Opening hours Monday to Friday, 9am-12 noon and 2-5pm. Emergency number: 06 85 06 38 32.

British Consulate: 11 Square Dutilleul, 59800 Lille; ☎ 03 20 12 82 72; fax 03 20 54 88 16; e-mail consular.lille@fco.gov.uk. Covers: Nord, Pas-de-Calais, Somme, Aisne and Ardennes. Opening hours: Monday to Friday, 9.30am-12.30pm and 2-5pm. Emergency number: 03 20 54 79 82.

British Consulate: 24 rue Childebert, 69002 Lyon; ☎ 04 72 77 81 70; fax 04 72 77 81 79; e-mail britishconsulate.mail@ordilyon.fr. Covers the regions of Auvergne, Bourgogne, Franche-Comté and Rhône-Alpes. Opening hours Monday to Friday, 9am-12.30pm and 2-5.30pm. Emergency number: 04 72 77 81 78.

British Consulate: 24 ave du Prado, 13006 Marseille; ☎ 04 91 15 72 10;

fax 04 91 37 47 06; MarseilleConsular.marseille@fco.gov.uk. Covers: Pyrénées Orientales, Aude, Hérault, Lozère, Gard, Vaucluse, Bouches-du-Rhône, Var, Alpes-Maritimes, Alpes-de-Haute-Provence, Corsica and Monaco. Opening hours: Monday to Friday, 9am-12 noon and 2-5pm. Emergency number: 04 91 15 72 10.

Financial Resources. As well as all the above, you need to have proof of financial resources. If you already have work, or have been offered a job, you can use your contract of employment; you can also ask your employer to make out a *Certificat d'Emploi* on headed paper, confirming your passport number, the date you started work, and your salary. If you plan to be self-employed, you will need some proof that you are a member of a professional body and that you have registered with the local *chambre de métiers* or *chambre de commerce*. If you are planning to stay in France without working, you will need bank statements, again witnessed by a notary. If your income is less than the French minimum wage or SMIC – about £8,000 a year – you will probably be refused a *carte de séjour*. The authorities seem to accept that two people can live together on this amount. Whether you own your property or not is irrelevant.

Proof of Residence. If you have bought a property, your notary can supply a *certificat* giving proof of residence. If you rent, then rent receipts will be adequate proof. If you are staying with friends, and not paying rent, then your friend will need to supply an *attestation d'hébergement* and proof of their identity. Naturally, if you are paying someone rent and they are not declaring it, then no *attestation d'hébergement* is likely to be forthcoming. Further proof of residence includes phone or electricity bills (from EDF/GDF) with your name and address.

Local officials can react in very different ways to applications for a *carte de séjour*. As is the way here, much depends on the whim of the official. You need to be well-prepared, and patient if obstacles seem to be put in your way. Getting irate with the local petty officials will make future contacts a lot more difficult.

DOCUMENTS REQUIRED FOR THE *CARTE DE SÉJOUR*

- Passport, with copies of the main pages, stamped as *copie certifiée conforme* by the *préfecture* or *town hall*.
- Four passport photographs of each member of your family.
- Birth certificate, with an official translation if requested, notarised by a French Consulate or French lawyer.

- Marriage certificate/divorce papers/custody papers (officially translated and notarised only if requested).
- Certificate from the town hall stating that you are living in *concubinage notoire* if you live with a common-law partner.
- Proof of residence: *certificat* from the notary who handled your house purchase, or rent receipts, or *attestation d'hébergement* from the person you are staying with.
- Proof of entry. Your travel ticket may be sufficient; or ask the immigration police when you enter the country.
- Proof of employment.
- Proof of financial resources.
- You may be asked for proof that you have no criminal record.
- Medical certificate (for non-EU citizens).

Renewing your residence permit. The first *carte de séjour* is for one year. You need to apply for a renewal before it runs out. EU citizens will usually receive a 10-year residence permit as long as they are in regular employment in France. You will have to prove that you have paid all your taxes. The permit is then renewed again for five or ten years at a time. The same documents as above are required, except that you will not need to produce your children's or parents' birth certificates. Certain categories of residents do not automatically receive a 10-year residence permit:

- Students or anyone who has been unemployed for more than 12 months: a one-year permit. If you are still unemployed after the permit has expired it may not be renewed.
- If you become unfit to work, other rules will apply.
- Economically inactive persons (mainly pensioners): a five-year permit.

If you change address within France, you are required to inform the police in your new place of residence, so the address on your *carte de séjour* can be changed.

Remaining in France

If you have worked in France and want to stay on you should fall into one of the following categories:

- You are of pensionable age in France, and you have worked for at least the last 12 months and lived in France on a continuous basis for more than three years.
- You have lived in France on a continuous basis for more than two

years, and have stopped working as a result of permanent disablement resulting from an occupational accident or illness that entitles you to a pension paid by the relevant French body, and you fulfil other residence requirements.

O After living and working in France for three continuous years you become a frontier worker (*frontalier*) and remain resident in France.

O You come to live in France after retiring in another EU state, or you come as an economically inactive person: you need proof of income and adequate social security cover (see above).

Residence Permits for Non-EU Nationals

Non-EU citizens require a Schengen visa to enter France: normally this allows you to stay for up to three months (*visa de court séjour*). You can also ask for a multiple entry visa that allows you to remain for 90 days out of six months for up to five years (*visa de long séjour*). Citizens from some countries – in particular, the USA, Canada, Australia and New Zealand – do not need to apply for the visa in advance, it is given at the port of entry. Regulations can change, so it is wise to check before setting out. You are not allowed to look for work as a tourist in France.

WORK PERMITS

EU citizens do not require work permits; they only need to follow the same regulations as French citizens as regards self-employment and business formation. They have exactly the same rights as French workers. Non-EU citizens need to apply for a work permit well before they take up employment in France. This can only be done through an employer who has offered you a post in France. You may try to enter France as a student, au pair or trainee, which will allow you to work legally. Your local French consulate will be able to advise you. If you want to start a business in France, you will need a *carte de commerçant étranger,* obtainable through a *chambre de commerce.* For more information see the French government website: www.service-public.fr.

Useful Addresses

French Embassy in London: 58 Knightsbridge, London SW1X 7JT; ☎ 020-7201 1000; www.ambafrance-uk.org.

French Embassy: Cultural Department, 23 Cromwell Rd, London SW7 2EL; ☎ 020-7838 2055.

Visa enquiries should be sent to the French Consulate:

French Consulate: Service des Visas (Long Stay Visas), 6A Cromwell Place, PO Box 57, London SW7 2EW; ☎ 020-7838 2048. Open 9-10am for long stay visa applications only. Closed on UK bank holidays and French public holidays.

French Consulate General: General Inquiries, 21 Cromwell Rd, London SW7 2EN; ☎ 020-7838 2000; fax 020-7838 2118; www.ambafrance-uk.org. Open 9am to midday Monday to Friday; also 1.30-3.30pm Tuesday to Thursday.

French Consulate at Edinburgh & Glasgow: 11 Randolph Crescent, Edinburgh, EH3 7TT; ☎ 0131-225 7954. Open daily 9.30-11.30am for visas.

French Embassy & Consulate General: 4101 Reservoir Rd NW, Washington DC 20007; ☎ 202-944-6195; www.ambafrance-us.org.

British Embassy and Consulates in France. Documents are issued from Paris. The Consulates-General can issue forms, which you then send to the British Embassy in Paris. The Consulates-General can issue emergency passports valid for one journey. Addresses of Consulates-General are given above.

British Embassy: 35 rue du Faubourg St Honoré, 75008 Paris Cedex 08; ☎ 01 44 51 31 00; fax 01 44 51 32 34; www.amb-grandebretagne.fr.

British Consular Services Paris, 18bis rue d'Anjou, 75008 Paris; ☎ 01 44 51 31 00; fax 01 44 51 31 27.

US Embassy and Consulates

United States Embassy: 2 ave Gabriel, 75008 Paris; ☎ 01 43 12 22 22; fax 01 42 66 97 83; www.amb-usa.fr.

United States Consulate: rue St Florentin, 75001 Paris; ☎ as above.

Part II

LOCATION, LOCATION...

WHERE TO FIND YOUR IDEAL HOME

REGIONS OF FRANCE IN ALPHABETICAL ORDER

WHERE TO FIND YOUR IDEAL HOME

CHAPTER SUMMARY

- **Administrative Organisation.** France's ancient provinces were reorganised by Napoleon to combat regionalism.
- **Local Traditions.** Every area of France has its own building traditions, as well as the local cuisine and wine.
- **Prices.** Prices vary tremendously, between derelict barns that are virtually given away free, to multi-million pound mansions on the Riviera.
- **Renovation.** The supply of properties for renovation has dried up in some popular areas, while in others there have never been many properties for renovation.
- **Up-and-coming areas.** These include: Deux Sèvres, Vendée, La Creuse, Haute Vienne, Ariège, Hautes Pyrénées, and Pyrénées Orientales.
- **Exclusive Properties.** The most expensive properties are on the coast, or near ski slopes, and in central Paris.
- **Location.** The proximity of airports, motorways and TGV is a crucial factor if you want to have visitors.
- **Avoiding the Reefs.** It is strongly advised to rent a property in your chosen region for a few months to see how it is out of season.
- **Learning the Language.** Being able to speak French is the key to settling in.
- **Retirement.** It is easy to retire to France as long as you have a minimum income of £800 per month.

ADMINISTRATIVE ORGANISATION

France is divided up into 100 *départements*, or provinces, including four overseas *départements*, known as the DOM-TOM (*Départements d'Outre-Mer et Territoires d'Outre-Mer*). Each *département* has a two-figure number, used for postcodes and car licence plates. The present system of *départements* only dates back to 1789 and the French Revolution: most of them are named after rivers or mountain ranges. The new system was intended to divide the country into more or less equal-sized provinces, while discouraging anti-revolutionary regional movements. As a gesture towards reviving more of a sense of regional identity, 22 *régions* with directly elected assemblies were set up from 1972. The new rightwing government elected in 2002 has embarked on a process of decentralisation. All local *communes* now have to join up in *intercommunalités,* within the limits of their competencies, and these will come under 'supermayors'. The regions are being given more powers in the areas of culture, tourism and economic matters. The departmental prefects are still the intermediary between Paris and local administration. When one considers that there are already 56,000 intercommunal organisations in France, the potential for chaos is obvious, and the more republican-minded French are not that happy with the current government's experimentations with decentralisation.

There are in addition more than 200 *'pays'* (smaller regions) which you will be constantly reminded of as you drive around France. The locals will tell you they come from such-and-such a *pays*, not from a *département.*

The regions are considered here from the aspect of their scenic and cultural attractions, accessibility, the value of property and the likelihood of finding employment.

THE REGIONS OF FRANCE

Information Facilities

Tourism is France's biggest money-earner – generating 12% of GDP – and every region has lavish brochures on offer to advertise its uniqueness. If you can, it is worth visiting the French Government Tourist Office, where there are brochures for every part of France, otherwise you can order the information by e-mail.

Since the SNCF took it over from British Rail, Rail Europe has run from the same building as the French tourist office in London, so you can book a train ticket at the same time as looking at brochures. The main city in every region has a *Comité Régional du Tourisme* who organise information facilities. *Départements* have a *Comité Départemental du Tourisme,* which may be more informative than the regional office. Towns and cities have their own *Office du Tourisme*; in smaller places the equivalent is the local *Syndicat d'Initiative,* which may have a small welcome office, but their opening hours are generally shorter than those of the Office du Tourisme, and their function is more to promote business in general in their area. The *syndicats* are still not all on the web. For more practical information about living in France, the best starting point is the French Embassy's website: www.ambafrance-uk.org. Each *département* has its own website: just search on Conseil Général + the name of the *département*. The regional websites are under Conseil Régional.

Useful Addresses

Maison de la France Great Britain: 178 Piccadilly, London W1V OA1; ☎ 0891-244 123; fax 020-7493 6594; e-mail info@mdlf.co.uk; www.franceguide.com *or* www.tourisme.fr *or* www.tourism-office.com.

Maison de la France USA: 444 Madison Ave-16th floor, New York, NY 10022; ☎ 410-286-8310; fax 212-838-7855; e-mail info@francetourism.com; www.francetourism.com.

Maison de la France Ireland: 10 Suffolk St, Dublin 2; ☎ 1 679 0813; fax 1 679 0814; e-mail frenchtouristoffice@tinet.ie.

Maison de la France Canada: 1981 Avenue McGill College, suite 490, Montréal H3A 2W9, Canada; ☎ 514-876-9881; fax 514-845-4868; e-mail mfrance@attcanada.net.

ALSACE

CRT: 6 ave de la Marseillaise, 67005 Strasbourg; ☎03 88 25 39 81; fax 03 88 52 17 06; e-mail frachedi@tourism-alsace.com; www.tourism-alsace.com; www.strasbourg.com.
Percentage of population: 2.88%; percentage of GDP: 2.88%.

Alsace borders Germany in the northeast of France, and has its own very particular traditions, and its own Germanic language, Alsatian or Alle-manic. The locals consider themselves neither French nor German, but Alsatian. After being incorporated into France in 1681 by Louis XIV it was re-absorbed into Germany after the Prussian victory of 1870, only to be returned to France in 1918. During World War II, 140,000 young Alsatian men were conscripted into the German army to fight on the Russian front and many never returned. The use of French was also forbidden in the region for the duration of the war. These days the Alsatian language is still widely used. Lutheranism is the established church here.

There was a vogue in the 1990s for Germans to buy properties near the border and commute to work in Germany. Many of them have now gone back to live in Germany, disappointed to find that Alsace is not as Germanic as they had hoped. The French, on the other hand, go across to Germany to shop where it is easy to see that prices are cheaper because of the euro. The greatest appeal of Alsace lies in the Vosges mountains, good for skiing in winter and walking the rest of the year. Fishing and horse-riding are also popular. The region is 45% forest; the climate is fairly wet.

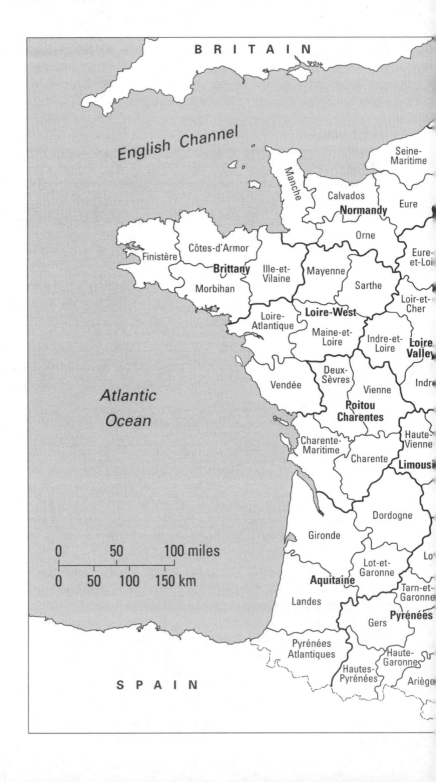

Regions and Departments of France

BELGIUM

GERMANY

LUXEMBOURG

Nord-Pas-de-Calais
Pas-de-Calais
Nord
Somme
Picardy
Oise
Aisne
Ardennes
Meuse
Moselle
Lorraine
Alsace
Paris
Seine-et-Marne
Marne
Meurthe-et-Moselle
Bas-Rhin
Région Parisienne
Paris et Région
Champagne-Ardenne
Aube
Haute-Marne
Vosges
Haut-Rhin
Loiret
Yonne
Haute-Saône
Belfort
Côte-d'Or
Franche Comté
Burgundy
Cher
Nièvre
Doubs
SWITZERLAND
Saône-et-Loire
Jura
Allier
Ain
Haute-Savoie
Creuse
Puy-de-Dôme
Loire
Rhône
Corrèze
Auvergne
Savoie & Dauphiné
Savoie
Cantal
Haute Loire
Rhône
Isère
ITALY
Ardèche
Drôme
Hautes-Alpes
Lozère
Aveyron
Gard
Vaucluse
Alpes-de-Haute-Provence
Alpes Maritimes
Côte d'Azur
Tarn
Languedoc
Provence
Bouches-du-Rhône
Var
Hérault
Aude
Haute-Corse
Pyrénées-Orientales
Corse-du-Sud

Mediterranean Sea

Alsace consists of two *départements*, Bas-Rhin (67) and Haut-Rhin (68) both bordering onto Germany, with the Rhine on the eastern side. The main city, Strasbourg (pop. 388,000), houses the plenary sessions of the European Parliament, as well as being home to the Council of Europe, but the MEPs only stay for 10 days at a time. Both Strasbourg and Mulhouse have very high crime rates. There are flights from Strasbourg to London.

Cuisine. The cooking draws heavily on the fish that are caught in the local rivers. The term *à l'alsacienne* means 'with sauerkraut', or *choucroute*. Alsace has a great tradition of producing white wine (and to a lesser extent rosé), such as Gewürztraminer, but the area is equally known for its beer, of which Kronenbourg is the best-known.

Property. The classic Alsace house has half-timbering (*fachwarik*) with a hipped and sometimes mansard roof. The massive German style with all the functional spaces under the one roof is common. Houses are generally well looked-after and tidy. For protection against the weather farm walls are sometimes covered with shingles. The town houses are similar to those over the border with Germany, typically with dormer windows, windowboxes, and decorative shutters. Generally one is limited to a choice between apartments and large houses.

There is only a limited second homes market in Alsace; houses to renovate are few and far between. Property is expensive compared with most of France. Reckon on paying a minimum of €100,000 for a 2-bed apartment.

AQUITAINE

CRT: Cité Mondiale, 23 parvis des Chartrons, 33049 Bordeaux cedex; ☎05 56 01 70 00; fax 05 56 01 70 07; e-mail tourisme@crt.cr-aquitaine.fr; www.crt.cr-aquitaine.fr; www.bordeaux-tourisme.com; Percentage of population: 4.85%; percentage of GDP: 4.24%.

The Aquitaine region covers a large and diverse area of southwestern France, stretching from the borders of the Massif Central down to the Spanish border and the Pyrenees. The regional capital, Bordeaux, also the prefectural town of the Gironde (www.tourisme-gironde.cg33.fr), has a long and close association with the UK and Ireland. The city (pop. 700,000) stands next to the Garonne river, where it turns into the Gironde estuary. It was the capital of the Dukes of Aquitaine in the 11th century and the city became an ally of the English in their wars with the French kings until it finally came under the French crown in 1453.

The British demand for Bordeaux wines, or 'claret' led to the expansion of the port, and made this a rich city. It was again substantially rebuilt in the 18th and 19th centuries with classical-style buildings and boulevards. It is the gateway to the world's most prestigious wine-producing region, but also well-known for its excellent cuisine. The port is not as important as it was when France had an empire; the city is a centre for high-tech industries, aerospace, wood-based products and food processing. It has been rated second for economic dynamism and quality of life after Toulouse in a survey conducted by *Express* magazine amongst managers.

Aquitaine has five *départements*: Pyrénées-Atlantiques (64), Landes (40), Gironde (33), Lot-et-Garonne (47), and Dordogne (24). Pyrénées-Atlantiques is certainly the least typical *département* in this region, as it incorporates the French Basque country bordering on Spain. The Basques in this area are not particularly militant; their main demand has been for the creation of one Basque *département*, but all they have gained is the status of a territorial collectivity. The most militant acts these days are spraying graffiti in Basque, or defacing road signs. Basque villages, with their *pelota* courts (a rougher version of squash), banana trees, and red peppers drying on the balconies, present more an image of Spain than France. The churches are also redolent of Spanish-type Catholic fervour. By comparison with the French, the Basques are rather introverted and supposedly surly, but outsiders find them friendly enough. They appreciate it if you try to pronounce Basque words correctly: z is pronounced as 's' and x as 'sh'.

Biarritz, close to Spain, is a popular and expensive resort for surfers, once popular with British royalty. The prefectural town of Pyrénées-Atlantiques is Pau, well-known for its rugby team. The main attraction is the mountainous scenery, excellent for walking and camping.

The Landes (www.tourismelandes.com) is a rather empty region of forests and sandy soil which can boast the longest and straightest beach in Europe, the Côte d'Argent, stretching from the Gironde estuary down to Biarritz. The flatness of the landscape makes it ideal for cycling, and camping.

The Dordogne and Lot-et-Garonne are two *départements* strongly associated with second homes for Brits; the latter is rather cheaper than the first. It is estimated that the presence of foreigners looking for second homes has pushed prices up by some 30% over what they would be otherwise. Lot-et-Garonne is an agricultural region about half the size of the Dordogne, and not that well-known. The main Bordeaux-Toulouse railway and motorway bisect the *département*.

Cuisine. The Gironde around Bordeaux is home to some of France's great vintages. To the northwest, Médoc produces only red wines, the most prestigious being Château Margaux. The St Émilion/Pomerol/Fronsac region near Libourne is famed for superior reds. The Entre-deux-Mers, actually between the rivers Garonne and Dordogne, specialises in white wines. To the southeast of Bordeaux as far as Langon, lies the Graves region, with red and white wines that formerly had a poor reputation but which have now regained some credibility. Past Langon you come to the Sauternes and Barsac region, world-famous for its sweet golden dessert wines; the use of 'noble rot', allowing the grapes to shrivel before picking them, gives the wine its powerful taste. Wine is very much an industry; only the expensive *appellation controlée* wines are picked by hand these days. Part of the Armagnac (brandy) region extends into the Lot-et-Garonne – the Ténarèze around Nérac and Mézin, and into the Landes; most production is in the Gers.

The cooking of the Landes and Gironde is rather overshadowed by the wines. The main dishes are the oysters cultivated in the Arcachon basin, lampreys, and lamb cooked over vine leaves. The prefectural town of the Lot-et-Garonne, Agen (pronounced *azheng*), is world-famous for its prunes; duck cooked with prunes and similar dishes are the local speciality.

The Basque country offers Bayonne ham, *palombes* (pigeon), tuna and a strong ewe's milk cheese, *tomme* or *gasna*. Red peppers can be seen drying on many housefronts; *pipérade* is an omelette with chilli peppers, ham and tomatoes; *piquillos* are sweet red peppers stuffed with cod. The Pyrenean potato and cabbage soup – *garbure* – is an everyday item. Seafood is often on the menu, e.g. stewed squid, *txiperons,* and fish soup, *ttoro.*

Property. The styles of construction are closely related to the building materials available. The western Landes and Gironde is an area with very little stone, but plentiful forests. The typical farm building is made of closely set wooden beams filled with *hourdis* – tiles set in mortar. The surface area is very substantial; all the storerooms and animals sheds are set under one low-pitched roof. In some *landaise* farmhouses the main entrance leads directly into the stables, or *court*, where you formerly dismounted from your horse. The downside of this type of design is that it is not really possible to add any extensions to the building, as they would spoil its appearance. The *landaise* is copied in modern villas; otherwise one finds the usual rather uniform ochre-washed holiday bungalows with Spanish tiles. Properties are most expensive on the coast, particularly at Arcachon, the high-class yachting resort. The up-market wine regions are also expensive.

The Pyrénées-Atlantiques has one typical style, the Basque villa, which became popular after 1920, and copies features of the traditional local farmhouse, the *labourdine*. The *maison labourdine* is similar to a Landes farmhouse, except that it generally has two or even three storeys. The base is stone, with half-timbering on the upper floors, and painted shutters. The roof is low and double-pitched. This type of house is similar to the *landaise* insofar as the front entrance goes directly into a garage or storeroom, called an *eskarratza*, and the living quarters are often all on the first floor. Animals were once housed on the ground floor. The design was adapted for the neo-Basque villa; these are all whitewashed and the timbers painted red or green, in the Basque national colours, making for a rather monotonous effect. Ornately carved galleries and shutters are added for decoration. Rather different in style are the Edwardian holiday villas in Biarritz and all along the coast.

In the Hautes-Pyrénées one finds an entirely different kind of design – the *type basse Navarre* – a massive stone-built farmhouse, with four-pitched roof, and a second farm building at right angles to it. At the lower elevations the abundance of pebbles on the river beds is put to use to make walls of geometrically arranged pebbles in mortar.

Dordogne

The Dordogne (www.perigord.tm.fr/tourisme/cdt) was the first area of rural France to be invaded by British second-home owners. After the first discoveries of human bones belonging to the Cro-Magnon people in the valley of the Vézère river in 1868, British prehistory buffs started to buy properties around the small railway town of Les Eyzies, between the departmental capital Périgueux and Sarlat. Dordogne even has its own English monthly newspaper, *The News*, published from Périgueux, but covering the whole of France.

The Dordogne is known as Périgord to the French; foreigners tend to use the word Dordogne for a wider adjoining area. Certain areas of the Dordogne are being taken over by foreigners, the heaviest concentration being around Ribérac northwest of the capital Périgueux, Sarlat to the southeast and Eymet in the southwest (the latter even boasts its own cricket team). The Ribérac area originally became popular because it was cheaper than the southern Dordogne, and now it probably has the most foreigners. In the village of Bouteilles-St-Sébastien, outside Verteillac in Périgord Vert, 60% of the houses are owned by foreigners, but 90% of these are rented out to holidaymakers and remain shuttered in winter. In the wake of this invasion, some Brits have bought bars and hotels, or started art galleries or antique shops. The large properties that outsiders want are becoming scarce and expensive; some Brits are even buying smaller houses in the towns; old barns or watchtowers are optimistically put on the market in the hope that someone will be brave enough to do them up.

The French locals view the foreign invasion with resignation. The kinds of properties that foreigners buy are generally beyond the means of the locals anyway. In one sense the outsiders keep the countryside alive, but the locals are less happy if they try to bypass the local economy entirely. The Périgourdins are naturally friendly and sociable, and this has certainly been a factor in drawing foreigners here, rather than to some other areas of central France where people are more difficult to get to know.

Périgord is remarkable in that it has evidence of continuous human occupation going back to 500,000 BC. The cave paintings of Lascaux are no longer open to visitors, but there is a respectable recreation at Lascaux II. The appeal of the Vézère valley for cavemen is easy to understand, as they could find easy shelter under the overhanging limestone cliffs called *abris*. Périgord is geologically complex, but about half of it is limestone, as is much of south-central France, easily cut through by rivers to form the typical gorges and limestone plateaux called *causses*. The region is on a slope going down from the Massif Central towards the plains of the Landes; the bottoms of the river valleys are only a few feet above sea level.

Four Colour-Coded Regions. Périgord is divided into four different areas: Purple, Black, White and Green. In the south is Périgord Pourpre (www.bergerac-tourisme.com) named after the grapes that are grown here, with Bergerac at its centre. Monbazillac, a little to the south, is famous for its sweet white apéritif wine. Bergerac is known for robust red wine as well as dry whites; the town has no connection with the well-known English detective series. There are direct flights to London Stansted.

East of the purple country is Périgord Noir (www.tourisme.fr/module3/sarlat/), which takes its name from the dark oak forests here. This *pays negré* or 'black country' was a place of refuge during the wars that have often been waged around the area. The main town, Sarlat, is a tourist trap in the summer, understandably thanks to its superbly preserved Renaissance architecture. Les Eyzies, an unpretentious little town with a fine museum of prehistory, is the gateway to an area of well-preserved prehistoric caves along the Vézère river which leads up to the market town of Montignac, near Lascaux.

Périgord Blanc (www.ville-perigueux.fr) cuts a swathe across the *département*, with Périgueux at its centre, but is the least touristic area of the *département*. The departmental capital, Périgueux, is rather dull, and most tourists try to leave as fast as possible.

Finally, there is the northern area of Périgord Vert (www.nontron.net), where most foreigners aspire to buy property, an area of lush countryside dotted with maize fields, but not as hilly as the south. The Friday market in Ribérac is well-known, and you will meet a large section of the foreign population here. There are quite a few Dutch and Germans in the area. The chocolate-box town of Brantôme, west of Ribérac, is built on an island in the Dronne river, and is always overrun by tourists in the summer. Just across the border with Charente, also on the River Dronne, the area of Aubeterre is very popular with the Dutch. The northern part of Périgord Vert has not been so heavily taken over by foreigners, but probably soon will be.

Probably more than anywhere else, the Dordogne offers the possibility of making a living offering services to other foreigners. There is, in any case, precious little work outside of agriculture and tourism. The climate is warm and humid much of the year, although it can occasionally snow on the hills in winter.

Cuisine. The culinary traditions of Périgord are a main factor in drawing foreigners here. Périgord is well-known for its agricultural products: nuts, apricots, strawberries, truffles, *foie gras* and even tobacco. The richness of the soil – the *terroir* – is reflected in the cooking. This is a land of truffles, odd fungi that only grow underground on the roots of oak trees, which have to be dug out using a sniffer sow or dog to locate them. While truffles cannot be cultivated, oak trees have been planted over the years, and they are carefully kept clear of weeds. A large truffle can fetch over £10,000. The only explanation for such prices must lie in the truffle's reputed aphrodisiac powers. The great French cookery writer, Brillat Savarin, remarked: 'Truffles make the ladies loving, and the gentlemen gallant.' While most of Périgord produces some truffles, the best come from around Sarlat, Verteillac and Sorges.

Paté is another speciality: geese are force-fed with cooked maize until their livers reach a kilo in weight. Opinions are divided on whether the geese enjoy the process. Preserved goose or duck (*confit d'oie/canard*) goes into making *cassoulet*, a dish of beans, *confit*, pork and sausage. The Périgourdins are also keen on game or *gibier*: one favourite dish consists of larks, thrushes and quails. Chestnuts are also an important ingredient in the local cooking; for poorer families they were a staple part of their diet. Périgord produces very little cheese, as there is little dairy farming.

Property. The types of properties foreigners look for in the Dordogne are generally traditional and may be in need of renovation, although there is less available in the latter category than there used to be. The demand is so great, however, that even new houses in the towns on estates (*lotissements*) are being bought by foreigners. The typical massive farmhouses or *périgourdines* are built from rough-hewn limestone, anchored with quoins (*chaînes d'angle*) at the corners from shaped stone, with massive oak beams running through them. Dormer windows are not that common in older property, but it is a tradition to have a couple of little V-shaped decorative openings called *outeaux* in the roof. One step up from the *périgourdine* is the *gentilhommière,* a gentleman's residence, usually with one or two separate wings, more recent and constructed from cut stone.

In the somewhat drier southern part of the Dordogne, one can also find Provençal-style *mas,* or manor houses, with flat tiled roofs and arcades. Newer holiday homes reflect the prevalent liking for the Provençal style of ochre rendering and Spanish tiles.

Because of the price inflation in Dordogne, foreigners are prepared to consider doing up any building that is still standing up, and the locals are quite happy to try to offload a collapsing barn (*grange*) for an apparently paltry sum on an unsuspecting Brit. Damp and woodworm are prevalent in old properties.

As far as finding property goes, there are several foreign-run estate agents (see list), so there is less scope for agents who might act as intermediaries between you and the *immobilier.* One could try the Wednesday or Friday edition of the regional newspaper *Sud-Ouest Périgueux.* There is no shortage of agents in the UK who can put you on to the kind of property you want.

AUVERGNE

CRT: 44 ave des États-Unis, 63057 Clermont-Ferrand Cedex 1; ☎04 73 29 49 49; fax 04 73 34 11 11; e-mail documentation@crt-auvergne.fr; www.crt-auvergne.fr; www.auvergne-tourisme.info.
Percentage of population: 2.18%; percentage of GDP: 1.77%

Auvergne includes four *départements*: Allier (03), Cantal (15), Haute Loire (43) and Puy-de-Dôme (63); the region sits on the Massif Central, a thinly-populated region, much of it above 3000 feet. The typical landscape features are the dome-shaped extinct volcanoes (*puys*) that litter the area. With its high moorlands, interspersed with oak, beech and birch, or man-made pine plantations, it has its own peculiar charm, especially with the mists settling in between the hills. To the French it conjures up an empty landscape where hard-bitten *ur*-peasants struggle to survive against the elements. Historically, the Auvergnats have been hostile towards central government; their strong sense of self-sufficiency and rebellious streak led many to convert to Protestantism during the Wars of Religion. As with the rest of the central France there is a flight from the land towards the cities by young people, and there is every likelihood that the population will fall in the coming years, while the countryside becomes more and more a preserve of the elderly.

The Auvergne has a number of interesting landmarks. The most well-known, the Puy-de-Dôme, is one of the highest points in the Massif Central (4791 ft/1452m), but it has lost some of its mystique as you can drive all the way to the top. Where the Romans had a temple to Mercury, there are now radio antennae and an observatory. You can reputedly see 70 extinct volcanoes from here on a clear day. Near Puy-de-Dôme are the springs from which Volvic and other mineral waters derive: the extinct volcanoes in the area act as a perfect filter, and half of all the mineral water in France comes from the Auvergne. The western half of Auvergne is covered by the Parc des Volcans d'Auvergne, spreading all the way from Vichy in the north to Aurillac in the south.

Clermont-Ferrand, the regional capital, was originally two cities: Clermont and Montferrand, but the former won out. Michelin tyres has its headquarters here. The symbol of the city and of Michelin guides, the Michelin man, real name Bibendum, was dreamt up in 1898 by a cartoonist called O'Galop.

In the *département* of the Haute-Loire, the main town of Puy-en-Velay (on the Loire) has a lot of charm, and an amazing church built on a rock, the Aiguilhe St Michel. The Loire actually rises in the Ardèche *département* east of Le Puy. North of here, Vieille-Brioude is spectacularly located in a gorge near the modern town of Brioude and is worth looking at if you want to buy in this region.

Among the man-made attractions of the Auvergne, two stand out: one is the Viaduc de Garabit, a 125-metre high railway bridge, designed by Gustave Eiffel, in the Cantal near St Flour, also a very attractive little town built on the outcrop of a volcanic plain. The other is the Forêt de Tronçais, an 11,000 hectare forest of oaks and other trees planted under Louis XIV to provide wood for the French navy. The forest lies in the northwest of the Allier, near the town of Cérilly and is open to the public.

Cantal is well-known for the cheese of the same name (www.cdt-cantal.fr). The departmental capital, Aurillac, specialises in making umbrellas; horse-traders from the Auvergne brought back cotton cloth from Spain to make into umbrellas. The other distinguishing feature these days are the cattle markets.

North of Clermont-Ferrand is the spa town of Vichy, which has unfortunate connotations of wartime collaboration, but is actually a very pleasant spot, with abundant hotels for those who want to take the waters. Vichy is only a sub-prefectural town, the capital of the Allier *département* being Moulins further north. Allier is cereal and cattle-farming country. Before the Revolution this was the Duchy of Bourbonnais. It is particularly rich in Romanesque churches.

The main attractions of the Auvergne for property buyers are cheapness and space, the main drawbacks remoteness and poor public transport. Railway lines have been replaced by buses in many areas. There are direct flights from London to Clermont-Ferrand and St Étienne, some way to the east.

Cuisine. Auvergne was once an important wine region, but the phylloxera epidemic of the 19th century virtually wiped the industry out. The vine-yards are making a slow comeback; the Côtes d'Auvergne stretches from north of Riom to the south of Issoire. The area is famous for its cheeses, such as Bleu d'Auvergne, Salers, Saint-Nectaire and Cantal. The typical local dish is *potée auvergnate,* a hot pot of vegetables and pork. The term *à l'auvergnate* means with cabbage, bacon and sausage. *Truffade* is a hearty dish of potatoes and Cantal *tomme* cheese. The other speciality of the area is ham; *pounti* is a terrine based on ham, pork breast, prunes and beet leaves. The town of Puy has trademarked the local green lentils; this was the first French vegetable to gain an *appellation controlée* mark.

Property. The French might say that the Auvergne is a place you would want to leave, rather than move to. The traditional image of the Auvergne is of a poverty-stricken region with fairly dire housing. There is not much of a market in holiday homes here, but on the positive side, prices are rea-sonable. In the Allier and Cantal, there are still derelict properties available for €15,000. One should bear in mind that it can be cold in winter on the higher ground, so good heating is essential. Village houses are sometimes built in terraces to save on building cost and to ward off the cold. Not sur-prisingly the most plentiful building material in the Auvergne is the local lava or basalt. Stone tiles with scalloped edges, or in the shape of fish scales, are used on older buildings in the mountainous parts.

The Allier, in the north of the region, has its own unusual styles of building. Large farms, known as *domaines,* are groups of houses in a U shape, which housed both the owners and their tenant-farmers. Smaller farms are called *locateries.* In the south one can find the *maison à galerie,* a house with a wooden gallery with the living quarters upstairs, as well as Spanish tiles, a sign of the nearness of the Languedoc. A *maison de montagne* or *maison auvergnate* is a cottage of rough-hewn stone with a tiled roof.

BRITTANY (BRETAGNE)

CRT: 1 rue Eaoul Ponchon, 35069 Rennes; ☎ 02 99 28 44 30; fax 02 99 28 44 40; e-mail tourism@region-bretagne.com; www.tourismebretagne.com; www.tourisme-rennes.com.

Percentage of population: 4.85%; percentage of GDP: 3.92%.

Brittany has for many years been one of the prime tourist destinations for the British. The area even has the same name as Britain; while Great Britain is Grande Bretagne, Brittany is Petite Bretagne. From the end of the Roman Empire in the 4th century until the 10th century, Celtic speakers emigrated here from Britain, thus keeping alive Celtic language and culture. Brittany became a full part of France in 1532; before that it was an independent dukedom that generally stayed outside the Anglo-French wars. The Breton language has been severely repressed by the central government in Paris, and it is mixed with French. Speakers of Welsh and Cornish can understand a good deal of Breton. There is also a Breton liberation front; up till now their most violent act was to bomb a McDonalds in 1999, accidentally killing one of the workers. Not many Bretons are now interested in independence.

The four *départements* that make up Brittany are: Finistère (29), Côtes-d'Armor (22), Ille-et-Vilaine (35), and Morbihan (35). The Bretons divide Brittany into Haute and Basse Bretagne (Upper and Lower Brittany); the dividing line runs between St Brieuc in the north and Le Croisic on the south coast. Ille-et-Vilaine is often called 'Haute-Bretagne'. The most popular tourist spots are along the north coast of Ille-et-Vilaine and Côtes-d'Armor, which has a ferry port at Roscoff with services to Plymouth and Cork. The main town of Ille-et-Vilaine (www.bretagne35.com), and regional centre, Rennes, was made capital when Brittany became part of France. These days it is a dynamic and trendy university city.

The old port town of St Malo, at the mouth of the Rance estuary, is a main tourist attraction, mostly for the great *citadelle* that overlooks the town. There are ferries to Jersey. Dinan (Côtes-d'Armor), 25km to the south on the Rance estuary has an equally superb *citadelle* or castle with a medieval town centre and well-preserved ramparts all the way around. West of St Malo, the small town of Dol was once a fortress barring the way to the Dukes of Normandy; there is still a cathedral. The rocky coastline around St Malo and the Paramé is a protected national park, known as the Côte d'Émeraude (Emerald Coast).

The *département* of the Côtes-d'Armor (www.cotesdarmor.com) was until quite recently known as the Côtes-du-Nord and appears as such on pre-1990 maps. The prefectural town of St Brieuc is more industrial than touristic. Further west, the coast between Perros-Guirrec and Trébeurden – the Côte du Granit Rose (Pink Granite Coast) – is outstandingly beautiful and a national park.

To the west is the most Breton *département*, Finistère (www.finisteretou risme.com), the only area where Breton is still a living language amongst the younger generation. The southern part of Finistère – which means 'end of the world' – is called Cornouaille. The port of Brest, at the western end of Finistère, was completely obliterated in World War II and only has modern buildings. The properties are some of the cheapest in France, but it would not be a place for a second home. Brest does have direct flights to London Stansted. Inland Finistère has the highest rainfall in France: over 50 inches a year. The area is subject to severe storms in winter.

Along the south coast is the fourth Breton *département,* Morbihan (www.morbihan.com). The port of Lorient holds the annual Inter-Celtic Festival where the Celts congregate. The prefectural town of Vannes was once the seat of the Breton parliament. It is rated as one of the best places to live in France. To the southwest is Carnac, Europe's most important prehistoric site, with hundreds of mysterious menhirs, or standing stones, aligned according to the moon and stars.

The appeal of Brittany for many lies in the ever-present Celtic spirituality. The area is rich in extraordinary superstitions; the natives still believe that they are in daily communication with the dead. The landscape is both rugged and beautiful, as are the houses.

Cuisine. For the French, Brittany symbolises *crêpes* or thin pancakes sprinkled with icing sugar. Every *crêperie* in France declares itself to be Breton. The other speciality in this line are buckwheat *galettes,* thick unleavened cakes. Buckwheat, or *sarrasin,* came back with the crusaders. The Breton rulers encouraged its use as a substitute for wheat, which was grown for export, so that the very poor would have something to eat. The locals call it *blé noir* (black wheat).

Brittany, with its long coastline, is a seafood paradise; the official authentic *plateau de fruits de mer,* is expected to have at least six kinds of shellfish, served on a bed of the local seaweed, *goémon.* Restaurants who meet the criteria have a symbol.

North-central Finistère – the Pays de Léon – is the main producer of artichokes in France. Brittany as a whole produces a lot of green vegetables, cauliflowers, broccoli and peas. The image of the Breton onion seller is well fixed in our collective memory. These days the Bretons can be found at markets in Britain selling a wider range of produce.

Cider is the main drink; there are no vineyards within the present-day boundaries of Brittany. The Muscadets of the Loire-Atlantique could be counted as Breton. Brittany was once full of vineyards, but they were torn up in the 16th century and replaced with orchards.

Property. Brittany was and is a poor region; the only good agricultural land is around Rennes. Although it is famous for its granite coast, very little granite was used for building except by the wealthy; its main use was for fireplaces and decorative features. Granite is in any case a porous rock that sucks up water, and not very suitable for such a wet climate. The typical building started with a double wall of schist or sandstone rocks filled in with mortar strengthened with ash, straw or animal hairs. The front of the house would face away from the prevailing winds from the west and south. Where houses face towards the west, one may see slates coming down to the ground floor windows.

The basic longhouse was divided between a cattle-shed, living quarters and stables. Grain was stored above the living-room, and hay above the stables. To start with families cooked and slept in one room; hay-lofts were converted into bedrooms. The most common roofing was at one time thatch, but this has been entirely replaced by slates because of the risk of fire.

In Ille-et-Vilaine, where there are more trees, upper storeys of houses were made of half-timbering filled with wattle and daub. The batons in between the beams are generally in a fishtail or cross pattern. Stone archways and quoins in red sandstone became popular in Brittany from the 16th century and are a recognisable feature of the architecture. Another feature is the irregular placing and size of windows, and the use of different coloured stones in elaborate patterns. The Bretons have always taken the trouble to make their houses as individual and attractive as possible.

Floors were once almost universally of rammed earth (*terre battue*) covered with clay and earth strengthened with ash and straw. There was at one time a tradition of inviting the neighbours to come and dance on your floor to make sure that it was well trodden down. In spite of the fact that rammed earth floors tend to break up or become muddy, they are still used in places. Mostly they have been replaced with flagstones or concrete.

Brittany is one of the most attractive areas of France, and some 20% of properties are second homes. The main drawback is the wet climate, especially in winter. Its remoteness is another drawback. The cheapest properties are in Finistère and Côtes-d'Armor. Reckon on a minimum of €30,000 for a 2-bed house.

BURGUNDY (BOURGOGNE)

CRT: Conseil Régional, BP 1602, 21035 Dijon; ☎03 80 28 02 80; fax 03 80 28 03 00; e-mail documentation@crt-bourgogne.fr; www.burgundy-tourism.com; www.ot-dijon.fr
Percentage of population: 2.68%; percentage of GDP: 2.34%.

Burgundy is a vast area where most of the prosperity is concentrated along the Saône river in the east, with vineyards that cling to the *côtes* or slopes, whose stony soils are particularly suited to producing world-class wines.

Vineyards were originally planted by monastic communities who were skilled in producing wine and brandy. Burgundy is one of the three main centres of French wine production; the other two are Bordeaux and Champagne.

There are four *départements*: Côte-d'Or (21), Saône-et-Loire (71), Nièvre (58), and Yonne (89). The regional capital, Dijon, was the seat of the Dukes of Burgundy, who were powerful enough in the 15th century to threaten the French king. The Burgundians were originally a Germanic people who migrated into the area after the fall of the Roman Empire. The last Duke, Charles the Bold, died at the siege of Nancy in 1477, tactically outwitted by the French king Louis XI.

The best wines are produced in the Côte d'Or region south of Dijon, that gives its name to the *département* of Côte d'Or (www.cotedor-tourisme.com). The most expensive wines come from the Côte de Nuits region, around Nuits-St-Georges and Gevrey-Chambertin. The Côte de Beaune specialises more in white wines, e.g. Meursault and Montrachet. Further down the Saône is the Challonais wine region, followed by the Mâconnais, between Mâcon and Tournus, in the *département* of Saône-et-Loire to the south; the name of Pouilly-Fuissé (named after two villages here) is well-known to wine-lovers. Burgundy wine brings with it a whole tourist paraphernalia, with visits to châteaux, wine-tastings and cookery courses for the enthusiasts.

The western part of Saône-et-Loire (www.cg71.com) is one of the more desolate regions of France; the soil is generally too poor for growing crops so this has become cattle country. The name of the best beef cattle breed, Charolais, originates from the town of Charolles between Macon and Digoin. Montceau-les-Mines was the centre of a coal-mining industry that has died out; miners were brought in from Poland in the 19th century and many stayed on. Digoin, to the west, is the centre of pottery manufacture in France.

The Morvan plateau, a desolate and underpopulated region, stretches over the northern half of the Saône-et-Loire and into the Nièvre next door. The emptiness and stillness appeal to those who like to leave the rat race behind. The creation of the Parc Naturel du Morvan in 1970 (www.parcdumorvan.org) has given the area a better image. The main attractions are fishing, canoeing and rafting.

The sub-prefectural town of Autun (www.autun.com), was founded by the Romans under Augustus, as Augustodunum, as a replacement for the Gaulish capital Bibracte, nearby, and was one of Roman Gaul's major cities for centuries. This is a city that seems to have been asleep since the Middle Ages; it hasn't grown much outside the medieval walls, which were built on Roman foundations, and there is a Roman amphitheatre. Autun has one of France's greatest Romanesque churches, the Cathédrale St Lazare, with perfectly preserved 12th century carvings of scenes from the

Bible. There is a TGV stop at Le Creusot, about 20 km away; the regular train service from Paris is scenic, but slow.

The *département* of the Nièvre (www.nievre58.com), west of Saône-et-Loire, is much the same: rather sleepy and with few inhabitants. The Nivernois is cereal and cattle-farming country. Nevers, the prefectural town, on the east bank of the Loire, is a pleasant spot, with a tradition of porcelain manufacturing, and regular jazz concerts.

The Yonne, north of Nièvre, is also quite thinly populated. The area closer to Paris has attracted some second-home owners from the capital. The prefectural town of Auxerre has two claims to fame: some of the oldest church architecture and frescoes (9th century) in France, and also one of the country's better football teams. The town of Poligny to the northeast, was a major monastic centre started by the Cistercians in the 12th century, but not much remains of the original monastic buildings; Thomas à Becket took refuge here to escape the wrath of King Henry II. The monks here also started the tradition of planting vineyards that produce the dry white wine called Chablis, named after the town a little to the south.

Cuisine. The Burgundy region is most of all known for its wines. Cooking in red wine has given rise to the standard dishes *bœuf bourguignon* and *coq au vin*. Anything *à la bourguignonne* is cooked in a red wine sauce with shallots, mushrooms and bacon bits added. To go with the beef, the Burgundians came up with Dijon mustard.

Snails (*escargots*) are cooked for hours in Chablis to make them edible – or not, depending on your point of view. The Morvan plateau is known for its hams, especially flavoured with parsley. Burgundy also has its local cheeses, none of which are very well known abroad, such as St Florentin, Epoisses and Chaource.

Property. Nièvre is an area rich in high-quality limestone as well as granite and schist in the east. Buildings are of stone with rendering; flat tiles are in use everywhere. In the wine-growing region a rather different type of building came into existence, the wine-grower's house, with storerooms on the ground floor and living quarters above, with wooden gallery and external staircase. Half-timbering has also been quite common in the wine-growing region between Dijon and Macon, an area poor in stone materials. The Morvan is limestone in the north and granite in the south; the typical farmhouse is of uneven stone.

The areas closer to Paris of the Yonne and Nièvre now have a high proportion of second homes, and there are opportunities for renovating old farmhouses. Southern Burgundy does not present the same phenomenon of flight from the land, and cannot be characterised as poverty-stricken. There are not that many derelict properties to do up. House prices are cheapest in Morvan. Prices are determined by the closeness to Paris, and the TGV. Expect to pay from €50,000 for a 2-bed house in an isolated area.

CENTRE (VAL-DE-FRANCE)

CRT: 37 ave de Paris, 45000 Orléans; ☎02 38 79 95 00; fax 02 38 79 95 10; e-mail crtl.centre@crtlcentre.com; www.loirevalleytourism.com; www.coeur-de-france.com.
Percentage of population: 4.06%; percentage of GDP: 3.5%.

The Centre region includes the pre-revolutionary counties of Touraine, Berry and Orléanais. For Brits this is 'the Loire Valley'. The main attractions are the châteaux and churches. The Loire has given its name to several *départements*, in several different regions; in the Centre you are never far from water, or marshlands. There is also the Loir river, which runs north of the Loire parallel to its bigger sister. The Centre counts six *départements*: Eure-et-Loir (28), Loir-et-Cher (41), Indre-et-Loire (37), Loiret (45), Indre (36), and Cher (18). Tourism is the main industry, along with food-processing, agriculture and manufacturing.

The prefectural capital of the Eure-et-Loir, Chartres, can boast one of the world's great cathedrals, a UNESCO world heritage site, most of it dating from the 12th and 13th centuries. The Loire Valley is most of all associated with châteaux and cycling holidays. The main city of the region is Orléans, which lies on the motorway from Paris to Toulouse. The Loire starts to make its massive curve towards the south at Orléans, eventually forming the boundary between the Centre and Burgundy. The Loire Valley evokes the struggle of the French to eject the English in the 15th century, and the extravagance of enormous châteaux built for the idle aristocrats of the *ancien régime*. The Loire Valley châteaux were developed as playgrounds for the aristocracy starting with François I (r.1515-47).

The regional capital, Orléans (population 245,000), is only an hour from Paris, and it is quite possible to commute to Paris for work. The city has an important place in French history; Joan of Arc, nicknamed the Maid of Orléans, lifted the siege of the city in 1429 and started the reconquest of France from the English.

The Loire represents the boundary between south and north as far as weather goes, and is often shrouded in mist; supposedly it presents a natural barrier to the clouds going further south. The Sologne area south of Blois straddles the Loir-et-Cher and Loiret, but as most of it is marshland or lakes it has little scope for house-buying. It is also the stronghold of the French hunting fraternity, and houses the world's biggest hunting museum at the Château de Gien on the Loire.

Further downriver, the city of Tours stands at the centre of the traditional county of Touraine (www.tourism-touraine.com), as well as being the prefectural town of the Indre-et-Loire. Here the clearest French is reputedly spoken. This was also the home of the great 15th-century writer François Rabelais.

Bourges, the capital of the Berry region, or Berrichonne, and prefectural town of the Cher, is another pleasant town with a cathedral that is listed as a world heritage site by UNESCO. The unfortunate *dauphin* Charles VII retreated here after Agincourt in 1415 until Joan of Arc gave him the courage to fight back.

Cuisine. The Centre is a fertile region, and produces more cereals than anywhere else in France. Soft fruits, such as strawberries and pears are also grown. The area of the Loire has no fewer than 22 AOC wines: Vouvray covers several types of whites; Bourgueil and Chinon are mainly reds; Sancerre is more known for whites. The Berry specialities are game, river fish and crayfish, and the AOC goat's cheeses, Pyramide St Pierre and Crottin de Chavignol. Loir-et-Cher has its own AOC goat's cheeses, Selles-sur-Cher and Cendré de Vendôme.

The Orléanais is the home of the favourite French dessert, Tarte Tatin or 'upside-down tart', made with pears or quinces, discovered by two sisters called Tatin in Lamotte-Beuvron. Quince jelly – *colignac* – is a speciality of the Loiret. Pears are used a lot in cooking and for making the pear liqueur Eau-de-vie d'Olivet.

Property. There is an active market in second homes in the northern part of the Centre, particularly Eure-et-Loire, which is within easy reach of Paris. It only takes 45 minutes by train from Chartres to the Gare de Montparnasse. In spite of the competition from the Parigots, prices are not unreasonable. About 17% of properties are second homes. The relative flatness of the landscape is a factor in dissuading Brits from buying here, but there are plenty of cultural festivals to make up for the indifferent scenery.

The typical older property is the *longère angevine* or stone-built longhouse, with white coping stones at the corners for decoration and solidity. There are plentiful villas, bungalows and similar modern-style brick-built houses. If you want something a little unusual, you could try a troglodyte dwelling cut out of a cliff-face, used by the vineyard workers near the River Loire. The cheapest houses start at around €70,000.

CHAMPAGNE-ARDENNE

CRT: 15 ave du Maréchal Leclerc, BP 319, 51013 Châlons-en-Champagne;

☎03 26 21 85 80; fax 03 26 21 85 90; e-mail contact@ tourisme-cham-pagne-ard.com;   www.tourisme-champagne-ard.com;   www.tourism.fr/reims.
Percentage of population: 2.23%; percentage of GDP: 2.02%.

The name of the region says a lot, but there is much more to the region than just bubbly. In the 17th century a monk and cellar master near Eper-nay, Dom Pérignon, tried adding yeast to the bottles of fermenting wine in his abbey cellars; most of the bottles exploded but those that didn't made the cork pop when drawn. Large-scale champagne production didn't really get under way until the 19th century, when glass-making techniques had advanced enough to make stronger bottles. Dom Pérignon is also credited with coming up with the idea of blending the three different wines that go into the drink.

Champagne-Ardenne is a rather flat and wooded region that is overlooked by tourists and property buyers alike. The four *départements* are: Ardennes (08), Marne (51), Aube (10), and Haute-Marne (52). The Ardennes borders on the Belgian provinces of Hainaut and Luxembourg. The dense forests of the Ardennes traditionally specialised in metalworking and slate-quarrying, but these are dying industries. Agriculture doesn't thrive here either. The prefectural town of Charleville-Mézières is the world centre for marionettes, and there is a large festival every three years devoted to them. The main attraction of the area is the stillness of the forest, and the fact that properties are cheap. Access to the UK is also fairly quick. Brussels and the Channel ports are about three hours away.

The regional departmental capital, Reims (pronounced 'Rengss') has a great history; 26 of France's kings, going back as far as Clovis in 496, were crowned in the Gothic cathedral. Reims is also the capital of champagne; the tourists can go round the great *maisons* such as Heidsieck, Taittinger and Veuve-Clicquot for *dégustations*. The real centre of champagne-production is the town of Epernay, 26km to the south of Reims, where the best-known name, Moët et Chandon has its *maison*.

South of the Marne is the Aube, a region of undulating wheatfields that rises up to the Plateau de Langres on the border with Burgundy. Troyes, the traditional capital of the champagne region and prefectural city, is architecturally very rich, with half-timbered houses, Renaissance mansions and a fine Gothic cathedral. In most respects the Aube is a rather deserted region, and not much visited by tourists. One can get from Troyes to Paris in about 90 minutes.

Cuisine. Most tourists visit Champagne-Ardenne for the fizzy drink. The Marne also produces still whites and rosés; one vintage goes under the name of Bouzy.

Champagne-Ardenne is not one of France's great gastronomic regions. There are the usual hams and pâtés; the most noteworthy local dishes are *boudin blanc* or white sausage from Rethel, and pig's trotters from St Ménehould. Troyes produces chitterlings, *andouillettes,* that are fried. There are some fine cheeses in the Ardennes: e.g. Grand Condé, Remparts and Rocroi. In the Haute-Marne there is the creamy Chaource and the strong cheese named after the town of Langres.

Property. The original building material of the Ardennes forest was, naturally enough, the local timber; clapboard or slate was attached to a wooden frame. More recent farmhouses are of shale with stone surrounds, and a heavy layer of rendering.

Traditional construction in the Champagne region was half-timbering, with closely positioned posts braced by long diagonal ties. Farmhouses have large square cart entrances with wooden lintels, called *porterue.* An unusual feature of Champagne farmhouses is the use of the space on the streetfront for storage.

The Ardennes has been more or less ignored by foreign buyers; its main selling point is the cheapness of the properties and the proximity of the Channel. Broken-down farmhouses can be picked up for next-to-nothing. Both Ardennes and Champagne are wet and humid areas, with a climate similar to southern England. There is never likely to be a great market for second homes here, but at least you won't be surrounded by English-speakers.

CORSICA

Agence du Tourisme de la Corse: 17 blvd du Roi-Jérôme, 20181 Ajaccio; ☎04 95 51 00 00; fax 04 95 51 14 40; e-mail ; www.visit-corsica.com.
Percentage of population: 0.43%; percentage of GDP: 0.34%.
The island of Corsica consists of two *départements*: Haute-Corse and Basse-Corse, although the division is rather arbitrary. Corsica (or La Corse) has more associations with Italy than with France, but has always had a strong antipathy towards foreign rulers. In reality, Corsica has never been independent since the time of the Romans. The local language is closely related to Tuscan in Italy. The French bought the island from the Genoese in 1768. The Corsicans staged a mass revolt but were defeated in 1769. Napoleon Bonaparte, born in Ajaccio in 1769, made the island a lot more noticed. Corsica's other famous son, Christopher Columbus, born in Calvi, is claimed by the Genoese as one of theirs.

Corsica is a mere 180km long and a maximum of 80km wide, is sparsely populated and very mountainous, with deep gullies and tree-covered slopes. The interior is covered with *maquis* (a mix of wild flowers, herbs and dense scrub). Viewed from the sea the island looks like a mountain. The 600-mile long coastline has Europe's finest beaches, which bring in the tourist hordes to the western coast in July and August. The east coast is uncomfortably hot in summer.

Corsica has little else but tourism to live from, but the profits go back to mainland France, fuelling the discontentment of the locals. The FLNC (Corsican liberation movement), has been in the habit of shooting up government buildings and dynamiting foreign-owned villas. France goes to great lengths to keep the Corsicans satisfied, by pumping in huge subsidies; the island also gets some €1 billion a year from the EU. The present trend towards decentralisation threatens to make the FLNC irrelevant; in any case, they spend as much time pursuing vendettas amongst themselves as they do fighting the French.

Corsica has exceptional natural scenery. The centre of the island is a national park, with the highest peak, Monte Cinto, reaching 8,943 feet (2,710 metres). For foreigners wanting to live and work here, the prospects do not seem that hopeful. About a third of the islanders work directly for the French state, but there is no work to be had for outsiders. You would probably have to pay protection money if you wanted to start a business. Recently, more and more Italians have been buying holiday villas, and they are better accepted than the French. The cost of living is considerably higher than in mainland France.

Driving between the main cities on the island is fairly easy; there is a limited railway network. The usual access to the island is by ferry from Nice, Toulon or Marseille. There are direct flights during the tourist season from London to Ajaccio and Bastia, on Air France. Otherwise one has to change at Paris or Nice. There is also an airport at Calvi.

Cuisine. The lowland areas grow all kinds of fruit: clementines, nectarines, peaches, avocados. There are the traditional chestnuts, olives and figs. The local cooking is strongly flavoured with the wild herbs that grow here in profusion. The national dish is *cabrettu a l'istrettu* (stewed kid goat). All kinds of game are found in the mountains, so you can taste wild boar, hare, partridge and wood pigeon. The local cheeses are *brocciu* – a soft cheese from ewe's milk – and a hard cheese, *fromage corse*. Sea fish and shellfish are available in abundance. The island also produces some decent wines: Santa Barba and Fiumicicoli reds and roses around Sartène in the south, and sweet muscat apéritif white wine from Cap Corse.

Property. Stone, found everywhere on the island, has always been the preferred material. The traditional Corsican village consists of tightly grouped houses without a central square which emphasises the closed nature of the society. The living room (*sala*) for entertaining guests traditionally has a rifle by the door; the bedrooms are protected by religious icons.

There are some properties advertised in French magazines, e.g. *Résidence Sécondaire* and *Particulier à Particulier*. One can pick up an apartment by the sea from €70,000.

FRANCHE-COMTÉ

CRT: La City, 4 rue Gabriel Plançon, 25044 Besançon Cedex; ☎03 81 25 08 08; fax 03 81 83 35 82; e-mail crt@franche-comte.org; www.franche-comte.org.
Percentage of population: 1.86%; percentage of GDP: 1.57%.

The Franche-Comté has four *départements* within its boundaries: Haute-Saône (70), Territoire de Belfort (90), Doubs (25) and the Jura (39). The region was historically not part of France until Louis XIV took it over in 1678.

The city of Belfort has changed hands many times over the course of history. From the 14th century it was a stronghold of the Austrian Habsburgs; in 1648, by the Treaty of Westphalia, it became French, and was ruled by the Princes of Monaco. It gained a special prestige by its resistance to the Prussian siege of 1870, and so escaped becoming part of the German province of Alsace in 1871. It was made a separate *département* in 1922, the Territoire de Belfort. The city is 10 miles away from the Swiss border, and there is naturally a strong Swiss influence on the architecture.

Besançon (www.besancon.com), the regional capital, stands on a bend of the River Doubs; it has preserved many of its original buildings, including a spectacular citadel. The city has traditionally specialised in clock-making. Besançon is also the departmental capital of the Doubs (www.doubs.org), a river that rises near the Swiss border south of Besançon at Saut du Doubs, and briefly enters Switzerland before making a hairpin turn back into France, eventually flowing into the Saône 200 miles to the west.

The Jura (www.jura-tourism.com) is in the pre-Alps, a green landscape of pastures and forests. It has something like the appearance of Switzerland; chalet-like houses with steep roofs and colourful windowboxes, interspersed with flowery meadows and pine forests.

Franche-Comté is is remote from the UK; the region is also devoid of airports or TGVs. This could be a region to live all the year round, but is not an ideal choice for a holiday home. On the plus side, there are areas close to ski fields, and one can enjoy white-water rafting, fishing and walking. There is superb scenery to enjoy, and more than half the region is covered in forests.

Cuisine. Franche-Comté is known for its *charcuterie* – cold meats – in particular for smoked beef (*brési*), sausages and hams. The semi-hard Comté is the most popular cheese in France. The majority of the local wines are whites. Four areas of the Jura have AOC wines: Arbois, Château-Chalon, Côtes du Jura and L'Étoile; they are not well-known outside France. Some are unusual, such as *vin de paille,* matured on a bed of straw, and wines flavoured with walnuts.

Property. The timber-framed farmhouse is standard in the Belfort region and the Haute Saône. In the Jura there are stone-built vinegrower's houses with the storerooms on the groundfloor. In the Vosges area of the Saône red sandstone is used, with red sandstone roof slates. The higher Doubs has inclusive farm building, with lower storeys of stone with white rendering, and planks covering gable ends for insulation. Some have a survival of the centrally-placed hearth: a pyramid-shaped hood over the whole kitchen that pierces the roof with a massive plank-lined stack. Building land is cheap. Houses start from about €70,000.

LANGUEDOC-ROUSSILLON

CRT: 20 rue de la République, 34000 Montpellier; ☎04 67 22 81 00; fax 04 67 58 06 10; e-mail contactcrtlr@sunfrance.com; www.crlanguedocrou ssillon.fr/tourisme; www.sunfrance.com.
Percentage of population: 3.82%; percentage of GDP: 2.87%.

The region consists of the *départements* Lozère (48), Gard (30), Hérault (34), Aude (11), and Pyrénées-Orientales (66). Languedoc derives from 'langue d'oc', that is the language – Occitan – in which the word for 'yes' is *oc,* or southern France, as opposed to 'langue d'oïl' or northern France, while Roussillon is another word for French Catalonia. Languedoc cannot really be defined as a precise geographical area; it covers anywhere where Occitan was once spoken. During the Dark Ages, the area was a refuge for the Spanish trying to reconquer Spain from the Moors. Generally, the idea of Occitan identity is still very strong here, but few people can speak the language, which was effectively obliterated by French with the introduction of universal education.

Catalonia first came into its own when the Counts of Barcelona became Kings of Aragon in 1137, and then joined up with the Counts of Toulouse to form a united front against the French. The Occitans and Catalans suffered a setback when Toulouse fell to the French in 1229; the Catalan kingdom split into two in the next century, with the Kings of Majorca ruling from Perpignan over the French area. After centuries of disputes, Louis XIV finally managed to gain control over Roussillon with the Treaty of the

Pyrenees in 1659, thus making the mountain range the border with Spain.

The heart of Catalonia is the Pic du Canigou (9180 ft), where a Catalan flag perpetually flutters from a wrought-iron cross; every true Catalan is expected to climb this mountain once in their lives. On the night of June 23-24, fires known as *feux de Saint-Jean* are lit and then carried to every village and town in Catalonia. This is the occasion for traditional Catalan *ferias* or festivals.

Pyrénées-Orientales. This *departement* (www.cg66.fr), formerly known as Pyrénées d'Or, includes part of the grape-growing region of Corbières in the north, and the former Catalan county of Cerdagne in the west, around Fort-Romeu. The sea-coast between the capital, Perpignan, and the Spanish border is known as the Côte Vermeille (Vermillion Coast). Generally, the coast has been over-developed. The picturesque town of Collioure, near Spain, gave the impetus for the colour experimentations of the painters Matisse and Derain in 1905, known as *fauvisme,* and there are Fauvist paintings everywhere. The city of Perpignan's main interest lies in the Palace of the Kings of Majorca.

Aude. The prefectural town of the Aude (www.audetourisme.com), Carcassonne, is one of France's most popular tourist destinations. The huge citadel, with its lists where knights jousted long ago, evokes the Middle Ages better than anywhere in Europe. Carcassonne lies on the Canal du Midi, a waterway running 240km from Toulouse to the sea at Agde which was conceived by a wealthy nobleman, Pierre-Paul Riquet, who spent every last penny he had on financing it. The canal was built between 1667 and 1681, and involved constructing 99 locks and 130 bridges, as well as diverting water from the mountains. Rather incredibly, it goes uphill for half its length and then downhill again. The canal had the desired effect of revitalising the local economy but was abandoned with the advent of the steam train. It is one of France's great tourist attractions; the poplar-lined canal with its classical buildings is a wonder of elegance and ingenuity.

On the western end of the Aude is the Lauragais, a farming region that spreads out into the Tarn, Ariège and Haute-Garonne. North of Carcassonne is the area known as La Montagne Noire (Black Mountain), whose people suffered severely during the anti-Cathar crusades of the early 13th century. The national park of the Haut Languedoc extends over the southeast of the Tarn into the Hérault and Aveyron; here you may come across the *mouflon,* the wild mountain sheep.

Hérault. Above the Aude is the *département* of Hérault (www.cdt-herault.fr), mostly arid vineyard and olive country at lower elevations, and deserted hills higher up. The prefectural town of Montpellier, is one of France's most dynamic cities, and has become the main centre for medical research. This is also the region's main city (it shares the title with Narbonne and Béziers) and focus of investment in new industries.

The surrounding country is known as *garrigue,* a stony landscape almost bare of trees, originally forest degraded by overgrazing and bushfires. The coastline of the Hérault, the Côte d'Améthyste, is equally arid. Saltwater lagoons separate the land from the sea, providing an ideal environment for breeding oysters and clams. The coastline is popular with sailors; much of it is unsuited for building, so overdevelopment is more of a localised problem.

Gard. The neighbouring *département* of the Gard (www.cdt-gard.fr) is noted for its Roman ruins, and has only a short coastline. The Gard does, however, have a part of the Cévennes national park. The prefectural city of Nîmes is well-known for its Roman amphitheatre, and the blue denim cloth named after the city. Visitors may be surprised to find out that this is also the centre of bullfighting in France. The Gard has always been popular with British property buyers, especially the pretty hilltop town of Uzès, northeast of Nîmes.

Lozère. North of the Gard, the Lozère (www.lozerefrance.com) has some of the country's finest scenery and includes most of the Cévennes national park, an area of forests and mountains, and few people. The *département* is one of France's most thinly populated, ideal for holidays, but rather bleak when the weather closes in. The southwestern quarter of the Lozère includes the Tarn Gorges – the Tarn rises at an altitude of over 5000 feet on Mont Lozère, and the headwaters of the Lot. The area consists of high limestone plateaux, known as *causses.* Geologically, the rest of the Lozère is more granite and schist.

The Cévennes is remote; it takes about two hours to drive from Nîmes airport. The northern Lozère is about 120 miles from St Étienne, which also has flights to London Stansted. Train and bus services are limited, but if you want to get away from it all this is the place to be. The area attracted hippies in the 1960s looking to set up alternative communities and some of them still remain.

In the Languedoc, as with much of southern France, the locals have traditionally rebelled against central domination. Having gone through the atrocities of the anti-Cathar crusades, they came out strongly in favour of Protestantism in the wars of religion; the Protestant guerrillas, the Camisards, started out from Ganges in 1702. In World War II, the people took a leading role in the Resistance against the Germans. In the 1970s the main focus of discontent was cheap foreign wine imports, and the necessary reorganisation of the wine industry.

Overall, this has traditionally been one of France's poorest regions; much of the land is only suitable for grazing goats and growing cork-oaks. A great deal of investment has gone into new industries along the coastal strip, which has attracted job-seekers from the rest of France. The region has plenty of sunshine – anywhere up to 300 days a year – and has preserved more local traditions than most parts of France. One of these is the *transhumance,* the practice of moving herds of sheep from the Alps across to the Languedoc every year, which has given rise to local festivals.

Languedoc-Roussillon has a distinctly extreme climate: although rainfall is adequate – around 25 inches per year – it tends to be infrequent and falls mostly in October and November. The Gard is particularly prone to flash flooding, caused by cold fronts from the Massif Central colliding with warm fronts from the south. They even talk here of 'horizontal rain', which can do serious damage to your roof. In September 2002, 27 people were killed and a large area between Nîmes and Alès was cut off from civilisation after several days of torrential downpours. Flooding is a real risk in the area and should be taken into account when buying property. During the winter and spring a strong cold wind, the *tramontane,* comes down from the northwest, blowing away the clouds, but also freezing everything in its path. In summer a pleasant breeze from the south, the *garbi,* brings rain and cools the land.

Cuisine. The Aude produces the best wines of the region. The reds that have achieved AOC status are Corbières, Minervois, Fitou and Cabardès. A *vigneron* in the town of Limoux south of Carcassonne claimed to have discovered how to produce *brut* or sparkling white wine. Crémant and Blanquette de Limoux are now AOC as well. The strong sunshine and short cold winters are ideal for the vines. Locally, sweet wines are very popular.

French Catalonia has cooking traditions similar to those over the border with Spain. The national dish is *boles de picolat,* pork and beef meatballs in olive sauce; other specialities are *cargolada* (grilled snails), *botifarre* (black pudding), and *fuets,* thin, dry sausages. Grilled peppers, aubergines and tomatoes combine with tuna and cod dishes or omelettes.

The coastal areas of the Languedoc tend to specialise in seafood, such as mussels, oysters and clams. Other typical dishes include *tapenade* (black olive paste), duck cooked in red wine, *foie gras* and *confits* from Lauragais. The Foreign Legion town of Castelnaudary calls itself the capital of *cassoulet,* the southern French dish of beans with duck and sausage.

Up and Coming Region: Pyrénées-Orientales

Pyrénées-Orientales is French Catalonia or Roussillon, rather than Languedoc. The typical older buildings are of Pyrenean granite. In the mountains one can find ski chalets. One can see the Catalan influence in the flat roofs and arched shutters. In the mountains there are even crude stepped gables, or *pignons à redents*. The hot and dry climate and Catalan culture have a lot of attractions for retirees. In summer one can go to take the waters at spas such as Amélie-les-Bains; in the winter there is skiing. There are direct flights from London to Perpignan; in other respects this is a remote area. The current property market is fairly flat, with not that many properties on the market, so one should not expect prices to rise. Expect to pay from €50,000 for a basic village house.

Property. Languedoc-Roussillon generally has few trees in low-lying areas, so few properties are built around wooden frames; termites are also a problem. Wooden rafters are used for supporting roofs, and some wood may be used for decoration on the exterior of houses. The main building material is granite, or limestone, where it is available (e.g. Corbières). Baked brick is generally only used for internal walls. Second homes make up 30% of the total housing stock in Languedoc-Roussillon.

Substantial houses are traditionally known as *mas* and some of them stand on the sites of Roman villas. The *mas* is a large farmhouse, also known as a *campanha* or *boria* in Occitan, with storehouses and cottages for the workers built on to it. These days, a new *mas* is a villa, usually with arched terrace and swimming pool. The wealthier wine-growers also used to build castle-like structures with stone towers. The farm-workers lived in *masets,* small stone-built cottages with two storeys and a chimney, but rather small for foreign buyers. It was also traditional to build a small stone structure – a *cabana* – next to the vineyards, to live in during the warmer season, and for picnics and parties. Another type of village structure is the wine-grower's house – *maison vigneronne* – typically with a large archway for wagons to pass through. Some have *celliers* or storerooms for the wine, attached. In the silk region of the Gard, a specialised stone building – a *magnanerie* – was used for breeding silk-worms. These have very large ground-floor windows, but only small openings on the first floor. The *magnanerie* would be heated and the windows sealed with paper while the silkworms were incubating on a wooden framework, and then opened up to the elements once they had emerged.

Traditional farmers' houses are sometimes built in modern material next to fields, and could be used as a basic holiday cottage. On the whole the Languedoc uses Spanish tiles (*tuiles canal*). Additional protection from the rain is afforded by several layers of half-tiles – *génoises* – set in mortar in a cornice along the edge of the roof. Roofs can be leaky, and may need lining.

The Cévennes has its own particular style of architecture: the granite-built houses are narrow with fairly thin walls (60-70cm), and often have three or more storeys. Roofs may be quite flat, the reasoning being that a thick layer of snow on the roof would act as insulation and stop water from going through the gaps between the tiles. Due to the narrowness of the houses, exterior staircases were sometimes built on to houses when there was no space for an internal staircase.

In the upland regions of the Lozère, the main building material is the local grey schist or granite, and the style is more that of the Massif Central, with the stone slates known as *lauzes*.

LIMOUSIN

CRT: 27 blvd de la Corderie, 87031 Limoges Cedex; ☎05 55 45 18 80; fax 05 55 45 18 18; e-mail tourisme@crt-limousin.fr; www.tourismelimou sin.com; www.crtlimousin.fr.

The western escarpments of the Massif Central consist of thinly populated river valleys, with forests of beech, chestnut, and birch, with oak at lower elevations, that clothe the region in superb autumn colouring. The countryside is sparsely populated and the roads are a pleasure to drive on.

The eastern Limousin is reputed as a desolate region where tough, dour farmers work hard to make a living from breeding Limousin cattle. Above 3,000 feet there is no arable farming, only pasture in between densely wooded valleys. The only other substantial industries are logging from managed pine plantations and gravel quarrying, with the attendant heavy lorries.

Tourism is a seasonal industry; the beauty of the landscape is the main attraction, although there are the usual cultural and gastronomic festivals. The Limousin is rather lacking in the literary connections the French find so fascinating. Auguste Renoir, the painter, came from Limoges. A more dubious celebrity is the current president Jacques Chirac who is from Sarran in Corrèze. There are plenty of Romanesque churches in the area; their granite block construction has barely weathered.

The regional government has poured money into new roads; the Paris-Toulouse motorway runs past Limoges. The east-west A89 from Clermont-Ferrand will eventually meet up with the A20 at Brive. The train services are scenic but limited; a lot of lines are only served by buses. There is an airport serving London at Limoges; there are also flights from Clermont-Ferrand.

The city of Limoges, whose inhabitants are called Limougeauds, is noted as a traditional centre of porcelain production. These days it is carried on for the benefit of the tourist industry; the museums are full of porcelain. Limoges is the prefectural capital of the Haute Vienne, and the regional capital of the Limousin. The limousine car takes its name from the all-enveloping shepherd's cape once worn around here, although there are not all that many sheep to herd these days.

As an industrial city, Limoges has a strong socialist tradition and has become a centre for refugees from the former eastern bloc. Whether one would want to live in Limoges is debatable; there is a verb in French – *limoger* – meaning to send someone to Limoges, i.e. give them the sack. The expression came about because Marshal Joffre sent an incompetent general to Limoges during World War I, to be rid of him. But if you are interested in porcelain or enamel then Limoges is the place to be.

The sub-prefectural town of Aubusson, in the valley of the River Creuse, along with neighbouring Felletin, had an international reputation as a centre of tapestry weaving, started around 1400 by immigrant Flemish weavers. There is still something of an industry in repairing old tapestries.

The northern half of the Limousin region corresponds to the pre-Revolution county of La Marche. South of Aubusson is the evocative-sounding Plateau de Millevaches, which sounds as though it should mean '1,000 cows' but actually means '1,000 springs'. The Plateau, at a height of between 1,650 and 3,250 feet, is the source of several major rivers, including the Vézère and the Vienne. The *département* of La Creuse (www.cg23.fr) is very green, and it is known as La Verte for this reason.

The southwestern corner of the Limousin tends to be lumped in with the Dordogne in the minds of the Brits. Brive-la-Gaillarde (Brive the Jolly Wench) is a main railway junction on the line from Paris, but not a place one would want to buy property. A little to the north, the town of Uzerche on the upper reaches of the Vézère is a lot more attractive. Tulle, the departmental capital of the Corrèze (www.cg19.fr), deep in the valley of the river of that name, is known for its stitched lace.

Cuisine. As a region with limited agricultural resources, the cooking here is simple and filling. The uplands are cattle-farming country. Hams are also a delicacy. The *cul noir* or black-bum pig of St Yrieix has its own festival. In the markets one can buy all kinds of cheese, from cows, ewes and goats. The forests yield wild mushrooms. Chestnuts are a local product in La Creuse. Corrèze has a *vin de pays;* there is also some cider production.

Up and Coming Region: La Creuse and Haute Vienne

These are two départements that are attracting increasing interest from foreign property buyers who have been priced out of the Dordogne and Lot. Southwest Haute-Vienne has been made into a regional park, the Parc Naturel Régional Périgord-Limousin. The area has strong associations with Richard the Lionheart; there is a route one can follow.

> La Creuse is a fairly empty region. There is just one golf course at Gouzon. Haute Vienne has three, and Corrèze two 18-hole courses. In La Creuse there are still small farms for renovation for as little as €15,000. Even the tourist town of Aubusson has some extraordinarily cheap properties in quite good condition. In the Haute Vienne the prices are a little higher. The main consideration is whether one would want to remain here all the year round. The valleys can be gloomy in winter with lingering fogs.

Property. The typical granite constructions with grey slates tend to accentuate the gloom; a certain amount of red sandstone is also used here and there, and you may even see the odd half-timbered house or *colombage*. The wetness of the climate can be gauged from the steeply tiled roofs and even the occasional northern-style slate-covered wall facing to the west.

The Limousin countryside has more to offer as a place a second home rather than somewhere to live all the year round. Rural depopulation is a serious issue here; property prices are about the lowest in France, and they are never going to rise by very much. One might also add that the rural population are rather suspicious of outsiders; if you are looking for Latin jollity and a warmer climate you might be better off a bit further south.

LORRAINE (LORRAINE-VOSGES)

CRT: Abbaye des Prémontrés, 54704 Pont-à-Mousson Cedex; ☎03 83 80 01 80; fax 03 83 80 01 88; e-mail crt@cr-lorraine.fr; www.cr-lorraine.fr. Percentage of population: 3.85%; percentage of GDP: 3.06%.

Lorraine is a region with strong Germanic influences, and was more or less independent for much of its history. The name Lorraine derives from Charlemagne's son Lothar who called his kingdom Lotharingia from 855. Lorraine split into two separate entities, Metz, Toul and Verdun on the one hand, and the Duchy of Lorraine on the other. The Dukes of Lorraine maintained their independence from the French until the end of the Thirty Years' War in 1648; Lorraine was finally incorporated into France in 1766. Parts of Meurthe and Moselle were annexed by Germany in 1871 after the Franco-Prussian War, and then joined with Alsace, but were returned to France in 1918.

As a frontier region Lorraine was heavily fortified by the French from the 17th century and there are still some massive fortresses, the most remarkable being the citadel at Bitche constructed by Vauban, in the northwestern corner close to Germany. The battle for Verdun in 1916 gave the French their greatest success in World War I, inasmuch as they blocked the German advance without the help of their allies, but at the cost of 400,000 dead. The Maginot Line, a sophisticated, but ultimately useless, defensive system meant to keep out the Germans after World War I, runs through Lorraine and is kept up in parts as a museum.

The conurbation of Nancy, with some 335,000 inhabitants, is less of an industrial city than it used to be, but has developed other industries such as banking and IT and has a major university. The designer Emile Gallé, known for his glass and ceramics, came from here, and started the Nancy School of Art Nouveau.

The other major town in the region, Metz, the departmental capital of the Moselle, has some 195,000 inhabitants. Lorraine has four *départements*: Meuse (55), Meurthe-et-Moselle (54), Moselle (57) and Vosges (88) in the south. As well as the main rivers, there is a canal connecting the Rhine to the Marne (Canal de la Marne au Rhin) and the Canal de l'Est, connecting the Meuse up to the Moselle. For 200 years the canals were major transport arteries for shipping coal, iron and steel from Lorraine to the west, but they fell into disuse with the coming of the railways, and are kept up now for holidaymakers.

The Meuse *département* (www.tourisme-meuse.com) is closely identified with Verdun and World War I; the departmental capital is Bar-le-Duc south of Verdun. Meurthe-et-Moselle (www.cdt-meurthe-et-moselle.fr) separates the Meuse and Moselle *départements*. The little town of Pont-à-Mousson on the Moselle supplies virtually all the manhole covers in France. Metz, the capital of Moselle (www.cg57.fr) is more or less due south of Luxembourg and there are regular trains to Germany. Lorraine does not have any direct air links with the UK, however, the nearest airport with flights to London being Strasbourg in Alsace.

The southernmost *département*, Vosges (www.vosges.fr) with the attractive town of Epinal, is a land of lakes, forest and spectacular gorges, and good skiing in winter. The southern part of the Vosges is a national park, Le Parc Naturel Régional des Ballons des Vosges. There is a tradition of taking the waters here, and both Vittel and Contrex mineral waters are produced in the area.

Cuisine. Everyone has heard of Quiche Lorraine, the local speciality; much of Lorraine is dairy-farming country. Because of the abundant rivers and lakes, Lorraine is also noted for its fish, such as pike, perch, trout and carp, typically cooked in white wine or cream. The area also shares the Moselle and its wines with Germany, mainly white wines such as Gris de Toul, Côtes de Meuse and Moselle, and some rosés. This is also the second beer-producing region of France. All in all, you can expect to eat and drink well here.

Property. Lorraine is generally rich in stone. The west is limestone, the mountains sandstone and granite. Stone and brick are the main building materials, but there are still a number of timber-framed houses with brick *hourdis* or pugging. More modern properties are brick-built with internal exposed beams and slate roofs.

Lorraine is unusual in that the traditional roofing was of Spanish tiles, with Flemish curled tiles in places. Overhanging roofs are another local feature. The typical farmhouse is the *usoir,* usually with an arched entrance for carts. Lorraine has a number of notable châteaux, if not the kinds of wrecks that Brits like to do up. As with Alsace, there is not a great market here for second homes, the main interest coming from the Germans. Houses start from about €80,000.

MIDI-PYRÉNÉES

CRT: 54 bvd de l'Embouchure, BP2166, 31022 Toulouse; ☎05 61 13 55 55; fax 05 61 47 17 16; e-mail information@crtmp.com; www.tourisme-midi-pyrenees.com.
Percentage of population: 4.25%; percentage of GDP: 3.6%.

Midi-Pyrénées covers a diverse area of mountain, high plateaux, lower-lying river valleys, and areas of rolling hills with rich, dark soil called *ter-reforts.* Most of it is situated within the former province Guyenne-Gascony, more or less the same as Aquitaine in its widest sense. In the 12th century the Counts of Toulouse presided over a federation of independent cities stretching as far as the Alps, with a tradition of tolerating all kinds of religious belief. All that was snuffed out by the Albigensian Crusade sent to stamp out the Cathars, a sect who considered themselves without sin: *katharoi* meant pure in Greek. The land was laid waste between 1209 and 1229 by the English warlord Simon de Montfort. The final act was the fall of the castle of Montségur in 1244. The County of Toulouse became part of France, and the great Occitan troubadour tradition disappeared overnight. The region suffered again from the English occupation during the Hundred Years War (1340-1453). More *bastides* (fortified hilltop villages) were built by both sides, until the English were finally booted out.

Most of the region, especially the Ariège, has experienced severe rural depopulation. It is reckoned that half of the houses in Ariège are now second residences. The region's capital, Toulouse, is one of France's most dynamic city in terms of economic opportunities and lifestyle, largely thanks to the effect of Aérospatiale and its European Airbus factory.

Midi-Pyrénées consists of eight *départements*: Ariège (09), Haute-Garonne (31), Hautes Pyrénées (65), Gers (32), Tarn (81), Tarn-et-Garonne (82), Aveyron (12), and Lot (46), all areas that should interest second-home buyers. Toulouse is in the Haute-Garonne (ww.cdt-haute-garonne.com). The Gers (www.gers-gascogne.com) is increasingly popular with British home-buyers.

The Lot (pronounced *lott*) covers a large part of the old county Quercy, a wilderness of gorges and limestone plateaux (*causses*) that has an irresistible appeal for foreign buyers (see www.quercy-tourisme.com/le-lot). Next to the Dordogne, the Lot, in its widest sense, is the place where most British buyers would like to find a house. The prefectural town, Cahors, on the Lot, is a typical sunny, sleepy southern town. North of Cahors lies the Causse de Gramat, a dry limestone plateau, and to the south the Causse de Limogne. The most attractive town in the Lot is Figeac, east of Cahors, on the pilgrimage way to Santiago de Compostela; in the past the main industry was tanning. The remarkable church on a rock pinnacle at Rocamadour is the other major attraction.

The prefectural city of the Tarn-et-Garonne, Montauban, was the first *bastide* – fortified town – built by the Counts of Toulouse against the English and French in 1144. At the eastern end of the Tarn-et-Garonne is the castle town of St-Antonin-Noble-Val on the Aveyron river, in the vicinity of the 'golden triangle' which has recently been seen by cinema audiences as the setting for the Resistance film, *Charlotte Gray*.

The Tarn is one of the most popular areas for British property-hunters; suitable properties in the so-called 'golden triangle' of Gaillac, Cordes-sur-Ciel and Albi are becoming scarce and expensive. Only the out-of-the-way corners of the Tarn have cheap properties nowadays. The remoteness of the area is both an advantage and a minus: it can take a good two hours to get here from Toulouse or Bordeaux airport. Most tourists head for Albi, the prefectural town, with its remarkable red-brick cathedral that resembles an ocean liner.

The Aveyron (www.cdt-aveyron.fr), east of the Tarn, is an area of steep hills and forests in the southern Massif Central, with few inhabitants, which is much in vogue for camping and walking holidays with the French. The prefectural town of Rodez has a fine Gothic cathedral in red sandstone; it stands at the centre of a remote and wild region, little frequented by foreign visitors, where properties are still cheap and fairly plentiful.

Cuisine. The higher elevations of the Midi-Pyrénées are the home of goats, which are kept for their milk to turn into small cheeses or *petits chèvres*. There are numerous other cheeses from cow's and ewe's milk, called *tommes des Pyrénées*. Ducks and all kinds of dishes from ducks, such as *magret, confit, foie gras* and so on are native to the region. The Ariège has its own version of the ever-popular *cassoulet,* known as *mounjetado,* cooked slowly over a wood fire at village festivals. Pork products are essential to *cassoulet* and used down to the last detail. In the Tarn you could try pig's ears and snout cooked in wine, or perch in nettle butter.

Tarn-et-Garonne produces 80% of the fruit in the Midi-Pyrénées.

Chasselas table grapes from Moissac are well-known, as are the local Reine Claude plums. Tarn-et-Garonne is also the second biggest producer of garlic in France.

The mountainous areas of the Pyrenees are too cold for vineyards. The rest of the Midi-Pyrénées has a vinegrowing tradition going back over 1,000 years; there are now some 14 *appellations* ranging from the Vin d'Entraygues et du Fel in the Aveyron, to the Gaillac wines, both red and white, and sparkling, to the popular rustic reds of Cahors of the Lot.

Up and Coming Region: Ariège, Haute-Garonne, Hautes-Pyrénées

Southwest of Toulouse, towards the Pyrenees, is an area with few estate agents that has plenty of potential for second-home hunters. The Comminges region, between Bagnères de Luchon and Toulouse, is likely to become popular soon; it tends to be overlooked by foreigners, but there are plenty of properties in good condition. All three départements are close to the ski fields of the Pyrenees. The rest of the year there is climbing, fishing, sailing and walking for the active.

The Ariège is generally tipped as one of the up-and-coming regions for British house-buyers, mainly because of the very sunny climate; with luck you can be sunbathing for 10 months of the year here. During the winter there is skiing in the Pyrenees. The property market is geared to outsiders; the failing economy has left the département virtually dependent on tourism. The dryness of the climate makes it especially attractive to retirees. The drawback of the Ariège is the smallness of the properties and their limited availability, but one may still find a house in the mountains for as little as €15,000. Land is very cheap in the foothills; a 10-hectare farm can be had for as little as €100,000. You may not the get the kind of view of the Pyrenees that you would like; generally properties are built to avoid the excessive heat from the south and the prevailing winds from the northwest.

Hautes-Pyrénées has very cheap property on the plains around Tarbes; closer to the ski-fields expect to pay €150,000 upwards for renovated properties.

Property. The Midi-Pyrénées has 260,000 second homes out of 1,320,000 units. The property market around Toulouse has generally been transformed by the opening of the A20 motorway from Toulouse to Limoges and Paris, and cheap flights to the UK. Aveyron and Tarn have recently become fairly expensive, and one has to look in the more out-of-the-way areas for a bargain. There are farms in the higher plateaux for as little as €50,000.

The Midi-Pyrénées is rich in various rock types and traditionally an area of stone building. There is also a lot of red-brick building between Toulouse and Albi, one of the few areas of France with no local stone for building. One of the distinctive features of the Midi-Toulousain is the use of brick door- and window-surrounds and quoins even in stone buildings. Wood was scarce and expensive in the past due to deforestation in the mountains, and was mainly used for balconies, haylofts and internal framework of houses. One can find some half-timbering with *torchis* or cob – a mix of plaster and woodshavings called *massaca*. Farmhouses in the Haute-Garonne and Ariège are sometimes partly built into the rockface; the cellar walls are bare rock. Higher up, roofs are of slates; smaller houses of the lower country use tiles. Around river valleys one may see another type of construction, using layers of pebbles set in mortar alternating with brick or with brick quoins. The local nobility built *maisons de maître* which they tried to turn into something like châteaux. These are on four storeys with servant quarters at the top. There is a great vogue for *pigeonniers* – purpose-built pigeon towers in stone with nests out of clay pots or wood. These served a useful purpose for manure and pigeon meat. They were also a status symbol; only those of higher social rank could have a *pigeonnier* or *colombier*.

NORD-PAS-DE-CALAIS

CRT: 6 place Mendès, 59800 Lille; ☎03 20 14 57 57; fax 03 20 14 57 58; e-mail contact@crt-nordpasdecalais.fr; www.crt-nordpasdecalais.fr; www.northernfrance-tourism.com.
Percentage of population: 6.65%; percentage of GDP: 5.25%.

A triangle of territory running with the Belgian border in the north and the English Channel on the west is made up of the two *départements* that give it its name: the Nord (59) and the Pas-de-Calais (62). This is one of the smaller regions, but very densely populated. Historically it was a border-land between Flanders (a powerful state in the Middle Ages) and France. Louis XIV brought the area under French rule from 1668. Flemish culture mainly survives in a small triangle in the northwest of the Nord *départe-ment* (www.cdt-nord.fr); place-names and family names are Flemish, but the language has all but died out in the last fifty years. Lille came under French rule earlier. The regional capital, Lille, joins up with the towns Roubaix and Tourcoing to form the only real urban sprawl in France, spilling over into Belgium. The Lille conurbation counts as France's fourth largest city, with 960,000 residents.

Pas de Calais (www.pas-de-calais.com) is well-known to the English as the entry point to France if you come through Calais, Boulogne or Dunkerque. In most ways, it tends to be overlooked by tourists and property-hunters who are looking for the sun and mountains. The Côte d'Opale has fine flat beaches, particularly suitable for families, but is fairly wild when the weather closes in from the sea. South of Le Calaisis and Le Boulonnais is the area of Canche-Authie, with the high-class resorts of Montreuil-sur-Mer and Berck-Plage. Le Touquet to the north was once popular with wealthy holidaymakers from the UK in the 50s and 60s, who would fly over from Kent. The golf course is still one of the best in France, and there are several others in the vicinity.

Inland is the ancient county of Artois and part of French Hainaut. In a corner of Artois one can visit Azincourt, the site of the Battle of Agincourt in 1415. The prefectural town of Arras was at the centre of World War I trench warfare; the nearby Vimy Ridge has been given to the Canadian people in perpetuity in recognition of their sacrifices. Historically, Arras produced fine wall hangings: an *arras* is another name for a wall hanging.

The Nord has one great advantage in that it is easy to reach from London: only two hours by train from Lille. Moreover one can get to Brussels in 40 minutes, and Paris in 60. TGVs from Lille go virtually everywhere in France, bypassing Paris. The French would also say that the people are very *sympathique*. They are generally less excitable than average French people, thanks to the calming influence of the slow and solid Flemish.

Cuisine. French Flanders is the centre of beer-brewing in France; you can find many of the finest Flemish beers in the cafés of Lille and round about. The cuisine is also distinctly Flemish, for example, *potje vleesch* (meat in aspic), *moules frites* (mussels and chips), *carbonnade flamande* (beef cooked in stout) and *poêlée d'endives* (fried chicory). The local spirit is *bistoul* or gin.

Property. Styles of construction are influenced by Flemish tradition: red brick is used a lot, along with a variety of coloured brick for decorative effect, and there is the same tradition of whitewashing farmhouses. Flemish stepped gables – *pignons à gradins* – are also in evidence. Close to the Belgian border the houses are indistinguishable from those in Belgium. Pas-de-Calais shares the same styles of building with Picardie. On the downside, the Nord-Pas de Calais is France's most industrialised region, but there is still enough countryside left to find some attractive properties, particularly along the canals. Naturally, the coast is expensive.

NORMANDY

CRT: Le Doyenné, 14 rue Charles Corbeau, 27000 Évreux; ☎02 32 33 94 00; fax 02 32 31 19 04; e-mail normandy@imaginet.fr; www.normandy-tourism.org.

While Upper and Lower Normandy are officially two separate regions, they have a great deal in common, and are treated together here. There is a strong possibility that they will be combined into one region in the next few years.

Upper Normandy
Percentage of population: 2.97%; percentage of GDP: 2.83%.

Upper Normandy – Haute Normandie – is a region rich in history linking it to England. Probably more than any other region in France it is connected with major writers and artists, who were inspired by its rural life whilst appreciating its being conveniently close to Paris The best-known painter of the area, Monet, grew up in Le Havre from the age of five; his house at Giverny with its brightly coloured flowers and lily pond provided subjects for many of his best-known paintings. The shifting light on the frontage of Rouen cathedral inspired some of his greatest work.

Upper Normandy is very much dairy country; the rolling hills are reminiscent of southern England, of which it is an extension. Although it doesn't have quite the cachet of the landing beaches in Lower Normandy that will go on attracting Americans for many years, Upper Normandy's closeness to England and the good ferry connections from Dieppe and Le Havre make it a popular location with Britons, particularly with those who want to keep working in England or who can work from home some of the time in France.

Upper Normandy comprises only two *départements*: Eure (27) and Seine-Maritime (76). Rouen, the capital of the region, was designed by the first Duke of Normandy, Rollo, a Viking who forced the French king to recognise his claim to Normandy in 911, on the site of the Roman Rotiomagus. Opinions are mixed on the attractiveness of Rouen, a city of 380,000 souls. The central streets have been carefully preserved in a uniform half-timbered style that makes a very attractive whole. Anywhere outside the centre and you are in dull industrial suburbs with nothing much to see.

To see the real beauties of the Seine-Maritime (www.seine-maritime-tourisme.com) it is best to head towards Honfleur, a picturesque port whose narrow streets are thronged with tourists most of the year. The coastline was much appreciated by the Impressionists; Renoir and Cézanne came here to visit Monet who loved to paint here. Further north Le Havre is France's second largest port, with 245,000 inhabitants, and is completely new as the original town was obliterated in World War II. Dieppe is conveniently close to Rouen and has regular ferries to Newhaven, but is not otherwise of much interest. The whole coast between Dieppe and Le Havre is known as the Côte Albâtre or Alabaster Coast, from the whiteness of the cliffs.

Upper Normandy's most attractive towns and villages are situated in the Eure *département*, east of Rouen (www.cdt-eure.fr). The best rustic architecture is at Lyons-la-Forêt. The woods around here are very popular with walkers. A little to the south, Richard the Lionheart built the Château Gaillard high above the Seine at Les Andelys to keep an eye on the locals. Only 15km away is Giverny, Monet's home. Évreux, the prefectural town, was heavily damaged in the war, but the outstanding cathedral of Notre Dame was saved, with its 14th-century stained glass, some of the finest in France.

Lower Normandy

Percentage of population: 2.37%; percentage of GDP: 1.92%.

Lower Normandy – Basse Normandie – has strong ties with both Britain and North America. Once you cross the estuary of the Seine over the futuristic Pont de Normandie you are on the Côte Fleurie or Norman Riviera with the twin resorts of Trouville and Deauville. These were popularised by the playboy Emperor Napoleon III in the 1860s. Wealthy Parisians come here for the casino and the racecourses. Overpriced and to be avoided.

Further west are the Côte Nacre and the Normandy landing beaches, with their lovingly tended military cemeteries. The city of Caen, inland from the ferry port of Ouistreham (ferries to Portsmouth) was virtually obliterated in 1944. Further west, Bayeux is famed for its great tapestry showing the successful invasion of England by William the Conqueror, whose birthplace was Falaise in the Orne. Bayeux was fortunate to be the first town in France to be freed from the Germans, so it came out of the war almost undamaged.

The *département* of Calvados, of which Caen is the capital, gave its name to a potent liqueur, also known as *calvados* or *calva*. All of Normandy is dominated by apple-growing and dairy-farming. The Orne *département*, to the south is the home Camembert, a bland cheese popularised by Napoleon III. At the very far western end of the coast is the great tourist attraction Mont St Michel.

To the northwest of Bayeux lies the Cotentin peninsula, also with strong World War II associations, which has found a place on the literary map in the series of humorous books by George East, such as *René and Me, Home and Dry in France,* etc. Although the Cotentin is rustic and remote, it does have a ferry port at Cherbourg.

Lower Normandy has some advantages over Upper Normandy: the climate is somewhat warmer, but it is also wetter. The annual rainfall in Cherbourg, in the Manche, is over 50 inches. For anyone who wants to start *gîtes* or *chambres d'hôte* prospects are good in Calvados if you are within reach of the *plages du débarquement,* the landing beaches, which guarantee you a steady stream of American tourists.

Cuisine. Norman cooking is rich in cream and butter as you would expect. The local drink is cider rather than wine, and the potent liqueur derived from it, *calvados*. It is customary to have a pause between courses in the copious meals for a *trou normand* (literally 'Norman gap') to knock back some *calvados*. Seafood is also eaten a great deal. All kinds of meat are popular, particularly ducks from Rouen, and *andouilles*, sausages made with cows' intestines. The apples and pears that are not turned into cider are put to use for apple tarts and cakes with cream.

Property. The archetypal Norman property is the half-timbered *longère* or farmhouse. Anything advertised as a *maison normande* will have half-timbering (*colombage*), even if it is only a token decoration. Another typical feature of all Norman farmhouses are the *lucarnes* or dormer windows, which are there partly for aesthetic reasons to disguise the massive size of the roofs.

Modest Norman houses were traditionally made of wood, the *pans de bois* style. First a wooden frame (*charpente*) is constructed on a foundation of sandstone, limestone or bricks. Massive vertical beams (*poteaux*) are fixed into the foundations about two metres apart. The *poteaux* are held apart by crossbeams known as *sablières*. Further massive beams of up to seven metres or more run from front to back. Batons are fixed into the spaces between the *poteaux* and *sablières*. The vertical batons are known as *potelets* or *colombes* and the latter has given the name *colombages* to this style of half-timbering.

The wooden framework is filled in with pugging (*hourdis*), consisting of clay mixed with straw or animal hair, soaked in water and then dried. Lumps of pugging are then attached to horizontal or oblique strips of wood (*palissons* or *éclisses*). Other types of pugging are cut-up tiles (*tuileaux*) fixed with mortar, arranged in geometric patterns. More rarely bricks are used. The wall is then rendered with lime rendering to protect against the rain. This type of construction is vulnerable to bad weather, so roofs tend to overhang by as much as 50cm. Construction in *pans de bois* (half-timbering) continued far longer in the Calvados, or Pays d'Auge, than in Seine Maritime, or Pays de Caux, reflecting the greater poverty of the Pays d'Auge.

Seine Maritime started using brick quite early on; light and dark bricks are used to create decorative effects, similar to the style of Pas-de-Calais. The *département* of the Eure still has many half-timbered houses. One step up from a *longère* is a *gentilhommière*, similarly constructed but of greater size.

The landscape is far more rocky to the west in the Manche. The traditional stone structure is of rough-shaped rocks or *moellons* placed on top of each other on two faces of a wall, with the gaps filled in with smaller rocks mixed with earth. Here and there a throughstone (*boutisse parpaing*) is inserted to give the wall stability. Quoins of cut stone hold the walls together at the corners.

Thatch roofs are becoming less common; the wet climate makes slates a more practical roofing material, and it is more expensive to insure thatch roofs. Thatching has to be replaced regularly, making it an expensive luxury. A house with thatching is a *chaumière* – although this is often translated as 'cottage' these are usually substantial dwellings. There is also a vogue for converting buildings used for cider pressing – *pressoirs* – into houses; they have single storeys, and rather disproportionately large roofs.

A wealthy farmer or lord of the manor generally preferred to build his *ferme-manoir* in limestone or granite. The entrance for coaches would be a grand arch, convenient for the main residence or *grange*. On three sides one may find storerooms (*celliers*), a cart-shed (*charreterie*), stables (*écurie*), bakehouse (*boulangerie*), dovecote (*pigeonnier* or *colombier*), milking-house (*laiterie*) and so on. These days they may be turned into garages and *gîtes*. The wealthier the farmer, the more architectural detail he would try to apply. The very well-off would add on a tower to the *grange*.

One may still find properties to do up in the Eure, and to a lesser extent, Seine-Maritime. There is competition from the Parisians for holiday homes. Starting prices are €50,000 in Eure, and €70,000 in Seine-Maritime. In the eastern Calvados and Orne there are plenty of half-timbered Norman longhouses or *longères* for sale, as well as other farmhouses with half-timbering. The Orne, on the other hand, is somewhat up-market. This is the centre for horse-breeding in France, with the national stud near Argentan. One should be wary of buying half-timbered houses in bad condition, even if they look very cheap. Only a specialist can deal with this type of construction. If you buy a listed building the renovation costs could be prohibitive. The cheapest properties are in Calvados, starting from around €30,000. In the Manche and the Orne there is not much under €75,000.

As a holiday area, most new construction in Normandy is for second homes. Prices of property depend on two things: the distance from Paris and the distance from the sea. A sea view adds 50% or more to the price. A good railway link to Paris is also a plus point. Note that the climate here is much like southern England. Good insulation is a must, as is an adequate heating system. Half-timbered houses are generally colder than stone ones.

PARIS AND ILE-DE-FRANCE

CRT: 91 ave des Champs-Elysées, Paris; ☎01 56 89 38 00; fax 01 56 89 38 390; e-mail crt@paris-ile-de-France.com; www.paris-ile-de-france.com; www.paris-touristoffice.com.
Percentage of population: 18.25%. Percentage of GDP: 27.3%

The nation's capital, with its surrounding area, forms one region known as Ile de France. The central core of Paris is home to 2.1 million people; the

Paris agglomeration has a population of 11.1 million, more than half as much again as Greater London.

Until 987 AD Paris was not a particularly significant place; in pre-Roman times the Parisi tribe had a small fortified stronghold on the Ile de la Cité (where Notre-Dame cathedral now stands) known as Lutetia, which was conquered by Julius Caesar in 52 BC. Paris became the centre of an embryonic French state when Hugues Capet made himself king of France in the 10th century, Ile-de-France as the only area that was really under his control. Most of the country was ruled by independent dukes and counts, who only paid lip-service to rule from Paris. Notre-Dame was begun in 1160 by Bishop de Sully and took nearly 200 years to complete.

Apart from Notre Dame very little of medieval Paris survives. A section of the Roman bathhouse which forms part of the extraordinary Musée du Cluny is the only real reminder of the earliest phase of the capital. The 'City of Light' was substantially remodelled in the 19th century, and turned into a homogenously magnificent metropolis worthy of its status as the capital of a world empire. To see how Paris looked in the time of Louis XIV you need to go to the Marais district, with its sumptuous *hôtels particuliers* (hotel also means an imposing private or public building). The Parisian taste for grandiose and daring building projects can be seen in the Eiffel Tower, the Beaubourg or Centre Pompidou, the first building to have all its pipes and escalators on the outside, and the fantastic Arche de la Défense to the west of the city, a modern echo of the Napoleonic Arc de Triomphe.

As with any huge urban conglomeration, Paris can seem overwhelming at first sight, but things are organised to make the city liveable. Unlike London, Paris has a well integrated public transport system, about half the price of London's.

The downside to Paris is partly to do with its size, and partly with the mentality of the Parisiens or 'Parigots' as the rest of the French call them. Along with all of France's national institutions, Paris has also concentrated every aspect of the country's social problems in the capital. Paris also has the reputation of being the least friendly city in France. Everyone is in too much of a hurry to talk much with you. Foreigners tend to stick together, and form their own social clubs. The negative image of the French as arrogant and xenophobic comes in part from foreigners' superficial contacts with Parisians. If a Frenchman is proud of his country, it follows that the Parisians are twice as proud of their city as the heart of francophone culture. If your heart is in the countryside, and you relish relaxed conversations in the local café, you might think twice about living here, but if you are looking for high excitement and a cutting-edge cultural experience, this would be the place to go for.

There is now a strong demographic tendency for the better-off to leave the centre of the city for the suburbs, while the city is more and more packed with immigrants and young people. Paris is by far the most expensive place to live in France. Prices of basic commodities in shops are roughly comparable with those in London, i.e. far more expensive than the rest of France.

Most people live in apartments; there are few houses on the market within the Boulevard Périphérique which delimits the city. Property prices are 40% to 65% of those in London, but there are vast differences between the 20 *arrondissements*. The *arrondissements* are arranged like a snail shell, going clockwise from the centre. The 1st and 2nd are the historical centre, with world-famous landmarks. The 3rd and 4th are trendy with a lot of bars and discos. The 5th includes the Sorbonne and the Quartier Latin. The 6th or 7th are the most expensive and exclusive, with government buildings and large open spaces. The 8th includes the shopping centre of the Champs Elysées; the 9th is an area of theatres, cinemas and department stores. The 10th has the Gare du Nord and Gare de l'Est; the 11th and 12th on the eastern side are being revitalised with large building projects. The 13th, 14th, 15th, 16th and 17th are residential. The 18th was very attractive in the past but has gone downhill with the spread of the red light area around Montmartre and Pigalle. The 19th and 20th are more downmarket areas. The relative standing of the *arrondissements* can be judged from the price per square metre for apartments, given below.

Outside Paris is a large area of suburbs as well as countryside. Central Ile de France is known as *la petite couronne,* and includes Hauts-de-Seine, Seine-Saint-Denis and Val-de-Marne. Paris is also a *département.* The rest of Ile de France is *la grande couronne,* comprising Seine-et-Marne, Yvelines, Essonne and Val-d'Oise.

Property. Almost all residential property in central Paris dates back to the 19th century. There are plenty of modern villas and mansions outside the inner city. The Ile-de-France has its own traditional architecture, characterised by white-rendered farmhouses with elaborate entrance arches, and *lucarnes* with pulleys for bringing in sacks of grain. Flat tiles (*pannes*) and slates are both common. More recent detached properties imitate various styles of regional architecture.

As far as Paris goes, the only property you could expect to afford would be an apartment. Houses rarely come on the market, and are worth millions in the upmarket *arrondissements.* Nevertheless, apartments are not that expensive, and anyone on a good income should be able to afford one near the city centre. Out in the suburbs, prices are very reasonable by British standards. A three-bedroom house in a good area can be had for £150,000. There are very expensive suburbs: wealthy Americans live in a sort of ghetto in St Cloud. Versailles, Fontainebleau and St-Germain-en-Laye are very up-market.

PAYS DE LA LOIRE

CRT: 2 rue de la Loire, 44204 Nantes; ☎02 40 48 24 20; fax 02 40 08 07 10; e-mail infotourisme@crtpdl.com; www.cr-pays-de-la-loire.fr, www.paysdelaloire.fr.
Percentage of population: 5.37%; percentage of GDP: 4.6%.

The western part of the Loire Valley has been made into a region covering the old counties of Maine and Anjou. The capital, Nantes (www.reception.com/nantes), was the traditional seat of the Dukes of Brittany – they are buried in the cathedral – but the city officially ceased to be part of Brittany in 1962. Duchess Anne brought Brittany under the French crown when she married King Charles VIII in 1491. In the past, Nantes prospered from the colonial trade (i.e. slavery) and ship-building, activities whose place has been taken by diversified industries, especially IT. Nantes is a pleasant place to live and offers reasonable job prospects for foreign workers. It was rated third in a survey of French cities by *Express* magazine, for economic dynamism and quality of life.

The *départements* of Loire-Atlantique (www.cdt44.com) and Vendée offer flat sandy beaches and excellent sailing and golf, but parts of the coast have been spoilt by overdevelopment. La Baule, west of St Nazaire – France's biggest shipbuilding port – is the most up-market (and therefore expensive) beach resort on the Atlantic coast. The Vendée has had an uneasy relationship with Paris; in 1793 the Vendéens unwisely backed a revolt against the Revolution and were soundly defeated. To dramatise the blood that was spilt, the town of Cholet (just inside Anjou) still turns out red and white striped handkerchiefs that are used all over France.

The *département* of Maine-et-Loire, corresponding to part of the old Anjou region, came under the control of the English when Henry I married his daughter off to Geoffrey Count of Anjou. His son, Henry II, was thus an Angevin. The area is dotted with castles recalling Richard the Lionheart and other romantic figures. The city of Angers and the area round about are worth considering for second homes; the proximity of airports and the TGV to Paris and Lille make it a convenient place for Brits. One could say this is an up-and-coming region.

In the north of the Pays de la Loire lies the wild and thinly populated *département* of Mayenne (www.tourisme-mayenne.com), reputed to have more châteaux per square mile than anywhere outside Paris. Rather confusingly, the departmental capital is not the town of Mayenne itself, but Laval further south, but they both lie on the River Mayenne. Agriculture is the main industry. Mayenne's remoteness makes it attractive to Brits who want to get away from it all without being too far from the Channel ports. Straddling the southern part of Basse Normandie and the northern edge of Loire is the Maine Normand national park. The Maine is both flat and somewhat arid, and lacks the kind of scenery that attracts foreigners.

The capital of the Sarthe *département* (http://tourisme.sarthe.com), Le Mans, lying on the motorway from Paris to Rennes, is rightly famous for its 24-hour race, but it also has an amazingly intact medieval centre, and the best-preserved Roman fortress walls outside Rome itself.

The Vendée (www.vendee-tourisme.com) is attracting a lot of attention now from foreign property buyers (see below). The fine sandy beaches and some up-market resorts attract Parisians in droves. There are two large islands of the coastline: the Ile d'Yeu (an hour by ferry from the mainland) and the Ile de Noirmoutier (connected by road), with strict planning laws about the size and design of buildings. The northern part of the Vendée coastline is known as Le Pays des Monts; along with the southern part, the Sables d'Olonne, this is an area thick with sandy beaches, dunes and holiday resorts, ideal for windsurfing, sailing, scuba diving, sand yachting and so on. There are four 18-hole golf courses. The southern Vendée includes part of the Marais Poitevin national park, a vast area of wetlands where the easiest way to get around is by punt. The town of Fontenay-le-Comte was rebuilt in Renaissance style by King François I. The inland part of the Vendée, the Bocage Vendéen, is also fairly touristic. The departmental capital, La Roche-sur-Yon, was built by Napoleon on a symmetrical plan to try to pacify the rebellious Vendéens and develop the local economy. It is rated as one of France's best places to live.

Up-and-Coming Region: Vendée

The traditional style of the Vendée is the low, whitewashed pisé or adobe farmhouse in the marshlands, and stone inland. The low, double-pitched roofs with their curled Spanish tiles testify to the dryness of the climate. The rainfall is as little as 24 inches per year. There has been a lot of new building on the coast to cater for Parisian holiday-makers, but this seems to have reached its limit as far as available land goes. Seaside properties are gaining rapidly in value, with annual rises of 20%. Anyone who wants to get away from the usual boxy developments by the sea, can find far cheaper properties inland. There is already a well-established British community. One could consider trying to set up a business relying on other expats. Angela Bird, the author of the guidebook The Vendée has set up a useful webpage for visitors and prospective buyers: see www.the-vendee.co.uk.

The main attraction of Vendée is the very mild climate, with sunshine on a par with the Riviera. Transport links are good, with direct flights to London from nearby Nantes, and TGV between Paris and Nantes.

Cuisine. The area around Nantes, near the mouth of the Loire, is mainly known for its light muscadet wines, which gain their particular flavour from the chalky soils. Saumur in Anjou specialises in a naturally sparkling white wine, the Saumur Brut. There is also the red Saumur-Champigny. A little to the south, around the Layon and Aubance rivers, some fine sweet dessert wines such as Coteaux du Layon have a worldwide reputation. The light, fruity wines of the Vendée, which go under the name of Fiefs Vendéens, are not well-known and hardly exported. Sarthe and Mayenne are more apple-growing regions.

Thanks to the long coastline, seafoods are plentiful in the western Loire, especially, mussels and oysters. The local sardines, anchovies and baby eels, called elvers, are well-known throughout France. The abundance of waterways in the region gives a wide range of freshwater fish, notably trout, pike, pike-perch (*sandre*) and carp. Free-range poultry from Challans in the Vendée and Loué in the Sarthe have their own *appellation,* the Label Rouge. The mild climate of the western Loire has led to the development of market gardens, growing small new season vegetables such as carrots, leeks and salads. There are all sorts of cow's milk cheeses; Port Salut from the Mayenne has a worldwide reputation.

Property. About 20% of properties are second homes in the region, mainly concentrated along the coast. Mayenne is well-known for its châteaux; there is scope for finding stone farmhouses to renovate. Sarthe is an area of small stone-built farmhouses. Habitable properties start from €50,000. One may also find something situated next to a river quite cheaply. Nantes, the regional capital, is one of the trendiest places to live in France, and is experiencing something of a housing shortage as a result, while Le Mans is a lot cheaper.

PICARDY

CRT: 3 rue Vincent Auriol, 80011 Amiens; ☎ 03 22 22 33 66; fax 03 22 22 33 67; e-mail contact@picardietourisme.com; www.cr-picardie.fr. Percentage of population: 3.1%; percentage of GDP: 2.46%.

The Picardy region has three *départements*: Somme (80), Oise (60) and Aisne (02). The name Somme naturally evokes World War I, and the senseless waste of human life that occurred at the Battles of the Somme starting from 1916 in which some 1,353,000 died in a vain attempt to win some land from the Germans, and relieve the French defenders at Verdun. The area is dotted with memorials and cemeteries of the combatants, particularly around the town of Albert on the road to Cambrai. The main British, Irish and Canadian memorial is at Thiépval, along with the Ulster Monument. Around the bay of the Somme, the region has one of the best stretches of unspoilt sandy coastline in France, ideal for sand-yachting. The coast drew the painters Seurat, Sisley and Dégas to try to capture its ever-changing light. The old holiday resort of Mers-les-Bains is noted for its *belle époque* (Edwardian) villas. The writer Marcel Proust enjoyed taking his holidays here.

The departmental capital, Amiens, will be familiar to anyone who travelled by train from the coast to Paris in the days before the Eurostar and cheap flights. Picardy is a land of gently rolling hills, criss-crossed by waterways and river, where the people are known for their love of flowers. Amiens has taken on the name of Venice of the North, thanks to the water gardens called Hortillonnages that can be explored in punts.

The Oise was the furthest south the Germans reached during World War I. The prefectural town of Beauvais specialises in the manufacture of tapestry, but is otherwise fairly uninteresting. It is only a short distance from here to Paris, and a short drive to Charles de Gaulle Airport at Roissy-en-France. There are flights from Beauvais to London and Birmingham. The Oise has one of France's finest châteaux, Chantilly, whose origins go back to the 12th century; the town of the same name is known for its lace, and, of course, cream.

The Aisne was heavily fought over in World War I; the front line stayed static here for most of the war. For anyone interested in cookery, Fresnoy-le-Grand, near St Quentin, should be a place of pilgrimage, as this is where cast-iron Le Creuset saucepans are manufactured. The Aisne has a short stretch of border with Belgium at the far northeast corner. Although Picardy was never under Flemish rule, certain traditions are similar, such as the popularity of archery, cards, skittles and other café games.

The region at one time had its own language, *picard,* one of the *langues d'oïl* (northern French dialects) that has fallen into oblivion. Its industrial and working-class traditions led Victor Hugo to use the area in some of his novels. Picardy generally prides itself on its literary traditions and holds some major literary festivals.

Cuisine. Picardy is not one of France's outstanding gastronomic regions. Its main contribution is the fresh produce from its market gardens. Apart from the Maroilles cheese, there is smoked river eel, lamb from the salt-flats of the Somme, and waterfowl. In the southeastern corner of the Aisne, there are champagne cellars, which produce 7% of France's output. There is also some cider production, and Colvert Beer, made at Péronne between Amiens and St Quentin.

Property. The agricultural plain of Picardy has traditionally been short of stone for building; brick is the most widely used material. Earlier buildings have timber-frames and clay and lath *torchis.* The more recent style is similar to Flanders, with low, tiled roofs, and whitewashed brick. It is not always obvious what material has been used as everything tends to be covered with a thick layer of rendering. Farmhouses are narrow; the farm buildings are usually arranged in a square, sometimes without any windows on the street side.

The Somme is one of the less interesting regions for foreign property buyers. The climate is wet and the landscape flat, and heavily farmed. The after-effects of the coal-mining industry are still in evidence, with old slagheaps that are gradually being reclaimed by nature. Away from the main roads to Paris the Aisne and the Oise have a lot more scope; generally they are more hilly and green, with more space.

POITOU-CHARENTES

CRT: 62 rue Jean-Jaurès, 86002 Poitiers; ☎05 49 50 10 50; fax 05 49 41 37 28; e-mail poitou-charente.tourisme@interpc.fr; www.tourisme-atlantique.com.
Percentage of population: 2.73%; percentage of GDP: 2.11%.

As the name suggests this is really two regions in one, the coastal area of Charente-Maritime and the inland Poitou. Poitiers, the capital, is well-known as the scene of a great English victory against the French in the Hundred Years' War, in 1356. This was also the seat of the Dukes of Aquitaine. The virtual reality theme park, Futuroscope, about 8 km outside the city, has turned Poitiers into a popular tourist destination for families. The building of the TGV station means you can get here from London with only one change of train at Lille; it also means fast connections to Bordeaux and Toulouse.

Aside from Futuroscope, Poitiers is not a tourist destination; there is a remarkable Romanesque cathedral started by Eleanor of Aquitaine. Out of the four *départements* of the region, Charente-Maritime (17) has the most tourism, Deux-Sèvres (79) and Vienne (86) are rather flat and agricultural, while Charente (16) is one of the popular areas with foreigners buying second homes, and borders on the Dordogne. As is often the case with poorer regions of France, the Vienne (www.vienne.org) has preserved a number of fine Romanesque churches, in particular the church of St Pierre, at Chauvigny, east of Poitiers.

The neighbouring small *département* of Deux-Sèvres (www.marais-deux-sevres.com) is poor agricultural land with low rainfall, like the Vendée. It includes part of the national park of the Marais Poitevin, the largest expanse of wetland on the western side of France, popular for the wildlife including otters, kingfishers, herons, and other rare birds. The Marais Poitevin national park extends into Vendée and Charente-

Maritime. The prefectural town of Niort is, rather surprisingly, the centre of the insurance industry in France. The other main town, Parthenay, has a number of Romanesque churches; it was on one of the main routes of the pilgrimage to Santiago de Compostela.

Charente-Maritime is a holiday region. The prefectural town, La Rochelle (www.ville-larochelle.fr), was once the main port for the trade with Canada and the West Indies; many colonists came from the Charente. Thanks to the policies of the local government, the town centre has remained largely unspoilt by uncontrolled building of holiday apartments that tends to blight much of the French coast. La Rochelle is linked to France's second largest offshore island, the 30 km-long Ile de Ré, by a modern bridge; the type of building and the traffic on the island are strictly controlled; it is naturally very popular with tourists in summer. There is a fortress here where prisoners were held before being shipped off to Devil's Island in French Guyana. South of La Rochelle, opposite the old naval base of Rochefort, lies France's largest island after Corsica, the Ile d'Oléron, also linked to the mainland by a massive bridge.

The coast of the Charente (www.poitou-charente-vacances) benefits from one of France's sunniest climates, over 2250 hours a year, on a par with Provence. Inland the climate is also quite sunny. After rain has fallen on Brittany and Normandy the clouds blow eastwards past the Loire. The prefectural town of Angoulême was once the paper-making centre of France. To the west, Cognac is the centre of the brandy industry; vast amounts are stored in *chais* – warehouses – that line the streets; they are sometimes put on the market for conversion. The grapes that go into making cognac can only be grown in the triangle between Royan, La Rochelle and Angoulême. This is one business that is never subject to recession.

Up and Coming Region: Deux-Sèvres

The small département of Deux-Sèvres, inland from the Vendée, is likely to see more interest from British home-buyers in the next few years. The climate is dry, and there are still farmhouses for renovation available. Small houses start from €25,000. This is an area of plentiful stone for building, mainly granite and gneiss. The improvements in communications make this a more easily accessible area than it was: there is a TGV as far as Poitiers, as well as flights from London. While the Vendée is becoming more and more popular with Parisians, Deux-Sèvres, which has no sea coast, remains cheap. There is the possibility of finding a house in the wetlands, next to water.

Property. Patterns of settlement in the past have depended on the presence or absence of water. In the marshlands of the northwest, houses were generally small and of wattle and daub, or mud, covered with bundles of rushes. The use of *pisé*, or adobe, meant that walls could not be built very high. This type of construction is more a historical relic, but the habit of using white rendering persists, and you will notice many low buildings. The rest of the region is rich in stone, and not much timber is used. This is generally a low-rainfall region; the water supply had to be drawn from very deep wells, so houses tended to cluster together close to the wells; village streets are narrow to try to diminish the effects of the strong winds.

Because of the shallowness of the soil, rocks were constantly dug up in the fields. Houses required only minimal foundations; the construction would be resting on rock in any case. The central swathe of the Poitou-Charentes consists of limestone and chalk, the rest of more ancient crystalline rock. In the roughest constructions the walls would be wider at the base and taper at the top. Since mortar does not adhere to limestone as well as to granite or schist, builders used cut stone quoins at the corners and inserted throughstones, and these can sometimes be seen protruding from the walls.

The Charente is already popular with foreign house-buyers; the area bordering on the Dordogne is the most attractive: Aubeterre-sur-Dronne is particularly expensive. Charente-Maritime, with its two large islands and seacoast is already well-established with Parisian holiday-makers.

PROVENCE-ALPES-CÔTE D'AZUR (PACA)

CRT: 10 place de la Joliette, Atrium 10.5, BP 46214, 13567 Marseille; ☎04 91 56 47 00; fax 04 91 56 47 01; e-mail information@crt-paca.fr; ww.crt-paca.fr; www.visitprovence.com.
Percentage of population: 7.51%; percentage of GDP: 6.62%

The Provence-Alpes-Côte d'Azur region, or PACA as it is usually called, has everything that the second home-owner might want in terms of sunshine and natural beauty. There is a sharp contrast between the overdeveloped coastal region and inland Provence, an area of poor agricultural land and high unemployment. There has been a recent trend for high-tech companies to move to the southeast, creating a sort of Silicon Valley around Nice, at Sophia-Antipolis. The success of Peter Mayle's books *A Year in Provence* and *Toujours Provence* in the 1980s set the trend for writing about one's experience of buying property in France, and probably led to Britons being priced out of a lot of Provence. One might also question whether one is really likely to have a Maylesque experience by moving here without having his fertile imagination.

The capital of the PACA region, Marseille (not Marseilles), is France's oldest city. After being founded by the Greeks in the 5th century BC the Romans took it over in 49 BC, when it was called Massilia. In the Middle Ages it was under the Counts or Kings of Provence; it finally became French in 1481. In the 19th century it took on more importance as the gateway to French North Africa. In recent years it has absorbed large numbers of immigrants. A sprawling, untidy city, it is regarded as not really part of France. It is certainly cosmopolitan, and a million miles removed from the expensive resorts of the Côte d'Azur. Counting its twin city, Aix-en-Provence, the population of 1.4 million makes it France's third city; it was once considered France's second city, but this honour now goes to Lyon. The surrounding area is one of the most industrialised in France. By some criteria, Aix-en-Provence is reckoned to be the best place to live in France.

The PACA attracts large numbers of outsiders from elsewhere in France, and from abroad. It is reckoned that the population will increase by 20% by 2020, because of high birth rates and immigration. The *départements* are: Vaucluse (84), Bouches-du-Rhône (13), Var (83), Alpes-de-Haute-Provence (04), Hautes-Alpes (05), and Alpes-Maritimes (06). The first four of these *départements* make up Provence; the region's capital was traditionally Aix-en-Provence, but this has been taken over by Marseille nearby. The Vaucluse represents one typical image of Provence: namely sunflowers and lavender fields, rich in Roman remains. The city of Orange has an amphitheatre that is still in use, and a Roman triumphal arch. Between 1559 and 1697 it was the domain of the Dutch Princes of Orange-Nassau.

The prefectural city of Avignon is more touristic, surrounded by its city walls, with the well-known bridge that stops halfway across the Rhône. Avignon was also the centre of Christendom for nearly 100 years. In 1309 Pope Clement V came here at the invitation of the French king to escape unrest in Rome. The Papacy returned to Rome in 1378, but another pope was elected in Avignon, starting the Western Schism; the situation was resolved in 1403 when the last Avignon pope fled the town. The magnificent Palace of the Popes is one of France's great tourist draws. The tourists also draw crime; Avignon has the highest rate in France.

Bouches-du-Rhône (www.visitprovence.com) is named after the delta of the Rhône which spreads out into the Camargue region, wild horse and cowboy country. The gateway to the Camargue, Arles, is a down-to-earth place that happens to have a Roman colosseum and amphitheatre in the middle of it. Being next to the Rhône it gets the full force of the *mistral*, a biting wind that blows down from the Alps for much of the year.

The Var (www.tourismevar.com), east of Marseille can boast the celebrity playground of St Tropez, and the Roman town of Fréjus, amongst other things. Sailing and beaches are two major attractions here. This is one of the sunniest regions of the south, with over 2500 hours of sunshine a year. This is also the stronghold of the neo-Fascist Front National.

The French Riviera. Les Alpes Maritimes (www.guideriviera.com) includes the main part of the Côte d'Azur, or French Riviera, stretching from Cannes to Menton on the Italian border. The region east of the River Var belonged to the kings of Sardinia who ruled over Savoie, and was incorporated into France in 1793, but then returned to Savoie after Napoleon's defeat. It became part of France in 1860, as a gift from the Italian government to France for her support in their war against the Austrians. The French Riviera is naturally synonymous with high living; as far as property prices go, the coast is in a league of its own, on a par with Paris and the most exclusive ski resorts in the Alps. Between Nice and Menton, lies the semi-independent principality of Monaco, stuffed to the gills with millionaires.

From around 1850, the Riviera became popular with wealthy convalescents thanks to the year-round warm climate, and lack of extreme weather. As Biarritz and the Atlantic Coast declined, so the Riviera gained in status. Overall, the coastal part of the Riviera may not be that attractive to British property buyers. The area suffers from high crime levels; the rich and famous have to employ armies of security staff to feel safe here. If you can do without the sight of the sea, an inland property has many advantages. For the price of a small apartment in Antibes you could have a large house inland.

Behind the Alpes Maritimes lies the *département* of Alpes-Haute-Provence (www.alpes-haute-provence.com), traditionally the route for invaders between the sea and the mountains. The prefectural town of Digne-les-Bains lies at a comfortable 1,800 feet above sea level. In 1980 a private company reopened the Digne to Nice railway; the Train des Pignes passes through pine forests up to 3,000 feet.

The border with the next *département* – Hautes-Alpes (www.hautes-alpes.net) – once marked the frontier between Provence and Dauphiné. Following the invasion of Dauphiné in 1692, Louis XIV ordered his military architect Vauban to build massive fortresses in the Hautes Alpes, at Briançon, Montdauphin and Fort Queyras. These no longer serve any military purpose, but are used for recreation and walking. The key to the French defensive system, Briançon, at 4,000 feet, is one of the highest cities in Europe; it is noted for its many frescoes and carved wooden doors, and some remarkable historic buildings. Hautes-Alpes is tourist country; ideal for water sports, walking, fishing, skiing, climbing and bird-watching.

Cuisine. Provençal rosés are good to drink in hot weather; the region is equally noted for its red wines, and a few whites. Inland Vaucluse along the Rhône has several vintage wines. The town of Châteauneuf du Pape is one of the great names in wine. The Côtes-du-Rhône around Visan, Séguret, Cairanne and Sablet are home to dark and heady wines. The Luberon and Mont Ventoux also produce some fine AOC wines. If you prefer something sweeter there are the Muscat dessert wines from Beaumes de Venise and Rasteau. The everyday drink is *pastis,* an aniseed-flavoured spirit that is drunk mixed with water.

Provençal cooking is one of the healthiest in France: a lot of fresh vegetables, fish and olive oil. The best-known dish is *bouillabaisse,* a fish soup, served with a red pepper paste, *rouille.* The garlic-flavoured mayonnaise – *aioli* – is well-known abroad. On the coast *fruits de mer* – mixed sea foods – is served in the better restaurants. The area around Nice has a more Italian type of cuisine, in particular ratatouille, small pizzas, ravioli, and a bitter salad called *mesclun.* The Camargue is the rice-growing region of France.

Local specialities of the Alpes de Haute Provence include *fumeton* (smoked leg of lamb), olives, truffles and herbs. There are some 200,000 sheep in the Haute Provence. The Hautes Alpes has some unusual dishes: *oreilles d'âne* (donkey's ears), which is actually wild spinach rolled in pastry and *tourton du champsaur* (potato or prune fritters). The Queyras area produces some classic cow's milk cheeses, such as Tomme d'Izoard, Bleu du Queyras and Gruyère Fontu.

Property. Provence is an area of stone building; the only exception is in the high Alps. There are numerous limestone quarries; the yellowish tint of the limestone is one of the defining features of Provence. Before the use of cement, dry-stone construction with mortar covering was common in the countryside. In the back country one will see many *villages perchés:* villages built up or on top of a hillside in a defensive formation with a small castle. Houses are built facing south, if possible, sometimes without windows at the rear and sides, to combat the effects of the *mistral.* You can have sunshine almost every day of the year, but you need to be sure that the prevailing wind isn't blowing through your front window. You can use the *mistral* as a mitigating circumstance if you murder someone in Provence.

The *maison de maître* or wealthy farmer's house here is the *mas,* sometimes with one or more defensive towers at the corners. The asymmetrical style of architecture is actually a throwback to Roman ground plans. Houses on the plain are generally surrounded by trees; higher up they may be quite exposed to the elements. Roofing is of Spanish tiles in the countryside. An original solution to combatting the sudden storms was to fix two or more rows of half-tiles (*génoises*) into mortar along the edge of the roof. You will notice that the roofs never jut out; this is to stop a strong shadow falling over the walls, which would look unattractive.

The Riviera around Nice is expensive as it is not subject to the *mistral* wind that affects the Rhône delta. The architecture of Nice and the former county of Nice has more in common with Italy than France. The back country of the Alpes Maritimes has many second homes. The population in the upper valleys has fallen by more than half since 1900, leaving plenty of abandoned old houses for renovation.

RHÔNE-ALPES

CRT: 104 route de Paris, 69260 Charbonnières-les-Bains; ☎04 72 59 21 59; fax 04 72 59 21 60; e-mail crt@rhonealpes-tourisme.com; www.crt-rhonealpes.fr; www.lyon.fr.
Percentage of population: 9.4%; percentage of GDP: 9.5%.

The Rhône-Alpes region revolves around two main natural features: the River Rhône and the Alps. The capital, Lyon, is France's second largest city population 1,600,000). Its main claim to fame is the high density of restaurants. Lyon suffers from its population growth, and parts of the city are not attractive, but the centre is still very impressive. Lyon does have excellent transport connections, the TGV runs through here on the way to Geneva, although very slowly beyond Lyon, and there are frequent flights to the UK from the Satolas airport to the east of the city.

Rhône-Alpes is a very varied region, stretching from the Massif Central in the west to the Italian border in the east, and down to Provence in the south. The Rhône is not so much an artery of commerce as a dumping ground for industrial effluent, and also serves to cool the nuclear reactors along its banks. Because of the concentration of chemical and other industry around the Rhône pollution is a factor here.

The region encompasses eight *départements*: Rhône (69), Loire (42), Ardèche (07), Drôme (26), Savoie (73), Haute-Savoie (74), Isère (38), and Ain (01). North of Lyon, in the Rhône, starting from Villefranche-sur-Saône, one enters Beaujolais country, named after the small town of Beaujeu. Properties in the wine region are hard to come by; the most active market is around Lyon itself. The Rhône (www.rhonetourism.org) is the smallest *département* in France after Paris; it is basically rural, and quite hilly.

The *département* of the Loire (www.cg42.fr) stands on the eastern edge of the Massif Central. The prefectural town of St Étienne has an airport with daily flights to London. The Loire does not stand out as a touristic region; it is more an extension of the wine-growing country of Beaujolais.

Ardèche (www.ardeche-guide.com) can be divided into two halves, the north and east with good transport connections to the outside world, and the rather remote western half. The northern end is a mere 50km from St Étienne airport and Lyon. The town of Annonay was the birthplace of the Montgolfier brothers, and holds an annual hot-air balloon festival. The eastern boundary of the Ardèche is formed by the Rhône; the prefectural town of Privas is a short distance from the river. The Gorges de l'Ardèche is one of France's main scenic sites; central Ardèche has been designated a national park, the Parc Naturel Régional des Monts d'Ardèche. The TGV from Lyon to Marseille runs on the other side of the Rhône.

Cuisine. The Valley of the Rhône is one of the premier vine-growing regions of France. North of Villefranche-sur-Saône, still in the Rhône *département*, lies the heart of the Beaujolais, centering around the village of Fleurie. South of Lyon, there is the Côte Rotie, a premier *appellation*. The quality of Ardèche wines is variable; the reds in the northeast are generally made from Syrah grapes, which require favourable conditions to ripen well.

In the Rhône, Lyon takes pride of place for its restaurants. The style of cooking favours cream and eggs in abundance, and is naturally based on all kinds of meat. Specialities are *quenelles* (meat or fish dumplings), cooked salads, and very rich cakes and desserts. Lyon is known for its pork *charcuterie,* and use of offal, such as tripe and calf's or sheep's feet.

The Ain has one particular claim to fame, the chickens from the Bresse region around Bourg-en-Bresse. The birds are especially patriotic, as they have blue legs, white feathers and red crests. The area of Bugey near the Rhône was the homeland of Brillat-Savarin, the great authority on cookery. It is noted for an onion and walnut tart, drunk with local wine, Le Manicle.

The Ardèche exports a lot of honey, especially from the southerly Vivarais region. It is also well-known for its candied chestnuts. In the Drôme one can find Picodon goat cheese from the pre-Alps, alpine lamb, walnut liqueur, and raviolis from Royans.

Property. The Rhône Valley is a vast region with a great variety in prices and types of property. In the Forez mountains of the Loire *département*, the architecture is similar to that in the Massif Central or Auvergne, using a bluish granite and slate roofs, thick walls and small windows.

The Lyonnais on the plain has, in the past, generally favoured the *pisé* method of construction: raw clay or concrete is pressed between wooden boards to make walls at least two feet thick. The walls are supported on stone or brick otherwise the rain would wash them away. More recent construction resembles what you would find in the Paris region.

The Ardèche tends to attract interest from foreign buyers who are looking for a permanent move to France rather than a holiday home, and there is a well-established British community. There are few cheap properties available now for renovation. Many properties are handled by estate agents in Montélimar, which is on the other side of the Rhône in the Drôme.

SAVOIE AND DAUPHINÉ

CRT: 104 route de Paris, 69260 Charbonnières-les-Bains; ☎04 72 59 21 59; fax 04 72 59 21 60; e-mail crt@rhonealpes-tourisme.com; www.crt-rhonealpes.fr.
GDP/Population: see under Rhône-Alpes.

Although officially part of the Rhône-Alpes region, Savoie and Dauphiné are quite different in character from the Rhône Valley, and so are treated separately here. Dauphiné was semi-independent until 1486, when the ruler had to sell it to the French to pay off his debts. It then became the personal property of the *dauphin* – the heir-apparent of France – and thus got its name. Dauphiné includes the *départements* of the Drôme and Isère. The Drôme (www.drometourisme.com) is a deserted and scenic region; south of the prefectural capital, Valence, you have a feeling of being in the Midi, the south of France. This is an area of vineyards and orchards, and olive-trees. Côtes-de-Rhône wine comes from here. Straddling the Drôme and the *département* of the Isére is the dramatic Vercors plateau, a centre for the Resistance in World War II and the scene of a massacre by the Germans just after D-Day, that has been made a national park. The Isère stretches from the Rhône to the Alps, with the prefectural city, Grenoble in the middle. Grenoble is considered as one of the best places to live in France. A survey of managers by *Express* magazines rated it ninth in terms of economic dynamism and quality of life. The downside is pollution.

Stretching northeastwards from Grenoble to Chambéry in Savoie lies the national park of the Chartreuse Massif, named after the Carthusians who started their order in the 12th century as a protest against the Cistercians' lax ways. Seventeen of their monasteries still subsist; many were devastated in the French Revolution. Ironically, the name Chartreuse these days mainly conjures up the image of the lethal colourful liqueur made by the monks.

Savoie takes in two-thirds of the French section of the Alps – the Alpes du Nord – including Europe's highest peak, Mont Blanc (15,719 feet) on the Italian border. Savoie was first a county, then a duchy and finally a kingdom, with its capital in Turin. In the 18th century the Kingdom of Savoie was linked with Sardinia under one crown. The final union of Savoie with France only occurred in 1860 after a referendum of the inhabitants. Chambéry, the gateway to the ski fields and prefectural town, was capital of Savoie for 200 years until 1583. Chambéry is on the TGV line to Paris and Lille. The ski scene has expanded since the 1992 Winter Olympics were held in the depressingly modern tourist town of Albertville. Tignes, on the Italian border, at about 13,200 feet, is the only place in France that can boast all-year-round skiing, if the weather is right.

The most spectacular scenery is closer to the Italian and Swiss border in Haute Savoie; the mountainous *massifs* attract the climbers, but virtually every part of the Haute Savoie is exceptionally scenic. The departmental capital, Annecy, is an up-market tourist destination. The star attraction, however, must be the old resort town of Mégève, stunningly located under the Alps. At the northern edge of Haute Savoie lies Lac Léman, known to the Swiss as Lake Geneva. The beauty of Savoie and the wildness of the weather in the mountain passes were an irresistible attraction to the English pre-impressionist Joseph Turner, who came here again and again for inspiration.

Cuisine. The Drôme, with the Rhône as its western border has some renowned wines on the *côtes* above Valence; most notably the Hermitage, and Crozes-Hermitages *appellations* (both reds and whites). There are also the *appellations* Côtes-du-Rhône Régionales and Villages, and the sparkling Crémant de Die. Virtually all the wines from the region are first-class. Montélimar, south of Valence, is synonymous with nougat. For the French, Dauphiné evokes *gratin Dauphinois,* a simple dish of thinly sliced potatoes with a browned covering of cream cheese and butter. The Isère is well-known for *noix de Grenoble* – walnuts – which are used in *gateau au noix* and other desserts. The local cheese, St Marcellin, is made into *marcelline,* slices of cheese with streaky bacon.

Perhaps reflecting its harsher environment, Savoie comes out less well gastronomically, as it has only given its name to a kind of cabbage in English. Savoyard cooking favours simple heavy fare, made from potatoes, bacon and cheese, rather like the Swiss; the term *à la savoyarde* means with a gruyère sauce. Savoie produces both white and red wines, as well as mineral waters like Evian.

Property. In Savoie one will see Swiss-style chalets, with richly carved balconies and steep roofs. At high altitudes houses were traditionally built around a massive wooden framework, with the ground level of stone. Traditionally the stables were next to the living quarters, with a hay loft on the first floor, providing natural insulation. It was also common to use pine shingles: about five or six layers are nailed to the roof – sometimes weighted down with rocks – to provide a weatherproof surface. Shingles or wooden panels may also be nailed to the walls, to increase heat-rentention.

At lower altitudes more German-style constructions are popular, with hipped roofs (*croupes*). Generally houses have a tidier appearance than in the more French areas. Whitewashing, decorative shutters and colourful windowboxes all give a rather alpine feel to the area.

Some of the most expensive properties in France are large ski chalets which can provide a high rental income, which will set you back over £300,000. Much of the ski accommodation is in unattractive concrete apartment blocks; they are a good investment but the initial purchase costs are steep.

WHAT YOUR MONEY WILL BUY

The following are given for guidance. The habitable surface area is given at the end of each entry, where available.

€6,900 – stone barn with land, for renovation, Picardie.

€7,700 – 3-room house, nr Rodez, Aveyron, for restoration. 65 sq.m.

€15,000 – small farmhouse with barn, for renovation, La Creuse.

€30,000 – 1-bed studio, Dives-sur-Mer, Calvados. 31 sq.m.

€38,000 – 12-bed hotel, restaurant, café, Baraqueville, Aveyron. 300 sq.m.

€50,000 – 2-bed stone house, nr Foix, Ariège, with 5000 sq.m. land. 90 sq.m.

€55,000 – stone barn for restoration, nr Bergerac, Dordogne, 3 hectares of land.

€60,000 – studio in Nice, no sea view. 30 sq.m.

€60,000 – 6-bed house in southern Aveyron, for restoration, with 11 hectares of land. 300 sq.m.

€80,000 – 4-bed village house with shop, Mayenne.

€96,000 – derelict stone farmhouse in Ardèche, for renovation. 150 sq.m.

€100,000 – Norman *longère* to renovate, with 1 hectare land, Normandel, Orne. 200 sq.m.

€110,000 – ruined church in the Gers, with 3000 sq.m. of land. 150 sq.m.

€125,000 – stone house with dependancies, for renovation, Drôme Provençal. 240 sq.m.

€148,000 – 4-bed house with double garage, Vichy, Allier.

€160,000 – small apartment with sea view, Carnac, Brittany. 28 sq.m.

€170,000 – 3-bed villa with swimming pool, near ski fields, Hautes-Pyrénées. 130 sq.m.

€175,000 – chalet with views of Pyrenees, near ski-slopes, Font Romeu, Pyrénées-Orientales. 137 sq.m.

€180,000 – 2-bed *fermette* with dependancies, nr Compiègne, Picardie. 130 sq.m.

€190,000 – 3-bed farmhouse, St Léonard-de-Noblat, Haute-Vienne. 230 sq.m.

€200,000 – restored farm nr Angoulême, Charente, with 8 guest rooms, and swimming pool. 700 sq.m.

€200,000 – 5-bedroom villa in the Landes, near sea. 240 sq.m.

€230,000 – 11-room 17th-century house, Ardèche, nr Valence TGV. 400 sq.m.

€240,000 – 3-bed holiday home, Pays de Monts, Vendée.

€270,000 – ancient town house in the Luberon, Vaucluse. 200 sq.m.

€280,000 – 3-bed holiday home, Paimpol, Brittany. 139 sq.m.

€366,000 – restored water-mills in the Hautes-Alpes, near Gap. 240 sq.m.

€408,000 – 4-bed restored farmhouse in the Drôme, with three hectares of forest. 180 sq.m.

€500,000 – 4-bed *maison de maître*, 8 hectares of land, nr Gaillac, Tarn.

€500,000 – 5-bed *périgourdine* on 9 hectares, near Les Eyzies, Périgord.

€600,000 – 18th-century chateau in the Gironde, with swimming pool. 290 sq.m.

€650,000 – Provençal *mas,* with swimming pool, views over Rhône Valley. 300 sq.m.+50 sq.m.

€717,000 – *maison de maître* with 75 hectares of land and forest, in the Gers.

€890,000 – restored *mas* in the Gard, with 1 hectare of land. 180 sq.m.

€950,000 – Belle époque villa, Villefranche, Côte d'Azur, with views over Cap Ferrat. 250 sq.m.

€1,250,000 – Art deco villa, Cap de Nice, with swimming pool and sea view. 250 sq.m.

€1,500,000 – Provençal *mas*, swimming pool, near Avignon TGV. 200 sq.m.

€2,450,000 – 17th-century 7-bed *bastide,* Uzès, Gard.

€3,200,000 – Renaissance château, Avignon, Provence.

PARIS APARTMENT PRICES

The prices are given by *arrondissement* per square metre.

1er	€4,404	11e	€3,054
2e	€3,462	12e	€3,154
3e	€3,884	13e	€3,185
4e	€4,485	14e	€3,663
5e	€4,538	15e	€3,734
6e	€5,473	16e	€4,413
7e	€5,348	17e	€3,461
8e	€4,289	18e	€2,520
9e	€3,300	19e	€2,428
10e	€2,594	20e	€2,555

Source: Compagnie des notaires de Paris. January 2003.

PRICES IN REGIONAL CITIES

The following are prices for average dwellings in city centres

	Apartments per sq.m.	Houses
Aix-en-Provence	€1,982-€2,287	n/a
Annecy	€1,677-€1,982	n/a

Besançon	€1,189-€1,281	€129,582-€137,204
Bordeaux	€991-€1,296	n/a
Caen	€1,372-€1,524	€152,449-€182,939
Clermont-Ferrand	€991-€1,372	€106,714-€129,582
Dijon	€1,250-€1,372	€131,106-€150,925
Grenoble	€1,296-€1,601	n/a
La Rochelle	€1,200-€1,372	€121,959-€182,939
Lille	€915-€1,372	n/a
Lyon	€1,524-€2,058	€182,939-€274,408
Marseille	€1,220-€1,677	n/a
Nancy	€762-€1,220	€137,204-€198,184
Nantes	€1,143-€1,524	€114,337-€152,449
Orléans	€915-€1,220	n/a
Reims	€1,296-€1,372	n/a
Rennes	€1,189-€1,601	€167,694-€228,674
Rouen	€1,067-€1,220	n/a
Strasbourg	€1,342-€1,906	€167,694-€274,408
Toulouse	€1,220-€1,448	n/a
Tours	€1,067-€1,372	€144,827-€175,316

n/a = not applicable since the vast majority of sales were of apartments not houses

Source: Crédit Foncier de France, 2002.

CHOOSING THE RIGHT LOCATION

Location is everything, as Conrad Hilton said. Nothing could be more true. The first thing to look at is where your potential property is in relation to airports and motorways. Properties near TGV stations are worth considerably more than those which are not. A property on a main road is generally cheap to buy, and very difficult to resell. Being within 5km of a motorway normally makes property useless for *gîtes* or *chambres d'hôtes*.

The next point to consider is whether there are any nuclear power stations in your area. There are 20 locations in France with nuclear reactors, some of them in tourist areas. See the website http://nucleaire.edf.fr to make sure you are not near one. Another point is to check whether there are any small airfields nearby. Noise from neighbouring farmyards can also be hard to cope with for city-dwellers.

Ideally, you need to spend several months renting a property in your chosen area to see how you like it out of season. Even the Côte d'Azur has wintry weather from time to time. French holiday homes by the coast can be awful places to live out of season. Buses may not run, and services may be reduced. Many shops and restaurants close down for the winter; there are few people about, and the place could be dead for several months.

A HOME IN

France

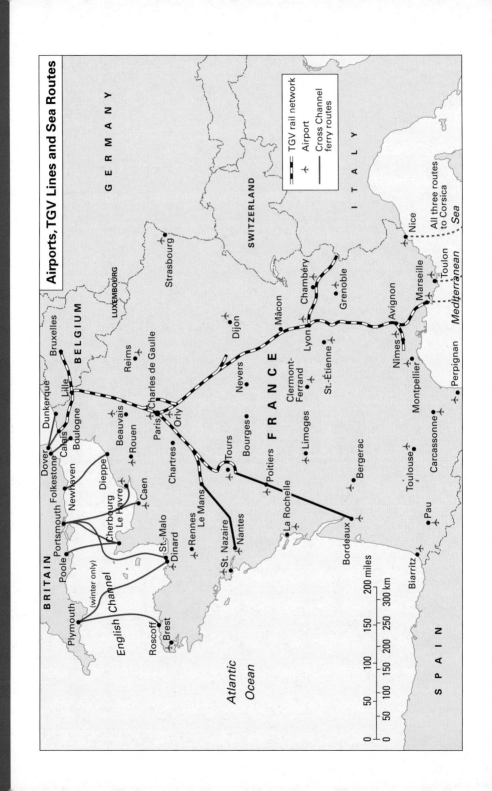

Airports, TGV Lines and Sea Routes

Legend:
- TGV rail network
- ✈ Airport
- Cross Channel ferry routes

BRITAIN

Dover, Folkestone, Newhaven, Portsmouth, Poole, Plymouth

English Channel

Roscoff, Brest

Dunkerque, Calais, Boulogne, Cherbourg, Dieppe, Le Havre, Caen, St.-Malo, Dinard, Rennes, St. Nazaire, Nantes, St. Nazaire, Le Mans

(winter only)

Atlantic Ocean

La Rochelle, Bordeaux, Biarritz

BELGIUM

Bruxelles, Lille

LUXEMBOURG

GERMANY

Strasbourg, Reims, Beauvais, Rouen, Paris, Charles de Gaulle, Orly, Chartres, Tours, Poitiers, Bourges, Limoges, Nevers, Dijon, Mâcon, Clermont-Ferrand, St.-Étienne, Lyon, Chambéry, Grenoble, Nîmes, Avignon, Montpellier, Perpignan, Toulouse, Carcassonne, Pau, Bergerac

SWITZERLAND

ITALY

Marseille, Toulon, Nice

All three routes to Corsica

Mediterranean Sea

FRANCE

SPAIN

0 50 100 150 200 miles

0 50 100 150 200 250 300 km

Left bank scene, Paris

Paris apartments at competitive prices

Normandy town house

Waterfront flats, Honfleur, Normandy

Window decoration, Colmar, near Strasbourg

Cottage on Brittany Côtes d'Armor

Village houses in Burgundy

Manor house with turret, in need
of renovation

Village houses in Oppede-le-Vieux

Town house, near Perpignan,
Pyrenées-Orientales

Windmill for conversion? Arles, between
Avignon and the coast

Chapel and farmhouse, Alpes de Provence

Harbour at Menton, Alpes-Maritimes

Potential Hazards

One should not be taken in by over-optimistic property agents who try to kid you that you will have no problems moving to France. Finding work in rural areas may be next to impossible. Naturally, if you are a writer or painter there is no problem at all, otherwise it is simply a fantasy to think that the local businesses are going to employ someone who doesn't speak French in preference to a local. The only possibility is to use your English as a selling point, or you could consider starting a business specifically to service other foreigners. You can always try to set up as an adviser to other foreigners buying property in your area.

Another major consideration is your social life. Some are happy with the company of a small circle of other foreigners, but in most of France you will have to find friends among the locals. Is your French good enough to talk about more than the weather and the price of vegetables? Isolation and the lack of clubs and societies can spell trouble. It is essential that both partners can drive. The availability of cheap alcohol is another of the 'reefs'. Relationships that are under strain can fall apart if one of the partners starts drinking, as happens all too often.

Everyone who has successfully settled down in France has two pieces of advice: learn French as soon as possible, preferably before you leave home, and do spend some time renting in an area before you buy.

RETIREMENT

France is in many ways an ideal country to retire to as the climate is near ideal in many areas and there is excellent health care provision. There has been a long tradition of the rich and famous retiring to the 'South of France', meaning the Côte d'Azur, now out of reach of all but the very well-off.

The area where you choose to retire is crucial. Most of northern France is as wet as England, and not really suitable; the greyness of the sky will soon pall. Normandy is muddy and foggy for much of the year. Brittany is subject to violent storms in the autumn and winter. The most obvious area to retire to is in the southwest, near the Pyrenees, where there is less rainfall and guaranteed sunshine for much of the year. Provence and the southeast are also attractive but subject to strong winds and violent storms. Anyone who suffers from arthritis or rheumatism will be better off in the drier parts of the south.

Location. This becomes more and more crucial as you get older. Being close to an airport is a must: it is estimated that if you live more than an hour from an airport, 25% of your potential visitors won't come; if you are more than one and half hours away, the figure rises to 50%. The eastern Pyrenees, in particular the up-and-coming Ariège, is an ideal area in this respect, since

there are cheap flights from London to Carcassonne, Perpignan and Toulouse. This is assuming that such cheap flights continue indefinitely.

You also need to consider accessibility by car. Although driving along
twisty mountain roads may be no problem when you're 50, by the time
you're 80 it may become a daunting challenge. Your family and friends are
more likely to come to see you if you are near a railway station.

Type of property. You need to think ahead regarding the kind of place
you want to spend your sunset years in. Bungalows – look for the word
plain-pied – in the adverts, are not all that common in towns, but there are
a lot in the countryside, especially on the Atlantic coast; there is nothing
to stop you from having one built to your specifications. Apartments may
not be that suitable for retirees; some older apartment blocks have no lifts.
You also need to consider whether the house you're buying has an adequate
bathroom. The term *salle d'eau* (SdE) in an advertisement rather than *salle
de bain* (SdB) should alert you that this is only a washroom with a primitive shower rather than a proper bathroom. Many properties only have a
shower, which cuts down on water consumption.

Size is an important consideration. The received wisdom from property
agents is to buy the biggest property you can afford: they would say that
of course. It is absolutely true that many older people regret not having
bought a four-bedroom house rather than a three-bedroom one, because
if they had, they could have more of their family to stay. The bigger your
house, the more popular you will be.

FORMALITIES

Retirees are subject to the same rules as anyone else, as regards residence
permits. After you have been in France for more than three months, or
much sooner if you know that you plan to stay in the country, you must
apply for your *carte de séjour* or residence permit. Pensioners are somewhat
better off than working people, in that they do not have to pay a fixed
amount for medical insurance every month, or social security contributions: they do on the other hand have to prove that they have a steady
income. The French authorities expect you to have at least £800 or €1,200
coming in every month, which is supposed to cover your rent as well: the
amount is the same as the minimum wage. They seem to believe that two
people can live on this sum of money.

Hardly anyone in France has a private pension plan, since the state
scheme is more than adequate. In 2002 the average French adult had
pension savings of €1,000, against €33,000 in the UK. If you want to know
more about French pension schemes, consult the website www.cnav.fr.

As regards medical care, retirees are very well off in France. You only need to be insured for the shortfall in your medical expenses which is not covered by the state, which is free over 65. You are not required to have additional insurance, but it would be unwise not to have it, since you will have to pay a part of your medical expenses – roughly 30-35% – which could mount up to a substantial sum if you become seriously ill. The additional insurance at age 60 is going to cost around £350 a year, and it goes up as you get older. Treatment for life-threatening conditions, and medicines for serious chronic conditions, are free, but you need some extra cover. The last thing you would want is to have to go back to the UK to a grim NHS hospital. On top of that, you can comfort yourself with the thought that you will probably stay healthier for longer in the balmy climate of southern France and drop dead playing tennis at 82, rather than shuffling around on a Zimmer frame in an English nursing home.

A salutary tale

Many Brits of slender means see retirement in France as a realistic option, but it is well to bear in mind the following tale before you sell up and leave it all behind. In 1998 there was a well-publicised case of a Belgian, Michel Cattier, who had been living quietly in the Lozère area of the Cévennes since 1991 in a broken-down old farmhouse with a leaky roof that he had taken a liking to. Michel – a French-speaking Belgian – never spoke to anyone and lived three miles from the nearest neighbour. Then one day he got into an argument with the owner of the land surrounding his house, which was used by hunters. The following morning the gendarmes were at his door asking to see his papers. Michel, age 57, had never bothered to get a *carte de séjour*, or medical insurance, although he always paid his *taxe d'habitation* and *impôt foncier* on time. He lived on £400 a month, which he had sent to him from Brussels, thus breaking the minimum income rule. After a 10-minute hearing the judge found him guilty of *séjour illégal* (being an illegal immigrant) and fined him £400. He also advised him to 'go back to Africa' since that was where he had spent his working life. Note that the rules for Belgians and British citizens are exactly identical.

Michel put his misfortune down to not bothering to go to the café and getting to know the locals. Ofcourse, his income was perfectly adequate to live on, since he owned his property, but the *maire* had to apply the rules. Clearly, it is best not to quarrel with your neighbours, or you could be out of the country.

BUYING FOREIGN CURRENCY FOR YOUR PROPERTY

If you're buying a property abroad for the first time, you've probably got enough to think about without worrying about exchange rates. You've found your dream home and secured the price of your property, and now all you have to do is look forward to your new life abroad. Right? Well, partly. Somewhere along the line you will have to change your pounds into euros, and that's where the dream can become a nightmare if you don't plan ahead. Whether you're buying a property outright or buying from plan in instalments, protecting yourself against exchange rate fluctuations can save you hundreds, if not thousands of pounds on the price of your new home.

Foreign Exchange markets are by nature extremely volatile and can be subject to dramatic movements over a very short space of time. In some ways it's all too easy to leave your currency exchange to the last minute and hope that the exchange rates fall in your favour. But if you don't take steps to protect your capital, you could find yourself paying a lot more than you bargained for.

As a matter of course, many people will approach their banks to sort out their currency, without realising that there are more cost-effective alternatives in the marketplace. There are a number of independent commercial foreign exchange brokers who can offer better rates and a more personal, tailored service. Their dealers will explain the various options open to you and keep you informed of any significant changes in the market. They will also guide you through every step of the transaction so that you are ultimately in control and able to make the most of your money.

If you're not still not convinced of how planning ahead can help you, take a look at the following example:

You've found your dream home and agreed the price of €200,000. When you signed your contract and paid your deposit in August 2002, the pound stood at 1.60. Just six months later when your next instalment was due, changes in the political and economic climate have caused the pound to weaken. You now only get 1.49 for your pound.

Agreed Price of Your New Home €200,000	Date	Rate	Cost in Pounds
	August 2002	1.60	**£125,000**
	February 2003	1.49	**£134,228**

In just 6 months the price of your home has **increased** by over **£9,000**.

Although changes in the economic climate may be beyond your control, protecting your capital against the effect of these changes isn't.

There are a number of options available to you:

- **Spot Transactions** are ideal for anyone who needs their currency straight away as the currency is purchased today at the current rate. However, if you have time to spare before your payments are due, it may be wiser to consider a Forward Transaction.
- **Forward Transactions** allow you to secure a rate for up to a year in advance to protect yourself against any movements in the market. A small deposit holds the rate until the balance becomes due when the currency contract matures.
- **Limit Orders** allow you to place an order in the market for a desired exchange rate. This has the advantage of protecting you against negative exchange movements whilst still allowing you to gain from a positive movement. Your request is entered into the system and an automatic currency purchase is triggered once the market hits your specified rate.

If you haven't had to deal with this kind of transaction before, this can all seem a little daunting. But that's where a reputable currency company can really come into its own. With specialists in the field ready to explain all the pitfalls and possibilities to you in layman's terms and guide you through each stage of the transaction, you can be sure that your currency solutions will be perfectly tailored to your needs.

Currencies Direct has been helping people to understand the overseas property markets since 1996. Specialising in providing foreign exchange solutions tailored to clients' individual financial situations, it offers a cost-effective and user-friendly alternative to the high-street banks.

With offices in the UK and Spain, Currencies Direct is always on hand to help you. For more information on how you can benefit from their commercial rates of exchange and friendly, professional service, call the Currencies Direct office in London on 020 7813 0332 or visit their website at www.currenciesdirect.com.

FINANCE

CHAPTER SUMMARY

○ The British are constantly amazed at how different banking and taxation are in France from the UK; it pays to find out as much as possible before you look for property.

○ **Banks:** Practices are very different from in the UK, but non-residents can open an account by post.

○ **Mortgages:** Your monthly repayments cannot exceed 33% of your income, and you will probably be offered 70% or less of the value of the property.

○ **Offshore Accounts:** These are becoming less popular because of new legislation requiring EU countries to exchange details of bank accounts held by non-residents.

○ **Trusts:** There is little legislation in France covering trusts, but they are still a useful tool to avoid taxes if set up in the right way.

○ **Tax:** France is a high-taxation country, and most taxes are raised through social security charges and Valued Added Tax, which cannot be avoided.

○ **Real Estate Tax:** The amount you will have to pay will probably be less than your council tax in the UK.

○ **Capital Gains:** Capital gains taxes in France encourage people to stay in one house for a long time, and penalise those who resell after a few years.

○ **Inheritance Tax:** It is vital to obtain professional advice about French inheritance laws before you sign a contract to buy a property.

○ **Importing Currency:** You can save thousands of pounds by using the services of a currency dealer rather than going through a high street bank.

○ **Insurance:** Third-party liability insurance is compulsory for home-owners and tenants.

○ **Wealth Tax:** A tax that does not exist in the UK, but which you should not try to avoid in the France.

BANKING

Sooner or later you will need to open a bank account in France. It is best to wait until you know where you are going to live before you open one. It may happen that an estate agent advises you to open an account when you are looking for property in a certain area, merely because he gets a commission from the bank for introducing new customers. Opening an account prematurely can influence your judgement if you are looking for property. Crédit Agricole Calvados has set up a service for non-residents who want to open an account without going in person called Britline: see below.

While you are still looking for property, you can withdraw money with a cashpoint card with the Visa or Cirrus symbol, or you can use a credit card. There is a charge for using your card to withdraw money abroad, and you may not get the best possible rate of exchange. Credit cards in France operate with a chip rather than a magnetic strip; you need to know your PIN code otherwise you may not be able to use your card. As far as changing cash in France goes, the same applies: you generally pay commission and the rate of exchange is very variable. The worst rates on offer are at railway stations. *Bureaux de change* in areas with large numbers of tourists do not necessarily offer bad rates. In Paris some of the best rates can be found around St Michel.

If you are staying in one of the major cities you may be able to open an account with a branch of a British bank. Barclays is the best represented. Lloyds has branches in Paris, Lyon, Cannes and Marseille; HSBC owns CCF. NatWest has no branches in France. British banks in France have to operate under French law; they mainly target wealthy expats with a lot of money to invest. Unless you have special requirements, you are probably better off having an account with a French bank.

Prospective house buyers in France often take out mortgages with UK banks in France; Abbey National, which has its main office in Lille, is particularly active.

The best tip for exchanging money on a longer-term basis is to come to an agreement with a UK resident with an account in France, whereby you pay equal sums into each other's bank accounts at the median exchange rate, thus completely avoiding the *agio*, the difference between selling and buying foreign currency.

Money Transfers

There will be situations where you need to send money to someone in France or vice versa. A transfer of money to or from France is a *transfert* in French, rather than a *virement*, a transfer within France. Telegraphic Transfer, via Western Union or American Express is the most expensive way, but may be unavoidable if you want to send money to the USA. The most usual system between banks is SWIFT, which takes a day or two, and costs from €25 upwards. A more cost-effective method is to open a post office account in France and a Girobank account in the UK. Transfers between post offices take three to 10 days, and there is only a fixed charge to pay however much money you transfer. The least effective way of transferring money is to send a cheque drawn on a foreign bank account; it could take a month to clear and the charges will be very high. If the amount is small it would be simpler to send cash with an International Registered Letter.

There is another possibility for making payments to French companies, which is to use a postal order, or *mandat cash,* obtainable in a post office. You pay a small charge in addition to the actual amount. The *mandat* is made out to a specific beneficiary; if for some reason you don't use the *mandat* or the beneficiary doesn't cash it, you will receive a notification from the post office so you can get a refund; if you lose the receipt then you have to go back to the post office where you originally bought the *mandat,* otherwise it is refundable at any post office in France.

To transfer large sums, i.e. for your house purchase, the best method is to use a specialised company, such as Currencies Direct: this is dealt with below under 'Importing Currency' below.

Credit Cards

Strictly speaking, there is no such thing as a credit card in France, rather there are charge cards with a deferred debit. Every thirty days the amount you owe is automatically debited from your bank account, meaning that you may pay for something the day after you bought it. In the UK the credit is for 30-60 days, in France for 0-30 days. In France if you want to defer payment you will need to open a sub-account which allows you to borrow money at a lower interest rate than you would pay in the UK on a credit card. There is an annual charge for credit cards in France. A Gold Card costs about €90 a year.

The national French debit card, the *Carte Bleue* (CB) can only be used in France. If you need a credit card that functions abroad, you can ask for *Carte Bleue/Visa* or *Mastercard*. Visa is by far the most widely accepted card in France; there are others of course. The credit card company and the bank are separate organisations. You are expected to clear your bill at the end of each month, unless you have arranged to borrow money.

Bank Accounts

Opening a bank account is not difficult. You don't even need to be a resident. If you are resident in France then you simply take along your passport, *carte de séjour* (or equivalent) and proof of your fiscal address in France. The basic form of bank account is the *compte de chèque* which comes with a cheque book.

When you open a bank account you will be offered a *Carte Bleue*, originally conceived as a substitute for writing cheques. The CB is a cashpoint card which can also function as either a debit card or credit card; you choose one of the two. CB also stands for *carte bancaire*, i.e. any kind of credit card. CBs work with a chip rather than magnetic strip; you key in your PIN number when making transactions in shops, so you need to remember it.

As well as the bank's own number, there is one central number for reporting lost bank cards: 01 45 67 84 84.

Resident and Non-Resident Accounts. Whether you are considered resident or non-resident, from the bank's point of view, depends on where you are fiscally resident, i.e. where your centre of interests lies. If you spend more than 183 days a year in France you will normally pay your taxes there, so you are fiscally resident. As a non-resident you can only open a *compte non-résident*. Correspondence will be sent to you in your home country. It is also possible to open an account by post through a French bank branch in the UK (mainly in London). After choosing your branch in France, you need to supply a reference from your UK bank, a legalised copy of your signature, photocopies of the main pages of your passport, and a draft in euros to start you off. If the bank has doubts about your creditworthiness, they may require proof that you have never been barred from holding a bank account in France (*non-interdit bancaire*). The main advantage is that you will have everything explained to you in English at the beginning, but there is no guarantee that anyone will speak English in the branch you have chosen. It is far simpler to open an account in person in France after talking to the local bank staff. For Americans it may be useful to open an account through the Banque Transatlantique which has an office in Washington DC: see www.transat.tm.fr.

Banking Practices

Banking services are not as sophisticated or as liberal in France as in the UK or US; the banks are not at all keen to lend money in a hurry. The main rule to remember is that you must never go into the red without prior arrangement, otherwise you risk becoming an *interdit bancaire* (see below). It is also worth bearing in mind that if you go into the red any standing orders that you have will automatically be stopped, so your telephone and electricity could suddenly be cut off. You need to anticipate standing orders so they do not make you go overdrawn.

When you open your account you opt for monthly or fortnightly bank statements, or whatever arrangement suits you. There are charges for most transactions, apart from statements. You can authorise utilities companies to debit your account automatically (*prélèvement automatique*) for bill payment, but this is not obligatory. This is not the same as a standing order (*ordre permanent/virement automatique*) although it might sound the same. If you have the internet, you can see what is going on with your account; the antiquated French version of internet, Minitel, is still used for some on-line banking services.

As far as statements go, watch out for underhand attempts to get you to borrow money: sometimes you may see a message such as 'You have €15,000 to buy a car', when in fact all it means is that the bank hopes you will borrow the money to buy a car. Banks are not allowed to pay interest on current accounts at the time of writing; the situation is likely to change in 2003, after a judgment by the European Union.

With your cashpoint card you can withdraw up to €300 per week from any cashpoint. You can always take out more by going in person to your bank. If you want to take out money above the limit from any cashpoint, you need to ask for a 'gold card' for which there is a charge. It is best to carry some cash in France, in case the cashpoint machine swallows your card and refuses to give it back; the simple solution is to carry two or three cards. There are card-operated filling stations and hi-tech hotels where you can only pay by card. Credit card theft and fraud are widespread in Paris and on the Côte d'Azur, where the mafia are very active.

Bank opening hours are a favourite gripe with foreigners in France; there is a law that prevents banks opening more than five days a week, so your bank may close on Mondays. Very small branches (*permanences*) in country areas may only open one morning a week. The internet is making things easier.

Cheques

Cheques are more widely used in France than in the UK, and there are no cheque guarantee cards, but you can be asked for other identification. Cheques are written out in a similar way to those in the UK, with the information positioned differently. Your bank will send you your first cheque book once there are funds in your account. The cheque book has to be returned to the bank if they demand it. French cheques are not negotiable to a third person. The basic form of cheque is the *cheque barré*, which is only payable to the payee (*destinataire*); the bank has to inform the tax inspectors if you want to use open cheques.

Bouncing Cheques. If you write a 'wooden cheque' (*chèque de bois*) you will be given 30 days to rectify the situation. The Banque de France is informed immediately, and you are not allowed to write any further cheques until matters are resolved. You not only have to pay money into the account to cover it, but also a fine of 12% of the amount, that goes to the French treasury. There is also a form to fill in, declaring that you have dealt with the problem or '*incident*'. If the money is not paid you are put on a Banque de France blacklist, and are barred from using an account in France for five years. Bank cards and cheques have to be surrendered to the bank. Any attempt to open a bank account within the five years will be reported to the police.

A cheque is considered the equivalent of cash and cannot be cancelled, unless it has been lost or stolen or is deemed fraudulent by the bank. A police report has to be submitted to the bank in both cases.

TIPS FOR HANDLING YOUR FRENCH BANK ACCOUNT

- Practise writing cheques in French.
- Use the French crossed '7'. The French '1' looks like an English '7'.
- Carry your cheque book separately from any ID.
- Never, ever go overdrawn.
- Keep a close eye on your standing orders.
- Remember that cheques take a long time to clear in France, up to 10 days, and plan accordingly.

French Banks

There are several types of bank in France: clearing banks such as Crédit Lyonnais; co-operative banks such as Crédit Agricole; corporate banks, e.g. BNP Paribas, and savings banks or Caisses d'Epargne. The Crédit Lyonnais went spectacularly bust recently and had to be bailed out by the French state; the clearing banks have all been privatised. The Crédit Agricole has an immense advantage in that it has the largest number of branches, 7,500 in France alone. The departmental branches of CA function as separate banks and issue their own shares. Other co-operative banks include the Crédit Mutuel and Banque Populaire; if you want to take out a mortgage with a co-operative bank you are usually required to buy shares in the bank, but not if you just want a cheque account. The post office, La Poste, has 17,000 branches in France and longer opening hours than banks, so it could be convenient to have a post office account, or Compte Courant Postal (CCP). The number of your post office account is a RIP rather than RIB; the number of an account with a Caisse d'Epargne is a RICE.

The French bank you choose will depend a lot on whether there is a branch near you, and whether you need specialised services. It is worth finding out if there is anyone who speaks English in your branch; where there are large concentrations of English-speakers some banks are trying to recruit English-speaking staff.

The Calvados region of Crédit Agricole has now started a service called Britline (with offices in Caen, Normandy), which allows you to open a bank account in France by post (☎ 02 31 55 67 89; fax 02 31 55 63 99; e-mail vincent.gray@ca-calvados.fr; www.britline.com). Britline has stalls at French property fairs. Banque Populaire in Nice has started an English-speaking service which has been a big hit (see www.cotedazur.banquepo pulaire.fr).

Major French banks
Barclays Bank SA: www.barclays.fr
Banque Populaire: www.banquepopulaire.fr
BNP Paribas: www.bnpparibas.fr
Britline: www.britline.com
Caixa Bank: www.caixabank.fr
Crédit Agricole: www.credit-agricole.fr; www.ca-[name of department].fr
CCF: www.ccf.com
Crédit du Nord: www.credit-du-nord.fr
Crédit Lyonnais: www.creditlyonnais.com
Lloyds Bank SA: www.lloydstsbiwm.com
Société Générale: www.socgen.com

MORTGAGES

French mortgages – *hypothèques* – work in a rather different way from those in the UK, even if they appear similar at first sight. The straight repayment mortgage is the usual type. Fixed-rate mortgages are by far the most common; it is also possible to mix fixed and variable rates. The amount you repay each month remains the same over the life of the mortgage.

There is also a basic difference in concept: the mortgage lender does not hold the deeds to your property as security; these remain with the notaire. All property and land is registered with the *cadastre* – the French land registry – and given its own unique number. This is given in the *acte de vente* which remains with the notaire, while you have a copy. Your mortgage is registered with the local *bureau des hypothèques*, and there is a fee to have the mortgage removed once you have paid it off. When you take out a loan (*prêt*) you give the lender a *hypothèque* or charge on your property, which allows them to auction it off if you default on the loan.

It is highly advisable to have an offer of a loan before you look for a property in France, whether you are buying something new or planning to borrow money to renovate. A French mortgage lender can provide you with a statement guaranteeing you a loan (*certificat de garantie*) for which there may be a charge. You don't have to take up the offer, but you will at least be ready to sign a preliminary purchase agreement if you see a property you like.

There are two possibilities: one is to remortgage your UK property, the other is to take out a mortgage with a French bank using a French property as security. UK-based banks will not lend money on foreign properties; the French branches of UK banks operating under French law in France will, as well as one or two other UK lenders.

It would seem far easier to deal with a UK lender, whom you may already know, where the transactions will be entirely in English, than to go to a French bank and deal with a system that is quite foreign to you.

Every French *département* has an organisation called ADIL (Association Départementale d'Informations sur le Logement) which offers free advice on the property buying process and mortgages. See www.adil.fr. There is also the national organisation ANIL: www.anil.fr.

UK and French Mortgages

Remortgaging or taking out a mortgage in the UK has advantages; fewer questions will be asked, and you will be able to borrow more than you would in France. Since UK properties are likely to go up in value far faster than those in France, there is rather less of a risk for the bank. If your income is in sterling, then it makes sense to have a UK mortgage. It is equally possible to borrow a smaller sum for a short period to cover the cost of buying your French property. The downside is that UK interest rates are about 2% higher than those in France, and there is every possibility that sterling will fall in value against the euro.

PROS AND CONS OF FRENCH MORTGAGES

For

○ French mortgage interest rates are lower than UK ones and are likely to remain so: at the start of 2003 minimum rates were: France 4%, UK 6%. The French rate is generally 2% higher than the Euroland interbank rate (EURIBOR).

○ The euro has appreciated in value recently and is likely to continue to appreciate. If the mortgage is in sterling, repayment could become more expensive.

○ If your income is in sterling, and you are not living in France you will lose something every time you send money from the UK to France.

○ You can benefit from French mortgage interest relief if you pay taxes in France.

Against

O Charges involved with setting up a French mortgage (*frais d'hypothèque*) are high.

O French banks may not offer you a mortgage until you are established in France, have a regular salary, and have completed all the formalities for French residence.

O Sterling might rise against the euro in the future.

O French banks rarely lend more than 80% of the value of a property; for non-residents the figure is 70% or less.

O There are strict rules about the maximum monthly repayments.

O The maximum term is normally 15 years.

The straight repayment mortgage is the only type in common use. One can choose between variable and fixed interest rates in France. The market is highly competitive: lenders advertise all sorts of attractive rates. One trick is to forget to mention the cost of death insurance – *assurance décès*. What you need to look at is the final rate – the *taux effectif global* or *TEG* – including insurance and charges. Lenders are required to furnish detailed information on the monthly repayments, the rate of repayment, and total amount repaid. You should not sign a mortgage contract until the small print has been explained to you, if necessary, in English.

The Loi Scrivener and Protection for Borrowers

Borrowers are generally well protected, but in spite of the strict rules defaults among foreigners are common, mainly because the borrower has spent too much doing up a dilapidated property, or hasn't worked out their business plan well. In the case of default, the property is compulsorily sold at auction and will fetch considerably less than if you had sold it yourself. The law generally favours owners, and it takes a long time before a forced sale can take place.

The Loi Scrivener – passed in 1979 and named after Madame Scrivener who promoted it – provides for transparency in the mortgage application process, and some protection for borrowers. The main provisions include:

1. The lending organisation must first state in writing: the lender's name and address, the type of loan, the property that is to be acquired, the rate of interest, total repayment and the time period of the loan, and the fact that the property purchase is dependent on obtaining the loan. There is a *délai de réflexion* (cooling-off period) of 10 days before the offer of the loan (*offre de crédit*) can be accepted and any funds transferred.

2. The initial offer of credit (*offre préalable de crédit*) will state in writing: the

identity of the lender and borrower; the type of loan; the amount of the loan; and the date from which funds will be available, and the repayment terms.

In the case of variable rate mortgages, the interest rate taken as a reference point, and the actual repayment rate, are stated. The offer also includes the insurance required by the bank, namely life/invalidity insurance; the guarantees and guarantors (if any) in case of default; the costs of early repayment, or transfer of the loan.

3. Once the offer has been received by registered post by the borrower and guarantors (if any), the borrower has 10 days to reflect before they can accept it. The acceptance can be sent by ordinary post. The offer of credit remains open for 30 days.

The Actual Loan Contract (*contrat de prêt*)

1. The lender cannot change the conditions of the loan offer for 30 days; during this time the borrower can look at other offers. Personal guarantors (*cautions personnes physiques*) may guarantee all or part of a loan. No money will be paid to the borrower, or any third parties until the offer has been accepted.

2. It will be stated in the *compromis de vente* that the purchase of the property will only take place on condition that the purchaser obtains a mortgage: the so-called *condition suspensive* (get-out clause). Once the prospective buyer has obtained an offer of a mortgage, they are obliged to go through with the purchase of the property, even if they turn down the mortgage. The buyer will be in breach of contract if they have not made efforts to obtain a mortgage within a reasonable time, or if they have made misleading statements about their income or assets. The *condition suspensive* cannot be used as a way of evading one's obligations.

3. The offer is accepted with the proviso that if the actual mortgage contract is not concluded within four months of acceptance, then the borrower is no longer bound by the contract. If for reasons beyond the borrower's control, the sale of the house does not go through within four months of acceptance of the mortgage, then they are freed from the mortgage contract. The borrower will, however, have to return any moneys, and pay a small compensation to the lender.

4. If the borrower becomes involved in litigation in connection with building work related to the house purchase, he/she may not stop repayments. This is only allowed with the authorisation of a magistrate. Once the case has been settled repayments recommence.

5. In the case of early repayment, the penalty cannot exceed the

equivalent of six months' interest, and never more than 3% of the total of the principal sum remaining. The amount can also be less.

6. If the buyer has stated in the *compromis de vente* that they do not intend to seek a loan, and then decide to ask for one anyway, they are no longer protected in the same way by the Loi Scrivener.

MONTHLY LOAN REPAYMENTS

In order to understand the likely amount of your monthly repayments, the following table gives monthly payments per £1000. Euros or dollars can be substituted for pounds.

Interest Rate % p.a.	Repayment mortgage with a term of *n* years: amount in pounds sterling*				
	5	10	15	20	25
1%	17.08	8.75	5.98	4.60	3.77
2%	17.51	9.19	6.42	5.05	4.23
3%	17.93	9.63	6.88	5.52	4.72
4%	18.36	10.07	7.35	6.01	5.23
5%	18.78	10.53	7.83	6.53	5.77
6%	19.21	11.00	8.33	7.06	6.33
7%	19.65	11.47	8.84	7.60	6.91
8%	20.08	11.95	9.37	8.17	7.51
9%	20.52	12.44	9.90	8.74	8.12
10%	20.95	12.93	10.44	9.33	8.75

*Interest calculated daily.

The above figures will vary slightly with different lenders. There is a useful French mortgage calculator on www.french-property.com. Most of the general property sites mentioned in chapter 5 have mortgage calculators, but these are entirely in French. For a UK mortgage calculator look at www.themarketplace.co.uk.

The Amount you can Borrow

French regulations mean that your monthly repayments cannot exceed 33% of your net income; if you are already repaying other loans these are subtracted from the 33%. At the same time, the costs and taxes associated with the property purchase, between 10% and 15% of the purchase price will also be taken into account. Mortgage lenders' websites will give you a rough idea of how much you can afford to pay (see www.adomos.com; www.guideducredit.fr; www.patrimoine.com). If you have a partner their income will be taken into account. It is less certain whether projected rental income will be taken into account; it is usually taken into account if you are purchasing a property through a leaseback scheme.

French banks will lend rather less for a second home purchase than for a principal residence. The amount may be only 50% of the purchase price. The greater the proportion that you can pay in cash (*l'apport personnel*) the more likely they are to go to the 33% ceiling on your personal income. They are not keen to lend if you are still paying off a UK mortgage, depending on how much there is to pay and your income. Any outgoings – e.g. loan repayments – that are likely to continue for more than six months must be taken into account when calculating your borrowing capacity.

CALCULATING HOW MUCH YOU CAN AFFORD TO BORROW (*CAPACITÉ D'ENDETTEMENT*)

Your net (joint) monthly earnings including investment income	£ – – – – – – –
take 33% of this amount	£ – – – – – – –
deduct rent, loan repayments, alimony payments, etc.	£ – – – – – – – £ – – – – – – –
The result is the amount that you can repay per month on a French mortgage.	£ – – – – – – –

Documents Required to Apply for a French Mortgage

- Copies of all the usual identification documents of all applicants: i.e. passport, birth/marriage/divorce certificates, and *carte de séjour* if resident in France.
- Notarised letter from your partner agreeing to a mortgage being taken out on the property, if they are not an applicant.
- Your last three months salary slips.
- Letter from your employer stating that you are employed.
- Tax returns/statements from previous year.
- Full accounts for three previous years, and current accounts, if you are self-employed.
- Proof of current outgoings, such as rent, loan repayments, alimony, child support payments, etc.
- Business plan, or projected rental income, if you plan to make money from your property.

- ○ Application form and fee.
- ○ Copy of the *compromis de vente* (preliminary contract).
- ○ Results of a medical examination (sometimes required).

Charges and Procedures Involved with French Mortgages

The amount, interest rate and payment terms of the mortgage must be the same in the *acte de vente* as in the mortgage contract. Any discrepancies should be rectified.

Charges:

- ○ The *frais de dossier* (lender's fees): approx. 1% of the loan.
- ○ Fee for opening the dossier (*ouverture de dossier*): €150-950.
- ○ Fee for valuing the property: about €300.
- ○ Fee for arranging insurance: 0.4-0.5% of the loan.
- ○ Notaire's emolument on a sliding scale: €889 on €100,000.
- ○ Fee for registering the mortgage with the Bureau des Hypothèques: 0.615%.
- ○ Further small charges and taxes.

The maximum fees come to about 5.9% for a loan of €50,000, or 3.5% on €200,000.

Some of the above fees are negotiable. French mortgage lenders generally only cast a rapid eye over the property to satisfy themselves that it is not about to collapse; they are well-informed about the property market and know better than foreign buyers how much money it is safe for them to lend.

You need to have money available in your French bank account to pay the fees given above when the *acte de vente* is signed, otherwise the deal cannot go through. Lenders require payments to be made by direct debit from a French bank account, which you will have to open before you apply for a mortgage in any case. The lending bank is not allowed to make you open a current account with them.

If your mortgage is in sterling or other non-euro currency, a revaluation clause (*clause de réévaluation*) may be inserted in the contract. The clause can work in favour of the lender or the borrower. If the euro has fallen in value against sterling during the repayment period, you will be required to make up the difference to the original value in euros. The borrower may ask for a clause protecting them against a rise in the euro.

Only once the *acte de vente* has been signed, and the mortgage registered, will the notaire arrange for the release of the loan funds. A different situation exists if you are having a new house built. Funds are released in stages (stage payments), depending on how far construction has advanced. You only pay interest on the amounts released, not on the whole.

Once the mortgage has run its course, there is a further two years to wait before it is automatically erased from the mortgage register. If you sell your property before this time, you will have to pay to have the mortgage cancelled. A property cannot be sold with a mortgage charge attached to it, unless the loan is about to be paid off.

MORTGAGE GLOSSARY

assurance décès/invalidité	death/invalidity insurance
assurance perte d'emploi	unemployment insurance
échéance modulable	variable redemption date
échéance fixe	fixed redemption date
échéancier	repayment schedule
frais de mainlevée d'hypothèque	fee for removing mortgage charge from registry
indemnité de résiliation	early repayment penalty
mensualités	monthly repayments
prêt à taux capé	capped-rate loan
prêt à taux fixe	fixed-rate loan
prêt à taux révisable/variable	variable-rate loan
prêt relais	bridging loan
remboursement	repayment; reimbursement
remboursement anticipé sans frais	penalty-free early repayment
résiliation	cancellation
TEG (taux effectif global)	APR; effective interest rate

Mortgage Insurance

Mortgage lenders generally insist that you take out death/disability insurance – *assurance décès/invalidité,* but it is not compulsory by law. About 90% of borrowers take out *assurance décès.* The type of insurance is *assurance décès temporaire,* running for the lifetime of the mortgage contract. The premiums are lost; there is no payout at the end. Another type of death insurance – *assurance décès vie entière* – which runs until the time you actually die, does have a payout. French life insurance – *assurance vie* – is another type of savings product, unrelated to mortgages. About 2% of applicants for death insurance are turned down, because of serious health problems; another 8% are only offered limited insurance; 90% are accepted. Insurance against unemployment – *assurance perte d'emploi* – is not compulsory, but is used quite a lot, since France has very high unemployment. You cannot be considered for unemployment insurance until you have been working for an employer for 6 to 12 months.

It is also possible to insure yourself against being forced to sell your house at a loss – *protection revente* – because of circumstances outside your control, such as divorce. The amount covered is only 10% of the purchase price or €15,000 euros at the most.

Renegotiating a Mortgage

Under certain circumstances it is possible to renegotiate the terms of a loan. If you are struck by a serious illness, or other circumstances beyond your control arise that make it impossible to meet your repayment schedule, you have a right to ask for a reduction in the interest rate of the loan. If the loan was taken out at a high rate of interest and rates have since gone down, you can try to negotiate with the lender for a reduction; you will probably be turned down. You can then cancel the loan and find another lender at a lower rate of interest. At the present time interest rates are low, and there is not much reason to expect them to go much lower.

How the French Buy Property

The French state has various schemes in place to encourage people to save up to buy a property. The most popular is the PEL (*Prêt d'Épargne Logement*); you are required to save up to a certain limit for four years, after which you are guaranteed a mortgage and you receive a premium from the state, up to €1,500. The scheme has been abused by some who collected the premium and never actually bought a property, but the loophole has now been closed. The LEL (*Livret d'Épargne Logement*) is a similar scheme but you only save for 18 months.

Then there is the so-called 1% loan, subsidised by businesses with more than 10 employees. A 0% loan is available to those who renovate properties over 20 years old, where the renovation costs exceed 35% of the price, but the loan only covers 20% of the purchase price. The state underwrites loans for properties over 20 years old, with certain conditions attached, the so-called *prêts conventionnés*. State functionaries are guaranteed loans at competitive rates. Anyone who is permanently resident in France could qualify for one of these loans.

There are other types of loans on the open market, which reduce the cost of borrowing. The *privilège de prêteur de deniers* (PPD) – a lender's guarantee – is not subject to the 0.615% registration tax; if you are already resident in France you can ask for this type of loan. Some loans are guaranteed by a mixture of PPD and *hypothèque*; the PPD cannot be used to borrow money for construction or renovation costs.

There is also the possibility of avoiding mortgage costs completely, by using a specialised co-operative organisation (*mutuelle*) to act as guarantor for the loan (for which there is a charge). Equally, if you work for the railways, post office, Air France, the education ministry, etc., then these bodies act as guarantors for your mortgage loan. None of this is of much comfort to foreigners, perhaps, but gives one some idea of the advantages that the French enjoy when it comes to borrowing money.

Mortgage Brokers/Advisors

Abbey National France: 70 rue Saint Sauveur, 59046 Lille Cedex; ☎ 03 20 18 18 89; fax 03 20 18 19 20; www.abbey-national.fr. Call themselves 'gentlemen-prêteurs'. Branches in Bordeaux, Grenoble, Marseille, Montpellier, Paris, Toulouse.

Axa-Baud: 5 rue d'Auray, 56150 Baud, Morbihan; ☎ 02 97 51 01 45; e-mail agence.herrmann@axa.fr. Mortgages, loans and insurance. Based in Brittany.

Banque Woolwich: 9 rue Boudreau, 75009 Paris; 01 42 68 44 33; e-mail mortgage.abroad@woolwich.tm.fr. Or call UK hotline: 020-8298 4400, and ask for brochure *Helpful Hints on Housebuying in France.*

Barclays France: Champs Elysées International Branch, 6 rond-point des Champs Elysées, 75008 Paris; ☎ 01 44 95 13 80; fax 01 42 25 73 60; e-mail champsint.france@barclays.co.uk.

Barclays France: Côte d'Azur International Centre, 2 rue Alphonse Karr, 06000 Nice; ☎ 04 93 82 68 02; fax 04 93 88 58 95; e-mail cotedazur .int@barclays.co.uk.

CCF: UK address c/o HSBC, 8 Canada Square, Canary Wharf, London E14 5RQ; ☎ 0800-085 8887; textphone 0800-028 0126; www.hsbc.co.uk.

Charles Hamer: Independent advisors on French mortgage finance since 1998. 87 Park St, Thame, Oxon OX9 3HX; ☎ 01844-218956; fax 01844-261886.

Conti Financial Services: 204 Church Rd, Hove, Sussex BN3 2DJ; ☎ 0800-970 0985 *or* 01273-772811; fax 01273-321269; e-mail enquiries@contifs.com; www.mortgagesoverseas.com. Well-established independent mortgage brokers.

 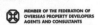

Michael Hackney: Independent mortgage broker who was MD of Abbey National France for four years; tel/fax 01869-277314.

Templeton Associates: French mortgage and finance experts, with offices in UK and France; ☎ 01225-42282; www.templeton-france.com.

IMPORTING CURRENCY

When buying property in France, you will, under normal circumstances have to pay in euros, the local currency. In the days of foreign exchange controls, before 1974, it was usual to take a suitcase full of pound notes over to France to pay for your property. Thanks to the Single Market, you can take as much cash as you like with you, but there is no advantage in doing so, and it is certainly risky. If you take more than €8000 in cash with you into France you are required to declare it. Taking a large amount of cash is not only risky; you could be suspected of being a drugs dealer or terrorist by the French customs if they find out.

Currency is nowadays normally sent using electronic transfer; the SWIFT system is the most well-known. There are charges involved at both ends so you need to know who is paying for them, and how much the receiving bank in France is likely to charge. The receiving bank should charge very little. The use of banker's drafts is not recommended as they are far too slow, and there is the risk of losing the draft.

Since the UK is not part of Euroland, anyone buying property abroad is confronted with the painful possibility that a percentage of their money is going to disappear into the pockets of a high street bank. Fortunately, this need not be the case, since a number of specialist foreign exchange companies have now started up to lessen the pain of the transaction.

A specialised company such as Currencies Direct (Hanover House, 73-74 High Holborn, London WC1V 6LR; ☎ 020-7813 0332; fax 020-7419 7753; wwww.currenciesdirect.com) can help in a number of ways, by offering better exchange rates than banks, without charging commission, and giving you the possibility of 'forward buying' – agreeing on the rate that you will pay at a fixed date in the future – or with a limit order – waiting until the rate you want is reached. For those who prefer to know exactly how much money they have available for their property purchase, forward buying is the best solution, since you no longer have to worry about the movement of the pound against the euro working to your detriment. Payments can be made in one lump sum or on a regular basis. It is usual when building new property to pay in instalments.

There is a further possibility, which is to use the services of a law firm in the UK to transfer the money. They can hold the money for you until the exact time that you need it; they will use the services of a currency dealer themselves.

OFFSHORE ACCOUNTS

While the idea of offshore banking sounds attractive, you need to be clear about what you hope to gain from it. Changes in EU law mean that lists of bank accounts held by EU citizens in other countries will be exchanged with the home country authorities, under the 'exchange of information' rules. It is becoming less and less feasible to open an account in another country and collect the interest without declaring it to the UK taxman. Negotiations are still continuing between the offshore tax havens of the Isle of Man, Jersey and Guernsey and the EU; Switzerland and other countries with strong banking secrecy rules are pressing for a flat-rate 35% withholding tax to be paid on dividends and interests, to be split with the UK, rather than allowing total transparency. The jury is still out, but the message is that tax-evasion using offshore accounts (at least in Europe) could soon be far too risky.

Bank accounts in Monaco are completely transparent as far as the French taxman goes. The French authorities can look at your accounts at any time. Even if you live in Monaco you may be treated as a French resident, so you will need some expert advice if you choose to become a tax exile there.

TRUSTS

The subject of trusts is a complex one. If you have substantial assets, then a trust of one kind or another (and there are many kinds) may be an effective way of reducing or avoiding French taxes, but this can only be done with expert advice. The concept of a 'trust' only exists in countries with common-law legal systems, e.g. the UK, USA, Canada and British colonies. French law is vague on this topic, so it is hard to predict how your trust will be treated by the French tax authorities. There are also moves by the government in the UK to make trusts less effective as a way of evading taxes.

The concept of a trust is simple enough: you give away or lend your money to a trust, and it is then treated by the taxman as though it were not your money. The trustees appointed to run the trust invest the money as they see fit. Income generated by the trust is taxed under a special regime in the UK, depending on the type of trust.

The two basic categories of trust are:

> ○ *Interest-in-possession trust:* this gives a person or people the right to income from the trust or the equivalent of income (e.g. the right to live in a rent-free property). The trustees have to hand over the income to the beneficiaries stated in the trust.

❍ *Discretionary trust:* the trustees decide which beneficiaries should receive income or capital from the trust. Where no money is paid out until the end of the trust, this is known as an *accumulation trust.* If money is paid out for the education, maintenance or benefit of beneficiaries until they get an *interest-in-possession,* then the trust is an *accumulation-and-maintenance* trust.

The French tax authorities make another distinction between *revocable* and *irrevocable* trusts. In the first case, the settlor, the one who sets up the trust, is also the beneficiary, and can revoke the trust. In the second case the settlor has entirely divested themselves of the assets in the trust, although they may still be one of the beneficiaries. The treatment of income and capital paid by the trust, and succession tax, depend in the first place on whether you have been tax-resident in France for six of the last 10 years or not. As a rule, life assurance products such as endowment policies are fiscally more favourable than other kinds of trusts, and easier to set up. In any event, it is far better to set up the trust before you become French tax-resident.

Trusts and French Taxation

French tax residents pay tax on their worldwide income, including gains or income from trusts. They also have to pay taxes on any income from offshore companies, trusts, accounts, shares and so on.

The French for a trust is *'trust'*; the term *fiducie* is used as well. As far as your French tax return goes, trusts come under *structures soumises hors de France à un régime fiscal privilégié,* a catchall term for assets held in countries with favourable tax regimes (Code Général d'Impôts, art.123). The tax authorities state that if you have more than a 10% interest in a foreign structure the gains or income have to be declared. The term 'favourable tax regime' applies if the tax withheld at source is at least a third less than the tax in France.

Assets held in a revocable trust must be declared for purposes of French wealth tax (ISF). If you make a loan to a trust this counts as part of your wealth. In general, irrevocable trusts do not need to be declared. If you are the beneficiary of a trust, any income or gains, or a life interest, have to be declared in your income tax return.

The French authorities take a dim view if a trust is used to deprive French nationals of their part of an inheritance. A French national who is a 'reserved heir' – i.e. entitled to a certain percentage of your estate – has the full weight of the law behind them in claiming their part of the inheritance.

For more information on the taxation of trusts look at *Living in France* by Bill Blevins and David Franks, or *Taxation in France 2002* by Charles Parkinson.

FRENCH INCOME TAX

French taxation is an extremely complex subject, and not something that one can easily summarise in a few pages. For this reason, if your tax affairs are at all complex, you are urged to seek professional advice before you go to France; a list of tax lawyers based in the UK, who specialise in French taxation, is given below. You may also require professional advice in France; a French accountant or lawyer may save you a lot of money, as they will know all the ins and outs of the system, which is far from transparent.

If you become French tax resident, that is, you spend more than 183 days a year in France, then you are taxed on your worldwide income in France, and you have to fill in a French tax return. If you only own a second home in France, you will still have real estate taxes to pay, and tax on rental income.

Before leaving the UK, it is important to plan your tax affairs and consider the most advantageous way to use the fact that you are moving to another country. It is even possible not to be resident in any one country for a whole year, although you can actually be considered French tax-resident without spending 183 days in France.

The methods by which French income tax is calculated give one the feeling that the French are a race of super-mathematicians. The whole thing has become increasingly complex because of all the exemptions that have been negotiated by different special-interest groups. Fortunately, you are only required to state your income; you do not have to work out your tax yourself.

While French income tax may appear exorbitantly high, this is not really the case, because of all the exemptions that are applied. Most taxes in France are raised through social security contributions and VAT, which are more difficult to avoid than income tax. Direct taxes account for less than a quarter of all tax revenues raised.

Moving to France

Procedure for UK Residents. The situation is reasonably straightforward if you are moving permanently abroad. You should inform the UK Inspector of Taxes at the office you usually deal with of your departure and they will send you a P85 form to complete. The UK tax office will usually require certain proof that you are leaving the UK, and hence their jurisdiction, for good. Evidence of having sold a house in the UK and having rented or bought one in France is usually sufficient. You can continue to own property in the UK without being considered resident, but you will have to pay UK taxes on any income from the property.

If you are leaving a UK company to take up employment with a French one then the P45 form given by your UK employer and evidence of employment in France should be sufficient. You may be eligible for a tax refund in respect of the period up to your departure, in which case it will be necessary to complete an income tax return for income and gains from the previous 5 April to your departure date. It may be advisable to seek professional advice when completing the P85; this form is used to determine your residence status and hence your UK tax liability. You should not fill it in if you are only going abroad for a short period of time. Once the Inland Revenue are satisfied that you are no longer resident or domiciled in the UK, they will close your file and not expect any more UK income tax to be paid.

If you are moving abroad temporarily then other conditions apply. You are not liable for UK taxes if you work for a foreign employer on a full-time contract and remain abroad for a whole tax year (6 April to 5 April), as long as you spend less than 183 days in a year, or 91 days a year averaged out over a four-year period, in the UK. If you are considered a UK resident and have earned money working abroad then taxes paid abroad are not deductible. If you spend one part of a year working abroad and the rest in the UK you may still be considered non-resident for the part spent abroad, the so-called split tax year concession; this only applies to someone going abroad for a lengthy period of time.

France has a double taxation agreement with the UK, which makes it possible to offset tax paid in one country against tax paid in another. While the rules are complex, essentially, as long as you work for a French employer and are paid in France then you should not have to pay UK taxes, as long as you meet the residency conditions outlined above. For further information see the Inland Revenue publications IR20 *Residents and Non-Residents. Liability to tax in the United Kingdom* which can be found on the website www.inlandrevenue.gov.uk. Booklets IR138, IR139 and IR140 are also worth reading; these can be obtained from your local tax office or from:

Centre for Non-Residents (CNR): St John's House, Merton Rd, Bootle, Merseyside L69 9BB; ☎ 0151-472 6196; fax 0151-472 6392; www.inlandrevenue.gov.uk/cnr.

Procedure for US Citizens. The US Internal Revenue Service (IRS) expects US citizens and resident aliens living abroad to file tax returns every year. Such persons will continue to be liable for US taxes on worldwide income until they have become permanent residents of another country and severed their ties with the USA. If you earn less than a certain amount abroad in one tax year then you do not need to file a tax return. The amount in 2002 was $7,200 for a single person; other rates apply for pensioners, married persons, heads of household, etc.

Fortunately the USA has a double taxation agreement with France so you should not have to pay taxes twice on the same income. In order to benefit from the double taxation agreement you need to fulfil one of two residence tests: either you have been a bona fide resident of another country for an entire tax year, which is the same as the calendar year in the case of the US, or you have been physically present in another country for 330 days during a period of 12 months which can begin at any time of the year. Once you qualify under the bona fide residence or physical presence tests then any further time you spend working abroad can also be used to diminish your tax liability.

As regards foreign income, the main deduction for US citizens is the foreign Earned Income Exclusion, by which you do not pay US taxes on the first $80,000 of money earned abroad (as of 2002; the amount has in recent times gone up by $2,000 every year). Investment income, capital gains, etc. are unearned income. If you earn in excess of the limit, taxes paid on income in France can still be used to reduce your liability for US taxes, either in the form of an exclusion or a credit, depending on which is more advantageous. The same will apply to French taxes paid on US income.

The rules for US taxpayers abroad are explained very clearly in the IRS booklet: *Tax Guide for US Citizens and Resident Aliens Abroad*, known as Publication 54, which can be downloaded from the internet on www.irs.gov. You can also ask for advice from the IRS office in Paris, at the American Consulate, 2 rue St Florentin, which is open from 9am to midday to personal callers. The office is generally very busy and may not be able to deal with your enquiry. You can try phoning on 01 43 12 25 55, or use the fax number: 01 43 12 47 52, or you can write to: IRS, c/o American Ambassy, 2 ave Gabriel, 75382 Paris, Cedex 8.

The US tax return has to be sent to the IRS, Philadelphia, PA 19255-0207; ☎ 215-516-2000. The IRS office in Paris will not accept tax returns or fill them in for you.

Aspects of Tax Residence

It is important to understand that the French authorities make no distinction between Residence, ordinary residence and domicile in the way the British tax authorities do. In the British sense, the country where you have your longest-lasting ties is your domicile; this is a concept not defined in the UK Tax Acts, but rather based on precedent. In French, domicile simply means residence, and is based on facts, such as the number of days you spend in a place, or where you have the main centre of your economic interests.

The French tax authorities define tax residence (*domicile fiscal*) somewhat differently from the British. If your household – *foyer fiscal* – is in France, e.g. your family live there, then you are tax resident there, even if you work in another country. The other test of tax residence is where you have your principal residence. If you spend more than 183 days a year in France then you are tax resident. You may even be tax resident in France if you spend less than 183 days a year there, if you have spent more time in France than in any other country. Whether you have a *carte de séjour* or not does not enter into the assessment. If the main centre of your economic interests is in France, or your main employment is there, then you are certainly tax resident there.

One may well ask how the French authorities can know where you have spent most time: it is remarkably easy for them to find out, since there are no rules preventing different agencies from sharing information about your movements, as there would be in the UK. Credit card statements, medical records, passenger manifests and bank records can all show where you have been. There is every likelihood that neighbours, or anyone you have fallen out with in your village, will share information about you with the authorities.

Although it might be tempting to try to avoid being tax-resident anywhere for a while, the consequences could be appalling for your heirs if you were suddenly to drop dead. The UK authorities will not accept that you have left their jurisdiction unless you can produce your French tax number.

Situations may arise where one married partner is tax resident in the UK and the other in France. Partners are considered separately as far as tax residence goes, even though the location of your household is the main criterion for establishing tax residence. In this case you have a choice between being taxed together in the usual way, or being treated separately, so that the resident spouse will declare their income to the local centre des impôts and the other to the *Centre des Impôts des Non-Résidents* in Paris. This is a possibility, since under French law, those married in the UK and US are assumed to come under the regime of separation of estates – régime de séparation des biens.

As a basic principle, tax is levied on a household as a whole – the *foyer fiscal* – rather than on separate persons. It is not usual for a husband and wife to pay tax separately, unless they are in the throes of divorce and have separate households, or are married under the separation of estates regime. If you have entered into a PACS – a civil partnership contract – you will have to wait for three years before you can be assessed as one household. If you are simply living together *en concubinage* you are treated as two separate households. Each of the *concubins* can have their own dependants, who will be taken into account when their tax is calculated.

How Income Tax is Paid

The French tax system works on the basis that you pay tax in instalments on your income for the previous year, calculated on the basis of your income in the year before that. There is, therefore, a delay before a foreign resident starting work in France for the first time pays any tax. No tax is paid in advance (except for those withheld at source on savings etc.). If you work for an employer, tax can be deducted at source through the year. You can either pay ten monthly instalments from January calculated on the basis of your previous tax return – the last two months are used to adjust the total tax paid – in which case you are *mensualisé;* or you pay in three instalments in February, May and September – the *tiers provisionnels.* Strictly speaking the first two payments are due on 31 January and 30 April, but it has become the custom to extend the deadline to 15 February and 15 May. Normally you will receive your final assessment during September. The final instalment is due on the last day of the following month. This is again extended to the 15th of the month after. Only after the 15th of the second month after you receive your final assessment will you have to pay the 10% penalty.

New legislation passed at the end of 2002 is likely to change this system somewhat. In future you would be required to pay within 45 days of an assessment. The 10% penalty cannot be applied before 15 September.

All French residents must be registered with the local *inspecteur des impôts.* You are liable for tax on your worldwide income from the day you arrive in France. It is up to you to request a tax return (*déclaration fiscale*) if you do not receive one automatically. The final date for submitting your tax return is 28 February. If you are non-resident, and live in Europe, you have until 30 April. If you file your tax return even one day late, you automatically receive a 10% penalty. The authorities take a very hard line with tax evasion, which is common with non-salaried workers.

Tax Returns. There are several different types of tax returns – *déclarations fiscales* – for different types of income. The basic form is No. 2042, the *déclaration des revenus.* If you are self-employed, have capital gains to declare, or rent out property, you also have to fill in No.2042C, the *déclaration complément.* If you are taxed as a *micro-entreprise* you also fill in No.2042P.

There are several more forms that one may be required to fill in:
   ○ Blue form No.2044 for *revenus fonciers* – property income.

- Pink form No.2047 for foreign income.
- Green form No.2049 for capital gains.
- Form No.2065 for corporation tax.
- Form No.2074 for capital gains on investments.

Calculation of Income Tax – Impôt sur le Revenu

Income tax is levied on a whole range of sources of income. Bank interest and income from some savings accounts and life insurance are taxed at a source.

TYPES OF INCOME THAT ARE SUBJECT TO INCOME TAX INCLUDE:

Wages, salaries, remunerations, pensions, life annuities	*Traitements, salaries, remunerations assimilées, pensions, rentes viagères*
Investment income	*Revenus de capitaux mobiliers*
Capital gains (short-term)	*Plus values à court terme*
Industrial and commercial profits	*Bénéfices industriels et commerciaux (BIC)*
Non-commercial profits	*Bénéfices non-commerciaux (BNC)*
Property income	*Revenus fonciers*
Agricultural profits	*Bénéfices agricoles*
Certain directors' remunerations	*Rémunerations des dirigeants de sociétés*

- Benefits in kind are taxed at the same rate as wages, salaries, pensions and life annuities, according to their market value. Employees can claim tax deductions for some expenses, include travel to and from work.
- Commercial profits – BIC – covers income from running a business, small-scale manufacturing and trading, as well as letting out shops or furnished properties. It is particularly relevant to those who run *chambres d'hôtes* and *gîtes*.
- Non-commercial profits – BNC – concerns income from liberal professions, i.e. doctors, architects, lawyers, and so on.
- Property income concerns the letting of houses, offices, factories, etc., agricultural land, lakes, forests, as well as hunting rights.

If your lifestyle is inconsistent with your declared income you may be investigated by the tax inspectors. If you possess a yacht, an expensive car, and so on, then these will be valued and taken into account. New assets can be assessed as income and taxed accordingly.

Exemptions

Certain kinds of income are exempt from income tax, notably:

- Rental income, if you rent out rooms in your own home, on a long-term basis, as long as the rent is considered 'reasonable'.
- Up to €760 rental income generated from short-term letting of *chambres d'hôtes.*
- Income from certain savings plans, and investments in industry, under certain conditions: e.g., PEP, PEA, CODEVI and *Livret A.*
- Social security benefits, some maternity benefits, disability benefits, incapacity benefits.
- Redundancy payments.

Although you may not pay income tax on the above, some of these items, namely investment plans, are still subject to social security taxes totalling 10%.

Deductions

Before any tax is calculated you are entitled to certain deductions, notably:

- Maintenance payments to parents and children, including adult children, if they can be shown to be in need.
- Child support and alimony payments to divorced partners.
- Voluntary payments to children up to a reasonable limit.
- Voluntary payments to persons over 75 living in your home.
- Some investments in French film-production or video-making.
- Losses in certain business investment schemes, qualifying for tax breaks.

If your income falls under wages, salaries, pensions, etc. there are further items to deduct from your gross income before tax is calculated:

- Professional expenses – including travel to and from work, meals, hotels, etc. – usually a flat rate of 10% of your gross income, up to €12,500. If your expenses exceed 10% of your income, more can be deducted, subject to proof.
- After deduction of expenses, there is a 20% abatement up to a limit of €23,800 in 2002.
- The interest on loans contracted in order to invest in a new company can be deducted from the salary paid by the company.
- Private pension contributions up to €40,000.

Note that any income that has not been voluntarily declared no longer

qualifies for the 20% salary abatement once you have received a first
warning letter from the French taxman.

Pensions. The French state pension is paid tax-free. If you have a *rente
viagère* or pension annuity, tax is paid on a sliding scale, on between 70%
and 30% of the pension, depending on your age. Private pensions, foreign
pensions, etc. attract an additional abatement of 10% before the above
deductions are applied.

If tax is or will be deducted at source in the UK from your pension,
you need to contact the Inland Revenue's *Centre for Non-Residents* and
ask for Form FRA2/INDIVIDUAL. Once the French tax office has
stamped it and you have returned it, the Centre will instruct your pension
provider not to deduct tax at source. You will then pay French tax on your
pension. Contact the *Centre for Non-Residents*, St John's House, Merton
Rd, Bootle, Merseyside L69 9BB; ☎ 00 44 151-472 6196 (from France);
fax 00 44 151-472 6392; e-mail non-residents@inlandrevenue.gov.uk;
www.inlandrevenue.gov.uk/cnr.

Methods of Calculation

The basis of the calculation is the total income of the household added
together. In order to compensate taxpayers with dependants or low earners
in their household, the French use a 'family quotient' system – *quotient
familial* – calculating tax according to *parts* assigned to members of the
family. The total income is divided by the number of parts, which has the
effect of calculating the tax as if each member of the family earned the
same amount. Once the tax has been worked out on a sliding scale, it is
multiplied by the number of parts to arrive at the final figure.

As a single person, you have 1 *part*. If you are married then you have 2;
if one partner is disabled the couple receives 2.5 *parts*; if both are disabled
3 *parts*. There are numerous different categories of *parts*. Dependants
(*personnes à charge*) are (to put it simply) children under 21, students under
25, children doing their military service, and disabled children whatever
their age. They are only accepted as dependants if they are based at home
and still require some support from you. In the first three cases they may
be 're-attached' to the household, even though they are living and working
away from home, and you will receive an additional 0.5 *parts* for each of
them. Since 2003, divorced or separated parents can receive 0.25% of the
parts if they share custody.

The French tax office allows foreign residents to benefit from the family
quotient system, on the assumption of reciprocity on the part of the British
Inland Revenue and other tax authorities, even though French residents in
the UK etc. do not actually benefit from the same system.

The most commonly used *parts* are given in the table below:

	Married couple	Single, widowed, or divorced
None disabled	2	1
1 disabled	2.5	1.5
1 dependent child	2.5	1.5
1 disabled dependant	3	2
2 dependent children	3	2
2 dependants including 1 disabled	3.5	2.5
2 disabled dependants	4	3
3 dependent children	4	3
4 dependent children	5	4

As a rule, each additional child or dependant gives a further 0.5 *parts.* Three children or dependants give 1 *part* apiece, plus 0.5 *parts* if one is invalid. There is a limit to the amount that you can save with this system. If your saving is more than €2,017 per half *part* above your base *parts,* then you do not qualify for the *quotient familial,* and your tax has to be calculated differently. Single parents and those with disabled dependants are treated more generously.

The Tax Calculation by tranches

The French tax system resembles other systems in that tax is calculated progressively on the amount per *part.* The amount per slice or *tranche* has to be multiplied by the *parts* to arrive at a final figure before tax credits and rebates are applied. The following figures apply to income earned in 2002.

Slice or *tranche*		Net income
1	0-4,191	0%
2	4,191-8,242	7.05%
3	8,242-14,506	19.74%
4	14,506-23,489	29.14%
5	23,489-38,218	38.54%
6	38,218-47,131	43.94%
7	47,131 and over	49.58%

Tax Credits

There are various tax credits and reductions, too numerous to go into in great detail. Note that these are all subject to conditions and limits. All are subject to having the correct paperwork. The more usual ones include:

EXAMPLE OF A TAX CALCULATION

Mr and Mrs Gallomane between them earn €50,000, and have no dependent children. Therefore they have 2 *parts*. They have no investments and have not realised any capital gains in the tax year in question. It is assumed that all social taxes and contributions have been withheld at source by their employers.

Income		€50,000
-10% employment expenses		(5,000)
		45,000
-20% abatement of salary		(9,000)
Taxable amount		36,000
halved for 2 *parts*		18,000
Tax on 0-€4,191 @ 0%	0	
on €4,192-8,242 @ 7.05%	285.59	
on €8,243-14,506 @ 19.74%	1,236.51	
on €14,507-23,489 @ 29.14%	1,018.15	
Tax per part		2,540.25
multiply by 2		5,080.50
Income tax		5,080.50

On the same income, a single person will pay €8,961. A married couple with two children who pay €5,000 for domestic help will pay only €582.

○ 50% of the cost of domestic help, child-minding, gardeners, cleaners, etc. up to a total credit for all employees of €5,000.

○ Child-minding expenses outside the home.

○ Charitable donations; but no more than 10% of your taxable income. Charities are not all treated the same by the authorities; you should check first to see what kind of tax rebate is on offer.

○ Renovations, extensions, repairs to principal home, and to tourist accommodation in certain designated rural areas, up to 15% of the purchase price of the property.

○ Investment in heavy equipment for the home, e.g. central heating, solar panels, etc.

○ Environmentally friendly vehicles.

○ One-off compensatory payments to divorced partners.

○ Life assurance premiums on policies taken out before 1996.

○ Investments in small and medium-sized businesses.

○ Lump-sum payment for children in school or college or higher education: €61-€183 per child.

The Décote

If your tax liability is below €760 you are eligible for a rebate – *décote* – of the difference between €380 and half the tax liability. Thus if your tax liability is €600, you will have a rebate of €80 and your liability is reduced to €520. If your liability is under €380 you pay no tax at all.

Complete Exemption from Income Tax

Certain persons are completely exempt from paying income tax. If your income after deduction of 10% professional costs is below €7,250 you pay no tax.

Social Security Taxes and Contributions

The basic tax is the CSG (*Contribution Sociale Généralisée*) which is applied at a rate of 7.5% after a deduction of 5% for professional costs (i.e. 7.5% of 95% of gross income). All earned and unearned income is subject to this tax, which is in many cases a withholding tax, except for sickness, unemployment and some other benefits. A contribution to repaying the social security system's debt, the CRDS or *Contribution pour le Remboursement de la Dette Sociale,* is levied at 0.5% on similar terms to the CSG.

All income is subject to an additional 'social contribution', the *Prélèvement Sociale* at 2%. Certain tax-free savings accounts, such as the *Livret A, Livret Bleu,* and *CODEVI* are not subject to the above social security contributions.

There are further social security contributions covering pensions and unemployment benefit, totalling some 9.3% of income, and then compulsory basic medical cover at 6.8% deducted before any tax calculation is made.

LOCAL/REAL ESTATE TAXES

Most local taxes are real estate taxes. There are some minor taxes that are not dealt with here in detail, namely, regional development tax, the tax to finance local chambers of commerce, and the refuse collection tax. The main real estate taxes come under three headings:

- *taxe d'habitation*
- *taxes foncières*
- *taxe professionnelle*

These are local taxes raised for the benefit of local *communes, départements* and *régions.* The rates of tax are set by the local administrative collectivities, up to specific limits set by the national government. The rate for your area can be found in the annual publication *Impôts Locaux,* published at the start of November. See www.guideducontribuable.com.

Taxe d'Habitation

The *taxe d'habitation* is payable by anyone who has premises at their disposal subject to the tax. This includes both principal residences as well as any secondary homes that are available for your use. Whether you rent or own the property, if you occupy the property on 1 January you are liable for the entire year's tax. It follows that if you move house during the year, the person whose dwelling you are taking over pays the tax for the year.

Any type of premises that are furnished so as to be habitable, as well as garages, parking spaces, gardens, staff accommodation and other outbuildings within one kilometre of the main building are assessed for the *taxe d'habitation*.

Some buildings are exempt from *taxe d'habitation:*

- buildings subject to the *taxe professionnelle*
- farm buildings
- student accommodation
- government offices

The tax is calculated by the local authorities on the basis of the cadastral value on 1 January, cadastral value being the nominal rental value of the property. If you own an empty habitable rental property, then you pay the *taxe d'habitation,* otherwise the tenant pays.

Exemptions. Those on very low incomes are exempt. Also exempt is anyone who is over 60, widowed, or disabled and unable to work. Anyone subject to Wealth Tax (ISF) cannot claim exemption. If you inherit a house which you intend to sell, and clear all the furniture out of it by 1 January (i.e. make it uninhabitable) you can escape the *taxe d'habitation* for one year. Caravans and mobile homes are exempt, as long as they have an engine or vehicle attached to them.

Reductions. The tax is reduced using the system of family *parts* outlined above; single persons do not qualify for this particular reduction. If the taxable income for the first family *part* does not exceed €16,290, there is a reduction of €3,533. There are further reductions for subsequent half *parts.* The family reductions only apply to principal residences, not to holiday homes.

The local *commune* may accord reductions to anyone whose principal residence is in the *commune,* and reductions for low earners.

Taxes Foncières

There are two land taxes, or *taxes foncières:*

- tax on unbuilt land
- tax on built-up land

Un-built Land

Agricultural land is subject to the element of the tax that goes to the *commune,* but not those parts that go to the *département* and *région.* There are exemptions for certain kinds of forests and tree plantations for fixed periods of time.

Built-up Land

Types of buildings and constructions subject to the *taxe foncière* include:

- Anything that has the character of a permanent construction.
- Warehouses.
- Private roads.
- Hard standings.
- Boats with permanent moorings.
- Grounds used for industry or commerce.
- Land with advertising hoardings.

Buildings used for farming or not-for-profit public services, are exempt. New buildings, or converted buildings, or extensions to buildings, are exempt from the tax for two years from the date of completion, as regards the regional and *département* element of the tax. As far as the *commune's* part of the tax goes, there may be a two-year exemption for new residential property, or the *commune* may collect the tax.

The owner of the property pays the *taxe foncière.* If the property remains empty through circumstances outside your control for more than three months, you may obtain a rebate of the tax proportional to the time it has stood empty. If you buy a property you can agree to divide the *taxe foncière* for the year *pro rata temporis* with the vendor, unlike the *taxe d'habitation.*

Built-up land is assessed on the basis of 50% of the nominal rental value, the *valeur locative cadastrale.* Un-built land is assessed at 80% of the cadastral value. There are exemptions for the over-75s and the disabled, subject to certain conditions.

Taxe Professionnelle

The *taxe professionnelle* is by far the most lucrative for the local authorities, and accounts for about half their income. The tax is levied on individuals (*personnes physiques*) and companies (*personnes morales*) that regularly carry on a non-salaried business. Members of partnerships and so-called fiscally transparent companies (whose members are assessed individually for income tax), are assessed in their own names.

There is a long list of persons exempt from the tax of which a few are relevant to foreign residents:

○ Writers, artists, and teachers.
○ Recognised private schools.
○ Artisans working alone, or in a co-operative.
○ Correspondents on local newspapers.

There are temporary exemptions for new businesses in some areas of the country. The most significant exemptions (if they are granted) are for people who rent out *chambres d'hôtes* and *gîtes*, who fall under the category of *loueur en meublés*. Rooms rented out in your principal dwelling to another person who uses them as their own principal dwelling are always exempt from the *taxe professionnelle*. The tax is calculated on the basis of the cadastral rental value of the premises, with some additions for larger business. There are reductions for artisans who employ no more than three salaried workers.

Taxe Locale d'Équipement

This is a tax payable on the completion of new buildings, and also on extensions and reconstructions. It is levied by *communes* with more than 10,000 inhabitants. Other *communes* may or may not levy it. The *Certificat d'Urbanisme* or outline planning permission will tell you whether you have to pay this tax, and what the amount is.

The tax is assessed at between 1% and 5% of the surface area of the building calculated on a fixed scale per square metre. One half of the tax is payable within 18 months of delivery of the building permit, and the second half within 36 months.

The main exemptions from this tax relate to building work done with certain state-approved loans, and buildings in certain zones earmarked for industrial development. The only exemption likely to apply to foreign residents or non-residents, is for rebuilding a house destroyed by a natural disaster. The local Division Départementale de l'Equipement can let you know if you are eligible for any reduction.

Taxation for Owners of Chambres d'Hôtes and Gîtes.

This subject is treated in chapter 12, *Making Money from Your Property*.

Non-Residents and Local Taxes

Non-residents who own property in France are liable for the *taxe d'habitation* and *taxe foncière* unless they qualify for an exemption. They would not normally have to pay the *taxe professionnelle*. As regards taxes on the letting of property, these are dealt with in chapter 12.

Taxation of Real Estate Owned by Foreign Companies

The French authorities have instituted an annual tax of 3% of the market value of real estate in France owned by non-French companies, more than 50% of whose assets consist of property, as a measure against tax evasion, and to discover the identities of the owners of the real estate. Since the UK has an agreement with France to combat tax fraud, this tax may not actually be applied in practice. It is, however, a serious disincentive to buying real estate in France through a UK company.

CAPITAL GAINS TAX OR CGT

In French CGT is known as *Impôt sur les Plus Values* or IPV. The tax is levied on the sale of:

- buildings
- land
- shares
- furniture and other movable goods
- antiques and works of art
- precious stones and precious metals

A distinction is made between short-term gains – *plus values à court terme* – made within two years of acquiring the assets, and long-term gains – *plus values à long terme*. In the following only the taxation of land and buildings will be dealt with. Companies 50% or more of whose assets consist of property are treated as properties.

Method of Calculation

The *plus value* on your property sale is worked out by deducting the original purchase price – *prix d'achat* – from the selling price – *prix de cession*. The costs associated with buying the property are added on to the original purchase price, thus reducing your liability. You may also add on the cost of building work, extensions, renovations, etc. to the purchase price. It is advisable to have all the original receipts and invoices from when the work was done. If this is not possible, a state-appointed expert may produce a valuation of the work, or you may opt for a flat rate 15%. If you or your family did the work yourselves this can also be taken into account, either using a valuation by an expert, or by multiplying the price of the materials you used by three. Secondary items, such as painting, wallpapering, carpeting, etc. will not be taken into account. Both the purchase price and the associated costs are indexed to the rate of inflation, thus reducing your liability further.

In the unlikely situation that you sell your French property within two years of buying it, or if it is repossessed, the gain from the sale of the property is added directly to your income tax liability, and the tax has to be paid immediately. In the more usual situation of a long-term gain, the capital gain is divided by five, and one-fifth is added to your income tax liability during the year you sell the property. The amount by which your income tax liability increases is then multiplied by five to arrive at your capital gains tax liability. The result is that those on low incomes who have made a small profit will pay little IPV, since their gain does not push them up into a higher tax band. The IPV can be paid over five yearly instalments, but you have to apply for this dispensation.

There are two main methods of reducing IPV. In the first place, the gain is reduced by 5% for every full year after two years since the purchase of the property. Thus after 22 years there is no more IPV to pay. Secondly, if you have owned your holiday home for more than five years, and have always had it at your disposal, then there is a deduction of €6,100 per married couple, and another €1,525 per child. A single person enjoys a deduction of €4,600. Everyone is allowed capital gains of €915 per year in any case.

Non-residents are taxed at 33.33% on their capital gains from the sale of property; or at 50% if they are trading in property. There are certain circumstances where you may not be liable for IPV on the sale of your French property as a non-resident:

- You do not own your principal residence.
- You have been tax-resident in France for at least one year in the past.
- You have had the use of the property for at least three years since you purchased it.
- You have not sold your principal residence within the two years of the sale of your second residence.

The application of the above rules depends on the type of double taxation treaty France has with the non-resident's country.

There is a complete exemption from IPV in some situations, e.g.:
- You are a pensioner not liable for income tax.
- The property has been your habitual principal residence since you bought it, or at least five years.

○ You have owned the property for more than 22 years.

If you can show that the sale of the property was forced on you by family circumstances or because you had to move to another part of the country, you can claim exemption. No IPV is payable if you receive the property as an inheritance, as a gift, or through a divorce settlement. If you originally received the property free of charge, the fair market value at the time you acquired it is taken as the purchase price; there are no deductions for any taxes paid at the time on the transfer of the property.

WILLS AND INHERITANCE TAX

The subject of succession tax (*droits de succession*) and gift tax (*droits de donation*) needs to be carefully considered **before** you buy a property in France. Failure to take the right steps before signing an *acte de vente* can have serious consequences for your heirs; it is difficult to make changes to the *acte de vente* once it has been registered. If your family situation is at all complicated – many foreign property-buyers have been married more than once – then legal advice is a necessity, and highly desirable even in straightforward situations. This means dealing with an English-speaking lawyer who understands French and UK law, which generally implies a UK-based lawyer. Several names are given below.

The French system of inheritance tax – strictly speaking 'succession rights' or 'succession taxes' (*droits de succession*) – is very different from the British one: you are not free to leave your assets to anyone you please. Blood relatives always come first, while your spouse or partner is treated almost as though they were strangers. The logic behind this is simple. Napoleon saw that too many men were leaving their properties to their mistresses, or their wives, so he instituted a system that would ensure that property remained with the blood family.

The first issue to consider is that of domicile, a concept that is not defined in the UK Tax Laws, but which rests on legal precedent. Domicile is something like nationality, but harder to lose. Loosely speaking, your country of domicile is the one where you have had the longest-lasting ties during your lifetime, or the country you intend to return to after living abroad. If you were resident in France on your decease, the French tax authorities will claim that your heirs should pay French succession taxes on your worldwide assets, or at the very least on your assets in France. The British tax authorities are very reluctant to concede that a British citizen is no longer domiciled in the UK. Foreign domicile can only be established after 'exhaustive enquiries', as they say.

There are potential advantages to being taxed in France as long as the inheritance exceeds £234,000. The top rate in France of 40% only kicks in on inheritances over €1.7 million (£1.2 million), while in the UK it starts at £234,000. If you are relatively wealthy, you will want to disperse your assets in good time, leaving as little as possible for the taxman. The good news is that there is a double taxation agreement between France and the UK concerning inheritances, so as long as you are open and honest about matters you will not have to pay inheritance taxes twice. There is also a general principle, however, that you should pay IHT in the country which has the higher rate.

Wills

Making a will in both the UK and France is essential. While it is possible to pay your IHT on a second home in France to the UK taxman, this may not be in your interests and could get you into trouble with the French authorities. One procedure is to make a UK will, after taking advice from someone familiar with French inheritance law, and have it translated into French and notarised, but having a will translated by an official translator can be very expensive, and the results may not even be that accurate. The other possibility is to make up a UK will with no mention of your French property; the French will only relates to your French assets. Before you make a will in France, you should take professional advice to make sure that it does not conflict with, or invalidate your UK will. Provisions in your UK will can be taken into account by the French authorities, as long as they are not in conflict with French law. Care needs to be taken if you make up another will at a later date: clauses such as 'this will invalidates all previous wills' can be disastrous if you have two wills.

You are strongly advised to leave copies of your will with a notary in France. One of the biggest problems that can arise is when your heirs do not know where your will is; locking it away in a safe deposit box in a French bank makes life difficult for everyone. You can help your heirs immeasurably by making sure that they have easy access to documents.

French Succession Taxes

Under French law, one part of your assets has to be left to specified members of your family (*la réserve légale*), while the rest is yours to do with as you please (*la quotité disponible*). Blood relatives are entitled to inherit in descending order:

RESERVED HEIRS
Children: 50% for the first child; 66.6% between two children; 75% between three and above. No distinction is made between children from a first and subsequent

marriage.

Parents: Where there are no children, parents receive 25% each. A single surviving parent can only receive 25%.

Spouses: Only become reserved heirs if there are no direct ascendants or descendants.

The grandchildren become reserved heirs if the children are no longer living. Brothers and sisters can be disinherited. They only inherit automatically if there are no descendants, ascendants or spouse. If deceased, nephews and nieces can inherit in their place. Children of the current marriage are treated equally with children of previous marriages, and children born outside marriage, including half-siblings of the deceased's children. The principle that children born out of 'adultery' have equal rights with their half-siblings has only recently been accepted in France. In the absence of the above then relatives take precedence over strangers, depending on their relationship to the deceased, up to the fourth degree. Relatives beyond the fourth degree are considered to be unrelated for the purpose of inheritance tax.

Inheritance and Gift Taxes. These are levied at the following rates. Note that 'spouse' only refers to your marriage partner; other rules apply to common-law partners. Children and parents benefit from a tax-free sum of €46,000; spouses from €76,000:

Tax percentage	Spouse	Children/Parents
5	the first €7,600	the first €7,600
10	€7,600-€15,000	€7,600-€11,400
15	€15,000-€30,000	€11,400-€15,000
20	€30,000-€520,000	€15,000-€520,000
30	€520,000-€850,000	€520,000-€850,000
35	€850,000-€1,700,000	€850,000-€1,700,000
40	€1,700,000 and over	€1,700,000 and over

Brothers, sisters and grandchildren pay at rates of 35% (0-€30,000) and 45% on the excess. More distant relatives up to the fourth degree pay at 55%. Anyone else pays at 60%.

Protecting your Partner

French law is far less favourable to partners than British law; to improve the partner's situation the law was changed in 2002, the main change being that the surviving partner has the option of remaining in the marital home for the rest of their lives (see below). The partner can also choose to move out of the property, and receive their part of the assets of the deceased. This is often the best solution where several children jointly inherit a property and want to dispose of it. It can be too much of a headache staying on in a property which is owned by children of your partner's previous marriage whom you do not get on with.

The law distinguishes between three types of partner: a marriage partner; a common-law partner or *concubin* with whom you live without entering into a legally recognised partnership, known as a *union libre*; and a partner with whom you have entered into an official notarised civil contract, the PACS (*Pacte Civil de Solidarité*). The latter was brought in in 1999 to improve the lot of gay couples; the contractants make themselves liable for each other's debts and agree to support each other; after three years they can file joint tax returns. Any two people who are not closely related can enter into one, whether they are couples or just live together. The PACS can be dissolved as well.

The following is an example of what a partner might expect to inherit on assets of €300,000, where there are no other heirs, and no provisions have been made to reduce succession taxes:

	Common-law partner	Spouse	PACS partner
Tax-free sum	€1,500	€57,000	€76,000
Taxable sum	€298,500	€243,000	€224,000
Rate of tax	60%	50% (-€1,500)	20% (-€2,630)
Actual tax	€179,100	€120,000	€42,170
Inheritance after tax	€120,900	€180,000	€257,830

The above graphically illustrates the usefulness of the PACS, and the value of marriage.

If you become resident in France, you can opt for different kinds of marriage regimes specifying how assets are divided on the death of one partner. If you go for the *communauté universelle avec clause d'attribution intégrale* your partner acquires all your assets on your death; your children will receive the entire inheritance when your partner dies. This is the option chosen by most French married couples. Another situation – the *participation aux acquêts* – is where the partners divide the assets acquired during the course of the marriage if the marriage comes to an end; this necessitates having precise records of what you owned before you married, and what you acquired after. A simpler solution is the *régime de séparation des biens* – separation of estates – where the marriage partners' assets remain separate. Marriages contracted in the UK, and many marriages in the USA, are assumed to come under the regime of separation of estates in France.

A common way to improve the marriage partner's lot is to make a *donation entre époux* (gift between spouses), an act which can be registered with a notary for a minimal cost (see below).

The other method that is favoured by the French for reducing succession taxes is the use of life assurance (*assurance vie*). These are long-term investments (at least seven years) which allow you to leave money to a named beneficiary, who will not have to pay any succession taxes on a sum under €152,500. The main limitation on using life assurance is that you cannot exceed the beneficiary's allowable percentage of the inheritance. Your family can challenge the beneficiary in court if it appears that you made excessive life assurance payments in order to reduce their inheritance. It is advisable not to inform the beneficiary that you have taken out life assurance, but to mention the life assurance in your will.

Buying En Tontine

The *tontine* was thought up by an Italian banker, Lorenzo Tonti, in the 18th century. It is more correctly called a *clause d'accroissement*. This is where two or more people whether married or not, acquire assets, on the understanding that the one who lives the longest acquires the whole, thus entirely cutting out the inheritors of the other members of the *tontine*. For legal purposes deceased members of a *tontine* – and, by extension, their inheritors – are treated as though they never had any share in the assets. The survivor is treated as though they owned the property from the day that it was bought. Acquiring property with a *tontine* clause was fiscally very advantageous before 1979, but these days it is much less so, unless you start a *Société Civile* (registered company) with a *tontine* element. Where the partners are unrelated, or *concubins,* the 'winner' of the *tontine* is subject to succession tax at 60% on half the value of the property, unless the property is worth less than €76,000 and it is their principal residence, in which case the survivor only pays 4.89% transfer taxes. If there is a PACS between them, the succession tax is only 50%. Married partners pay the usual succession tax applicable to them.

Partners cannot enter into a *tontine* unless they have roughly the same life expectancy and can therefore profit equally from the *tontine*. They should also contribute equal amounts to the purchase. It is not allowed to buy *en tontine* with your children as partners, or with someone who is likely to die soon.

A disadvantage of a *tontine* is that it is impossible to sell your part of the *tontine* since the buyer will lose everything if the person they bought their share from dies before the other members. If your partner in the *tontine* is also your spouse, then any dispute becomes very unpleasant. All the members have to agree to dissolve a *tontine* and it is still a costly and slow process.

The *tontine* is rarely used by French marriage partners, mainly because it is illegal for those married under the common ownership regime to enter into a *tontine* if they use commonly owned funds to buy a property. The main advantage is that it allows you to decide who will inherit your property. It is very effective in cutting the family of the partner who dies first out of the will. It is not actually tax-efficient (except for very cheap properties), since there is only one heir in this situation, and no flexibility as to who inherits. The *tontine* clause has to be put into the *acte de vente* before it is signed; afterwards is too late.

The Société Civile Tontinière. The best way to maximise the benefit of a *tontine* is to start a company for this purpose. The company owns the property, which can be bought and sold. The shares in the company cannot be sold for the reason outlined above. The advantage of the *Société Civile Tontinière* is that the transfer of the shares to the surviving member(s) is only subject to transfer taxes (4.89%), and not to gift tax. The value of the property is irrelevant. There is a very high likelihood, however, that sooner or later the French tax authorities will clamp down on this loophole, but this will not be retroactive.

Setting up a Société Civile Immobilière (SCI)

A potentially useful way of minimising succession taxes is to buy the your property through an SCI which you have set up yourself. You are then the owner of the shares which you can give to your children during your lifetime. This is best done at the start, otherwise you will have to pay transfer taxes if you sell the property to the SCI later. There are considerable costs involved; setting up the SCI costs on average €2500. There will also be Capital Gains Tax (*l'impôt sur les plus values immobilières*) to pay when the property is sold (see below).

If you already own a property and want to set up an SCI, the most effective method is to transfer only the *nue propriété* (ownership without *usufruit*) of the property to the SCI, which has a far lower value than the *pleine propriéte,* while retaining the *usufruit* for your lifetime. You would then give your child(ren) the shares in the company that correspond to the *nue propriété,* and pay a small amount of gift tax on the amount. Your children already have a minimum tax-free sum, and the tax on gifts made during your lifetime is half the usual inheritance tax.

The main requirement of the SCI is the holding of an annual general meeting. Decisions about the running of the company can be made by majority shareholder voting, thus avoiding the problems of the *indivision* where unanimity is required between all the partners.

The SCI is not ideal if you are planning to run *gîtes,* or *chambres d'hôtes.* By definition an SCI is meant to be non-trading, and it only owns property, not furniture. The solution is to rent the property out to another business structure, a SARL. There are also certain implications from the point of view of UK tax authorities, which concern directors' benefits-in-kind. If the authorities are aware that as a director you have the free use of a property in France for holidays then you can become liable for income tax on the assessed benefits-in-kind. The way around this is to ensure that shareholders are not managers – *gérants* – of the company.

You should seek expert legal assistance if you are thinking of setting up an SCI. If you engage a lawyer they should be fully conversant with UK and French law, and should have practised in both countries. The SCI is worth considering for expensive properties. It is also very useful where unrelated people wish to buy a property together, such as in the case of co-ownership.

Buying En Indivision

The concept of *indivision* is fundamental in French law. Where two or more persons buy a property jointly they automatically enter into an *indivision,* unless they opt for another regime, such as the *tontine* or the SCI. The term *indivision* came about because, while the members of the *indivision* have separate shares, the assets themselves are not divided up. Members of the *indivision* can leave if they wish, or ask to have the *indivision* dissolved through a court of law. Couples married under the regime of common property – *communauté des biens* – automatically have equal shares in a property, given that their names are on the *acte de vente.* There is also the possibility that only property that is acquired during the marriage is commonly owned. Under the regime of separate estates – *séparation des biens* – the property can be divided up unequally, or only one partner may own it.

Where two or more heirs inherit a property, they automatically enter an *indivision* and become *indivisaires,* until such time as the members decide to end the *indivision.* If you go to a notary and ask to see their portfolio of properties, you may see a file of 'problem' properties, where the owners are *indivisaires* or several people have some claim to a property. Often it is more convenient to rent the property out and leave matters alone. The *indivisaires* can decide to prolong the *indivision* for a certain length of time, and make up a *convention d'indivision,* a written contract. Once the members fall out with each other the only solution is to break up the *indivision.* Serious problems can arise if one member dies. The positive side of the *indivision* is that it is easy to enter into; no written agreement is required. Each member retains their share of the property and benefits proportionally from the income generated.

Buying En Achat Croisé

The *achat croisé* – meaning cross-purchase – is a simple way of protecting your partner so that they can stay in the marital home when you pass away. Each partner buys half the *nue propriété* (ownership without the use or profit of the property) and half the *usufruit* of the property. At the decease of one partner, the survivor then owns half the *pleine propriété* and half the *usufruit*. Succession tax is payable on the *nue propriété* element, but not on the *usufruit*. The idea is best represented in a diagram:

Situation at purchase		Situation on decease of A
A possesses	B possesses	B possesses
½ as *usufruit*	½ as *nue propriété*	½ as *pleine propriété*
½ as *nue propriété*	½ as *usufruit*	½ as *usufruit*

In rough terms, the survivor has 75% ownership, and a lifetime use of the property. This works in so far as such a disposition is not in conflict with the laws on reserved heirs.

Changing your Marriage Regime

One potentially effective way of protecting your partner is to change the regime you are married under to the *régime de communauté universelle*. In this situation the surviving partner acquires the partner's estate without any succession tax being paid; only 1% registration duty is payable. No declaration has to be made for succession purposes. Your children and other heirs then have to wait for the second partner's decease before they can inherit their rightful share. This solution cannot be used to disinherit children from the deceased's previous marriages. It is unsuitable for younger married partners, who may remarry in the future.

There are several disadvantages with this regime. Firstly, the children of the marriage will pay a higher rate of succession tax than they would have if they had received their inheritance directly. Secondly, each partner is liable for the debts of the other. Thirdly, the surviving partner can do what they want with the assets, and may use them to benefit his or her new partner.

Note that there is a similar-sounding regime – *communauté légale réduite aux acquêts* – where only the assets acquired during the course of the marriage are common property. In this case the surviving partner pays succession tax on half of the deceased's part of the common property.

Using Gifts to Favour your Heirs

Depending on your age, you can lighten the tax burden by giving away assets in good time. Gift tax – *droits de donation* – is payable at the same rates as inheritance tax. It has to be paid immediately, but the donor can pay the tax on behalf of the donee. Lifetime gifts enjoy two rates of reduction:

- ○ 50% if the donor is under 65.
- ○ 30% if the donor is between 65 and 75.
- ○ From 75 and above there is no reduction in tax.

Tax is also reduced if the donor dies more than 10 years after the gift is made. If you make a gift in the UK, it is tax-exempt if the donor dies more than 7 years after making the gift.

Grandparents can give grandchildren €30,000 tax-free every 10 years (as of 2003). Gifts that are not revealed to the tax office will not be subject to gift tax, but if their existence becomes known after the donor's decease then they will be treated as part of the inheritance and will be subject to full succession tax. The gift can be witnessed by the notaire, who will make up an *acte authentique,* a document which has legal force and which is recognised by third parties. The notaire can put certain advantageous clauses into the gift act, and there is then no risk of being penalised later when succession tax has to be paid.

If you wish to help your children during your lifetime, e.g. to go through university, you can give away the *usufruit* on a property you own for a set number of years. Your child collects the rent or profits from a property, and your tax bill is also reduced.

Donation Entre Époux/Donation au Dernier Vivant. These are two names for one type of gift. The gift can be written into the marriage contract in which case it is irrevocable; otherwise it can be revoked without informing the partner. The *donation au dernier vivant* means 'gift to the survivor'. The survivor only receives the assets on the death of their partner. Succession tax is payable above the basic allowance of €76,000.

The *donation entre époux* is of benefit to the spouse when the deceased leaves family members who are reserved heirs. Without the *donation entre époux* the surviving partner will receive less than they would have if their partner had made the *donation.* On the death of the partner the survivor can opt to continue to have the *usufruit* or benefits of the spouse's entire assets for the rest of their lives, while the children have the *nue propriété,* i.e. they own the assets without having the use or profit of them. The surviving partner can manage the deceased's portfolio of investments, but they can be challenged by the deceased's blood relatives if they appear to be mismanaging the assets.

The survivor can also opt to receive the part of the inheritance that they are allowed as *pleine propriété* (see *Reserved Heirs* above), without the *usufruit*, or to have 25% *pleine propriété* and 75% *usufruit*. This regime is particularly useful where there are children from previous marriages.

The *donation entre époux* is not an effective method of avoiding succession taxes; it is simpler and cheaper to put the provisions you want in your will. It is advisable to take legal advice before making a gift to ensure that this is best for you. This type of gift must be registered with a notaire. It is doubtful whether non-residents can enter into a *donation entre époux*.

Donation-Partage. One or both parents can make a gift to their children during their lifetime, and thus reduce the amount of taxes payable on transferring assets to their children or grandchildren. This is a method of dividing up and giving away your assets early. If the parents make the gift jointly – the *donation-partage conjonctive* – it is assumed for fiscal purposes that half the gift came from the father and the other half from the mother. Gift tax is payable on the *donation partage.* There is a reduction of 50% if the donor was aged under 65 at the time they made the gift, and 30% if they were between 65 and 75. If both parents make a gift jointly to their children, the children are allowed up to €46,000 per parent – i.e. €92,000 in total – free of tax.

It is possible for the donor to give away just the *nue propriété* of the property and retain the *usufruit,* and this can generate substantial tax savings.

The gift made under *donation partage* does not form part of the inheritance; ordinary gifts – *donations simples* – are reintegrated into the inheritance and evaluated for succession tax. The parents do not have to divide up their gifts equally between the children; normally the children agree that the gifts should be apportioned in a certain way. Children are not legally obliged to accept a gift, and this has no effect on their legal rights. They can challenge the distribution of the gifts after the parent's decease, if they believe that the gift has reduced their inheritance, e.g. they were not born when the gift was made.

Fraudulent Gifts. Certain types of gifts and loans are considered fraudulent by the tax authorities and are heavily penalised. These include:

- Interest-free loans to relatives.
- Fictitious loans.
- Selling a property below its market value to relatives.
- Selling a property to a relative without actually collecting any money.

◯ Giving away the *nue propriété* of the property, and then allowing relatives the *usufruit* as well.

These are treated as undeclared gifts and taxed accordingly, with penalties added on.

Disinheriting a Partner. Since 2002, it has become much more difficult to disinherit a partner entirely. As a minimum, the surviving partner should receive either 25% of the full property or the *usufruit* of the property for their lifetime. The surviving partner has an absolute right to remain in the marital home for one year from the decease, even when the home is rented. Although various provisions can be put into a *testament authentique* to try to prevent the surviving partner from continuing to occupy the conjugal home, these are not likely to stand up in a French court. A great deal depends on how many reserved heirs there are.

Disinheriting Other Family. If you want to favour your partner and provide them with an income for life, the simplest thing to do is to sell your property for a *rente viagère,* a pension annuity. The buyer pays an initial 20-30% of the price, and then an agreed annual sum to you and your partner, until your death. The contract includes a clause that your partner then receives the annuity until they die. The property then passes to the buyer. Your family cannot make any objections. The main inconvenience is that there are fewer and fewer buyers willing to enter this kind of arrangement, given the increasing life expectancy of sellers.

Taking Advice before Buying a Property

If you require advice about whose names to put on the property deeds, or concerning inheritance tax, it is best to go to a bilingual lawyer or tax advisor with experience of French law, rather than asking a French notaire. A notaire will know little about UK law, and may give quite unsuitable advice.

Types of Will

There are three types of will:

◯ Holographic (*testament olographe*): entirely in the person's handwriting, it is best done in French, and is generally not witnessed. If you choose, you can register it with the central register of testaments, the Fichier de Dernières Volontés. Most wills in France are in this form.

◯ Authentic (*testament authentique*): can be printed or written and has to be witnessed by two notaries or one notary and two other persons. Automatically registered with the Fichier de Dernières Volontés.

○ Secret (*testament mystique*): a will made up or dictated by a person who then hands it over in a sealed and signed envelope to a notary in the presence of two witnesses. The notary writes on it 'sealed document' or other comments. The testator either leaves it with the notary or keeps it themselves.

The holographic testament is generally the best, with the proviso that someone needs to know where it is kept. The secret testament has virtually fallen out of use.

Inheritance Procedures

Once someone has passed away, the family and/or partner need to visit the notary who dealt with the deceased's will as soon as is practically possible after registering the death at the town hall. The surviving partner, potential inheritors, the executor or creditors can request a *greffier en chef* (chief clerk) from the local civil court to put seals on the deceased's property (*pose de scellés*) if they believe there is a risk of theft or fraud. The *greffier* can make up a list of the goods and conduct a search for a will.

Legally, the reserved heirs, and anyone with a power of attorney, have the right and duty – known as *saisine* – to use the deceased's assets from the moment of death, to pay debts or bills as they arise. The deceased's bank account is automatically blocked, but money can still be taken out for bills, the funeral, and standing orders.

The names of the heirs are listed on the *acte de notoriété*, a legal document made up by the notaire or by a chief clerk of the court. This does not mean that heirs can immediately take their part of the inheritance, or that they are bound to accept an inheritance encumbered with debts. An heir can register the deceased's car in their name, with the right documents, and the agreement of the other heirs, before the estate is finally divided up.

A number of documents are required to start the inheritance process:

○ The death certificate.
○ A copy of the French will.
○ A copy of the British will, translated into French.
○ The names of all the potential inheritors.
○ Marriage/divorce certificates.
○ Death certificates of deceased former inheritors still mentioned in the will, if any.

In the course of time, you will need to produce documents relating to all of the deceased's bank accounts, investments and properties. The inheritors, and anyone who has received gifts from the deceased subject to gift tax, are required to file a *déclaration de succession* within a year. Interest is payable on the succession tax after six months if the deceased died in France, or 12 months if abroad. The *déclaration* is a form obtained from the French tax office, to be filled in in duplicate if the assets are over €15,000. Foreigners will find it convenient to mandate a notary to make the *déclaration*. The succession tax has to be worked out by the person filling in the *déclaration*. The tax authorities can challenge the value you place on a property, by comparing it with similar properties in the area. A small undervaluation is acceptable, but you can't go too far.

The tax does not come out of the inheritance; the inheritors are required to pay it together before they can receive the inheritance. It is possible to ask for a delay in payment of up to 10 years; you can also ask to pay in instalments.

It is possible to use an executor (*exécuteur testamentaire*) named in your will in France, but this is probably best avoided, unless you have reason to believe that your next of kin are untrustworthy or incompetent. Unless the executor is a notary, the French authorities may assume that the executor is actually an heir and charge them the maximum rate of tax: 60%. The executor is charged with filing the *déclaration de succession* correctly. They are entitled to payment for the work they do, which can come to a substantial sum, another reason to avoid using them.

Further Reading. For a detailed study of French succession law, see Henry Dyson's forthcoming *French Property and Inheritance Law,* to be published by OUP in 2003. This is a technical work written for lawyers. The author is an international legal consultant who can advise on property purchase and company formation; ☎00 33 04 93 62 70 70; fax 00 39 0184 67 24 79. For a general summary of inheritance in the UK and France, see Bill Blevins and David Franks' *Living in France.*

INSURANCE (ASSURANCES)

The French insurance market is very competitive and high profile. AXA and the state-owned GAN are household names in Britain. You can also add your French property to your UK insurance, as long as it fulfils French legal requirements. The received wisdom is that it is better to insure with a local company in France who are able to handle claims in English, so that you get a quick response in case of problems. Having your claim translated into French is expensive and time-consuming. There are English-speaking agents in many parts of France who can arrange insurance for you. There are agents who only sell policies for one company (*agents généraux*), and those who deal with several (*courtier d'assurances*).

House and Contents Insurance

The basic house and contents insurance is the *assurance multirisques habitation,* also often called *assurance multirisques vie privée* or *la multirisque.* This will include cover against natural disasters as a matter of course. Civil liability insurance – *responsabilité civile propriétaire* – is essential, in case an event on your property affects your neighbours. Your possessions also need to be insured. This kind of policy does not insure you against personal accidents, unless you ask for it. There are numerous formulas for the *assurance multirisques,* depending on your requirements.

If you are planning to build on a piece of land, an *assurance dommages-ouvrage* is legally compulsory, although you can get around this if the building is to be your family's principal residence.

It is possible to take over the existing insurance from the previous owner of the property you are buying; if you say nothing then it is assumed. If you do not wish to continue the same insurance policy – generally the wisest course of action for foreign buyers – you are required to present another policy to the notaire before you can sign the final *acte de vente.*

It is normal to insure the contents of your property as well. The current market value or *valeur vénale* of the items is used to work out the amount of cover; depreciation is taken into account. The insurers can insist on shutters being fitted to windows and bars on doors, and other security measures. You need to keep receipts, guarantees, photographs etc. of your possessions in a safe place for any claims. Read the small print in the policy, and watch out that you are not underinsured.

If there is nothing of value in your property you can take out a basic insurance against damage from natural causes, vandalism, terrorist acts, etc., known as an *assurance multirisques d'immeuble.* This is used by *copropriétés* and some owners of blocks of flats. This will be calculated by the square metre. There should be a clause in which the insurer agrees to rebuild or restore the property to its original state within two years in the same style.

Insurance and Tenants/copropriétés

If you rent a property for a long period the owner will ask you to take out an *assurance multirisques habitation* to cover the building and any risks that could affect neighbours, e.g. floods, fire, explosions. According to the laws governing tenancy, the Loi Quillot and Loi Méhaignerie, the proprietor can insert a clause in the tenancy agreement allowing him or her to cancel your tenancy immediately if you don't have adequate insurance. You should ask the owner whether you need insurance well before you sign a tenancy agreement. You are free to choose any insurance company you want.

In the case of a *copropriété* the building insurance will be taken care of by the manager of the property, and your share of the premiums will appear on the monthly charges. You are responsible for insuring your own possessions, and third party insurance for anyone visiting your premises.

Holiday Homes

Burglaries of holiday homes are common, especially on the Riviera, or any isolated area. An insurance policy for a principal residence is not suitable for a holiday home; there are usually clauses making the policy void if the house is left empty for more than 30 days. In order to get insurance cover, you will be expected to put in additional locks, shutters, burglar alarms and grills. Some owners go so far as to install webcams so they can watch their property being broken into. The longer you are away from the property, the higher your premiums will be, and the less likely the insurers are to cover valuables. Your premiums will be reduced if you install burglar alarms, electronic surveillance systems, and so on. Premiums vary widely around the country; they are highest in the southeast where there are more fires than in the rest of France. To give a rough idea: a €150,000 property in the Landes could cost €600 per year to insure, while in Aix-en-Provence it would be €1,200.

There is a particular risk of blocked or frozen pipes causing flooding, and every possible measure has to be taken to prevent this. You need to take sensible precautions: there has recently been a high-profile case of a woman who kept containers of kerosene in her flat, and received nothing when the place burned down. Insurers will take into account the condition of the property when they pay for repairs. If the original plaster or roofing was not that good then they will pay proportionately less to have it replaced.

Terms and Conditions

Thefts. It is a condition of insurance policies that you report thefts within 24 hours to the police, or as soon as possible, if you want your claim to be taken seriously. The police will give you a form – *déclaration de vol* – with the details of what you have lost. You need to inform the insurers within two working days of the theft and send the receipt of the *déclaration* by registered post (*recommandée*), with an *avis de réception* (AR) or receipt. It is advisable to telephone the insurer immediately and they will send you a confirmation. You then draw up a list of the stolen goods and send it by registered post.

Natural Disasters. There is a whole raft of regulations about which natural events count as disasters or *catastrophes naturelles*. The amount of time you have to report a disaster ranges from four days for hail to 10 days after a storm, if this has been declared a *catastrophe naturelle* in the official journal. Your house insurance should cover not only *catastrophes naturelles* but all kinds of other natural risks. You do not have to pay for cover against snow, unless you think it is necessary. Check that the policy covers damage to electrical items as well.

Checking the Small Print. Look carefully at the small print in the policy to see what conditions are set for reporting damage, thefts, etc., and any exclusions. Check for the *franchise* or excess, i.e. the first part of the claim that is not paid. Taking videos and photos of property is an eminently sensible precaution to make sure you are paid in full. You can use a court bailiff – *huissier* – or an insurance expert, to prepare a report on damage to your property (for a fee). The insurance company will normally send their own expert to draw up a report on your loss.

Policies are renewed automatically (*tacite reconduction*); you are given a period of time before the renewal date when you can cancel the policy. Once the date has passed it is too late to cancel. Premiums should be paid by standing order, within 10 days of the set date. You will receive a warning (*mise en demeure*) from the insurer. If you haven't paid within 30 days your policy will be cancelled, but you will still be liable for the outstanding amount and the insurer's costs.

Insurers may not take you on if your insurance has been cancelled for non-payment. Recent claims for damage through floods, avalanches and other major disasters make it difficult to get insurance.

INSURANCE GLOSSARY

assurance multirisques habitation	house and contents insurance
bris de glaces	window breakage
cambriolage	burglary/housebreaking
certificat de perte	police statement listing your losses
effraction	breaking and entering
franchise	excess (GB); deductible (US)
grêle	hail
incendie	fire
police	policy
protection juridique	legal protection
résiliation	cancellation
responsabilité civile	civil liability
risques locatifs	tenant's liability
store	heavy shutters
vol	theft
volet	shutters

Insurance of Schoolchildren

The state school system obliges parents to insure their children when they undertake voluntary activities. Private schools set their own rules. If one of your children goes to a state school and another to a private school you may be able to put them both on one policy. The *assurance scolarité* should cover not only harm that a child could occasion to third parties, but also any harm that could come to him or her (*garantie individuelle accidents*) which is not included in your usual house insurance. Without this insurance, your child will not be allowed to go on excursions. You can go further and insure your child's belongings, or against all sorts of disease; the sky is the limit.

Where to Find Insurance

Insurance companies are listed in the French yellow pages under *assurances;* some agents advertise in the French property magazines, such as *French Property News.*

Below are some insurance companies specialising in foreign homes, as well as other types of insurance:

Agence Eaton: Continent Assurances, 28 rue du Lt Col. Maury, B.P. 285, 56008 Vannes, France; ☎ 02 97 47 31 97; fax 02 97 47 98 94; www.french-insurance.com. Bilingual insurance bureau.

AXA Courtage: 26 rue Louis Le Grand, 75002 Paris; ☎ 01 49 49 40 00; fax 01 49 49 47 00; www.axa.fr. Large French insurer with branches in UK.

Azur Assurances: ☎ 02 37 33 83 83; www.azur-assurances.fr. House, car and health insurance.

Barlow Redford & Co: 71a High St, Harpenden, Herts AL5 2SL; ☎ 01582-761129; fax 01582-462380.

Cabinet F.X. Bordes: 11 rue Desportes BP 05, 24150 Lalinde; ☎ 05 53 61 03 50; fax 05 53 58 40 30. General agents for French insurance company; based in Périgord. Household insurance.

Copeland Insurance: The Andrew Copeland Group, 230 Portland Rd, London SE25 4SL; ☎ 020-8656 2544; fax 020-8655 1271; e-mail info@acopeland.com. Buildings and contents insurance for France and special scheme for UK-registered cars in France.

Europ Assistance: 32-38 Leman St, London E1 8EW; ☎ 020-7204 1444; fax 020-7204 1484.

Holiday Homes Insurance Services: PO Box 32, Romford, Essex RM1 2LU; ☎ 01708-730236; fax 01708-760717.

O'Halloran & Co: St James Terrace, 84 Newland, Lincoln LN1 1YA; ☎ 01522-537491; e-mail tpo@ohal.org; www.ohalloran.org.uk. Will arrange cover for holiday homes in Europe. Contact Linda O'Halloran.

Towergate Holiday Homes Underwriting Agency Ltd: Towergate House, St Edward's Court, London Road, Romford, Essex RM7 9QD; ☎ 0870-242 2470; fax 01708-777721; www.towergate.co.uk.

Tredinnick Insurance: 12 rue Dupuy, 16100 Cognac; ☎ & fax 05 45 82 42 93; e-mail insure@tredinnick-insurance.com; www.tredinnick-insurance.com. All types of insurance; based in Charente.

Woodham Group Ltd: Plas Kenrhos, Graig, Burry Point, Carmarthenshire SA16 0DG; ☎ 01554-835252; fax 01554-835253; e-mail bryandigby@woodhamgroup.com; www.woodhamgroup.com.

WEALTH TAX (ISF)

ISF or *Impôt de Solidarité sur la Fortune* only affects those with net assets over €720,000 if they are resident or have assets in France on 1st January of any tax year. The tax is levied on the *foyer fiscal* (fiscal household) defined as:

- Single persons, divorced, widowed, unmarried or separated from their partners.
- Married persons, including dependent children under 18.
- Persons who are known to be living together (*concubinage notoire*),

○ Those who have entered a PACS (partnership contract) and children.

The household's net assets as of 1st January are calculated by the householder him or herself; they include the assets of everyone in the household, including children under 18. The declaration, accompanied by payment in full, is due by 16 July for EU citizens, and 15 June for French citizens. Other foreigners (e.g. US citizens) have until 1st September to pay. Variations in the value of your assets during the year cannot be taken account when calculating your liability.

All your assets, including cars, yachts, furniture, etc. must be taken into account. You will need to produce receipts and insurance policies in order to justify your valuations. You are expected to calculate the 'fair market value' (*valeur vénale réelle*) of your property on the basis of prices in your area. The tax authorities have their own ways of assessing your net worth.

There are a number of items exempt from wealth tax, of which a few are given here in a simplified form:

○ Antiques over 100 years old.
○ Copyrights on works of art, literature, music.
○ Personal injury compensation.
○ Goods that you require to carry on your profession.
○ Shares in companies of which you are a director, with more than 25% voting rights.

It may be possible to have assets that you need to run *gîtes* or *chambres d'hôte* exempted from wealth tax. You are allowed a 20% reduction on the household's principal residence (not more than one house). You are not exempt from paying wealth tax on shares in French companies, or foreign companies owning property in France.

Since the basis on which ISF is calculated is your net worth, any debts can be deducted from the total. This includes any property loans. Any money you owe to builders or other tradesmen can be deducted, as can the taxes you owe for the previous year (including the ISF itself). Money that is owed to you is added to the total.

WEALTH TAX TARIFFS (AS OF 2003)	
Net Taxable Assets	Tariff
below €720,000	0%

€720,000–1,160,000	0.55%
€1,160,000–2,300,000	0.75%
€2,300,000–3,600,000	1.00%
€3,600,000–6,900,000	1.30%
€6,900,000–15,000,000	1.65%
€15,000,000 and above	1.80%

There is a further limitation on wealth tax, inasmuch as your total tax liability (including income tax) cannot exceed 85% of your net taxable income.

Payment and Penalties. Your wealth tax return and payment have to be made to the local Recette des Impôts by 16th July. If you are not resident in France payment is made to the: Recette des Impôts des Non-Résidents, 9 rue d'Uzès, 75094 Paris Cedex 02. If you reside in Monaco it is made to the Recette des Impôts in Menton.

In the unlikely event that you cannot pay the tax, you may give works of art instead. The penalties for submitting a false return, or late payment, are very high. Any assets that are not declared will be taxed under the inheritance laws as though they were gifts, and interest and other penalties will be levied. Since the wealth tax is not that onerous, it would be stupid not to pay it. From the point of view of the French state, it is useful as a way of keeping tabs on taxpayers' assets as much as a source of revenue.

Tax and Investment Advice
The law firms listed in chapter 8 under 'Lawyers' will give advice on how to plan ahead to benefit your heirs, or you can try the firms listed below.

There are several UK firms that specialise in giving advice to UK citizens who are buying or already own property in France. Some hold seminars in different locations in France. These are publicised in French property magazines and the monthly *The News* published from Périgueux.

Useful Addresses
Blevins Franks: Barbican House, 26-34 Old St, London EC1V 9QQ; ☎ 020-7336 1022; fax 020-7336 1001; www.blevinsfranks.com. Specialists in the expatriate financial sector. Offices and seminars in France.

Brewin Dolphin Bell Lawrie Ltd, Stockbrokers: Cross Keys House, The Parade, Marlborough, Wilts SN8 1NE; ☎ 01672-519600; fax 01672-515550. Services included international portfolio management with off-shore facility for those domiciled or resident outside the UK.

Hansard Europe Ltd: Enterprise House, Frascati Road, Blackrock, Co.

Dublin, Republic of Ireland; ☎ 01 278 1488; fax 01 278 1499; www.hansard.com. Expatriate financial services.

John Siddall Financial Services: Lothian House, 22 High St, Fareham, Hants PO16 7AE; ☎ 01329-288641; fax 01329-281157; e-mail invest ments@johnsiddalls.co.uk. Can help you build a pension fund geared to your needs and provides full investment, tax and inheritance planning.

PKF (Guernsey) Ltd: PO Box 296, St Peter Port, Guernsey GY1 4NA; ☎ 01481-727927; fax 01481-710511; e-mail french.tax@pkfguernsey.co m; www.pkfguernsey.com. Taxation advice and financial planning.

Siddalls International: Parc Innolin, 3 rue de Golf, 33700 Bordeaux-Mérignac; ☎ 05 56 34 75 51; fax 05 56 34 75 52; e-mail bordeaux.offi ce@siddalls.com.fr; www.johnsiddalls.co.uk.

Wiggin & Co Solicitors: 95 The Promenade, Cheltenham, Gloucestershire GL50 1WG; ☎ 01242-224114; fax 01242-224 223; e-mail law@wiggin.co.uk; www.wiggin.co.uk. Offices in London and Los Angeles.

M.S.

FINDING PROPERTIES FOR SALE

CHAPTER SUMMARY

○ **Agents and Estate Agents.** It is important to understand what kind of agent you are dealing with.
○ **Prices.** French Estate Agents should quote prices including their commission.
○ **Viewing.** Give yourself sufficient time to see a property, and take a checklist with you.
○ **Notaires.** Notaries' websites and leaflets are a good source of cheap properties.
○ **Adverts.** There are numerous websites advertising properties.

ESTATE AGENTS

The number of estate agents or *agents immobilier* in operation has grown rapidly in recent years. Most UK-based agents do not deal directly with properties themselves, but rather put you in touch with *immobiliers* in the area you are interested in, and generally organise your house-hunt for you. The advantage is that you do not have to deal directly with French *immobiliers*, and so your language abilities are not going to be so severely tested. Some – but not that many – French estate agents speak good English, and there are more and more British estate agents setting up in France, so whether you feel you need another intermediary is up to you. The need for agents arises because many British and foreign buyers do not have the time to search for properties during their holidays. Ideally, one would spend several months living in an area and looking for property, but this is not always possible.

The English-speaking agent receives a commission from the *immobilier* which can be as much as 50% of the total commission where there is a long-established partnership. Where agents are less well-established, their commission from the *immobilier* will be less and they will charge the customer 1% or 1.5% as an additional commission. It is important to be clear at the start how much commission you are paying any intermediaries. There will be a signing-on fee which is refunded in the event that you buy the property.

There are also a few conmen who pose as agents and try to trick customers into paying deposits in advance of seeing property. You should walk away from any so-called agent who makes unusual demands before you have actually seen any property.

Apart from agents, there are property consultants who do research for potential buyers, and offer every kind of hand-holding service, which can include arranging flights and stays in France and advice on dealing with the buying process. A consultant will be paid by the customer directly for their services.

French *immobiliers'* commissions vary from region to region, and are on a graduated scale depending on the value of the property. The minimum is around €2000. With very cheap properties the commission can be up to 20%; above about €250,000 the commission will not exceed 3%. A very cheap property naturally attracts a very high percentage in commission. Up-market properties in Paris or in tourist areas also attract high commissions; the normal range is 5% to 10%.

It is vitally important to find out at the start who is going to pay the *immobilier's* commission. It is usual for the buyer to pay. The asking price that is advertised must, by law, include the agent's commission if the buyer is to pay it. Some agents may try to quote you prices *net vendeur,* i.e. the price the seller will receive, so you need to be on your guard. Another dubious practice is quoting prices with all costs included, which allows the agency to slip in a few more thousand pounds unnoticed. You should always have a precise breakdown of all the components of the price.

Unlike in Britain, a French-based estate agent must have professional qualifications and have a licence from the *chambre de commerce.* According to the Loi Huguet of 1970, estate agents must have:

- O a diploma in law, e.g. DEUG
- O or a baccalaureate or other degree, and one year's work experience in an estate agency
- O or ten years experience in an estate agency.

Anyone who acts as an *immobilier* without a *carte professionnelle* is liable to a heavy fine and a jail sentence, and this has happened to some foreigners who, perhaps in ignorance of the law, have worked with *notaires* selling properties in France. They may have done a good job for their customers, but they still broke the law. The *carte professionnelle* has to be renewed every year. For an inside view of the estate agency business it is worth reading Alan

Biggins' *Selling French Dreams* and *A Normandy Tapestry* (www.normandy-tapestry.com). Biggins worked in a grey area of the law for a while before he had to concede that the regulations made it too difficult for him to be an estate agent in France.

Estate agents are required to display the following notices in their office:

- number of their *carte professionnelle*
- amount of their financial guarantee
- name and address of their guarantee fund
- name of their bank and the number of the account into which funds have to be paid
- amount and percentages of commission

Estate agents can choose to have a minimum guarantee fund or bond of €125,000 if they are members the national organisations of estate agents FNAIM or SNPI, as well as professional indemnity insurance. Members of FNAIM have indemnity insurance up to €2,500,000. The guarantee fund (*garantie financière*) ensures that you don't lose your deposit if the seller does a runner. If the agent does not have a guarantee fund, then you will not be able to pay your deposit to them, but only to a *notaire*, who will always have a guarantee fund.

Estate agents have negotiators working in their offices, but each main office must have a holder of a *carte professionnelle*. Some branch offices have an *agent de commerce* or a *fondé de pouvoir*, someone who is mandated by an *immobilier* to negotiate contracts on their behalf.

The *immobilier* has a time-limited *mandat* or mandate from the seller to negotiate on their behalf. It is common practice for a seller to give several agents a so-called *mandat simple* to sell property on their behalf. Where the agent has the exclusive right to sell the property you will see *en exclusivité* on the advertisement; the agent has a *mandat exclusif* which may give him or her the right to carry out the sale themselves, or to allow the seller to deal directly with the client. As a general rule of thumb, if a property is advertised with several agents for a long time, you can assume that it is difficult to sell, and you can offer a lot less than the asking price. You may see the same property photographed from different angles.

Only half of properties in France are sold through *immobiliers*. The rest are sold privately, through notaries or at auctions (see below). Going round villages asking if there are any properties coming on the market, or if anyone has died recently, can pay dividends. Even paying a local to act as a spy for you could save you a great deal of money.

Property Viewing

You may begin the process by looking on the internet at some adverts, or in some French property magazines, and contacting an *immobilier* who will, if you are lucky, send you some details of the properties they have available. French *immobiliers* do not go for the same hard-sell techniques as their UK counterparts, and their publicity materials are not of the same quality as in the UK. The role of the *immobilier* is to show people round the property. They stand to make a considerable sum of money if the property is sold through them. They will, not, however, put *A Vendre* (For Sale) on the property, for fear that potential buyers will trace the owner and deal directly with them. The For Sale sign will only be put up by private sellers, or if the owner is not easily traceable. You will not be given the keys to the property and sent to go and look for it, partly because you will probably not be able to find it, and secondly, because you may find the owner and negotiate a private deal. For this reason you are accompanied on your house-viewing visits by an agent or the *immobilier* him- or herself. They do not give out precise addresses of properties, but rather put 15 km from such-and-such a village. Since several properties in a village can have the same name, you will have a hard time finding the one you are looking for.

If you are taken around by an agent, you may be asked to sign a *bon de visite* at the start to prove that the agent has taken you to see the property, and that he or she is entitled to the commission if it is sold.

The main thing to watch out for is that you are actually shown the properties you are interested in. It happens all too often that Brits go out to France to look at a cottage and then find that they are being shown châteaux and barns, and everything but what they wanted, because that is all the agent has on their books. The other pitfall is to make sure that the property you specifically want to see has not already been sold to someone else. An attractive-looking property on the internet may not be available any more by the time you get to France. Agencies in the UK may be slow to find out whether a property has been sold.

Customers should also observe certain formalities in relation to agents. The British have gained a bad reputation for not turning up for meetings, or not leaving enough time to go and see a property. It is not possible to pack in several viewings a day when properties are so remote that it could take half a day to see just one. For this reason French estate agents may be reluctant to arrange meetings unless they have already seen you in person. They generally make a point of trying to find out if you are serious or not; they may well ask you straight off. It is sensible to let agents know if you are not going to be able to make it to a viewing. Having a mobile telephone so you can keep in touch will save a lot of trouble.

Marchands de Biens. As well as the *agents immobilier* there are also the *marchands de biens* (dealers in property), the main difference being that a *marchand de biens* buys and sells properties in their own name to make a profit, while an *immobilier* is legally not allowed to buy or sell in their own name. Anyone who makes a living from regularly buying and selling property or land has to register with the chamber of commerce; they are taxed according to a special regime, not on the basis of capital gains; and they pay VAT on the profit they make on selling a property. They are only subject to very low registration charges on the purchase of property as long as they resell the property within four years. It is common practice for a *marchand de biens* to make a downpayment on a property while looking around for a potential buyer, but they do have to own the property for three months before they resell it. They take the risk of having to pay hefty tax penalties if they don't find someone to buy the property within four years, or if, in the case of land, they do not start constructing a property.

List of Agents

The following agents are listed with the areas that they cover. Unless otherwise stated, they will mainly deal with properties in the western half of France, where most Brits are located, outside of the big towns. You should check to see if they belong to a professional organisation such as the NAEA or FOPDAC.

UK-based Estate Agents

Alpine Apartments Agency: Hinton Manor, Eardisland, Leominster, Herefordshire HR6 9BG; ☎ 01544-388234; fax 01544-388900; e-mail zigi@aaa.kc3ltd.co.uk.

A Home in France: The Old Anchor, Moat Lane, Wingrave, Bucks HP22 4PQ; ☎ 01296-688727; fax 01296-681433; e-mail info@ahomeinfrance.com. Contact Danielle Seabrook. All areas.

Beaches International Property Ltd: 3-4 Hagley Mews, Hagley Hall, Hagley,

Stourbridge, W. Midlands DY9 9LQ; ☎ 01562-885181; 01562-886724; e-mail info@beachesint.co.uk; www.beachesint.com. Haute Savoie.

Brittany Property Shop: 95 Farm Rd, Abingdon, Oxfordshire OX14 1NB; ☎ 00 33 2 96 86 61 06; fax 00 33 2 96 86 61 07.

Capital Mover Ltd: 20 Second Avenue, London W3 7RX; ☎ 07971-902 853; fax 020-8749 1077; www.capitalmover.com. NEW-BUILD.

Currie French Properties: 2 Fulbrooke Rd, Cambridge CB3 9EE; ☎ 01223 576084; fax 01223 570332; email cfps@ntlworld.com; www.french-property.com/currie.

David King Associates: ☎ 020-8673 6800; www.dkassociates.co.uk. Paris, West, South; over £150,000.

Domus Abroad: Maurice Lazarus, 4 Gardner Rd, Hampstead, London NW3 1HA; ☎ 020-7431 4692; fax 020-7794 4822; www.Domusabroad.com. Services for both buyers and sellers.

Dordogne & Lot Properties: 348A Woodstock Rd, Oxford OX2 8BZ; ☎ 01865-558659 *or* 513143.

Eclipse Overseas: 29 Stuart Rd, Highcliffe-on-Sea, Christchurch, Dorset BH23 5JS; ☎ 01425-275984; fax 01425-277137; www.french-property.com/eclipse. Normandy, Charente, Loire, Vendée, Brittany.

European Property Search: 9-11 St Cross Rd, Winchester, Hants SO23 9JB; ☎ 01962-853568; fax 01962-870008.

European Villas Sales: 618 Newmarket Rd, Cambridge CB5 8LP; ☎ 01223-514241; fax 01223-562713. Contact Adrian Medd.

Fourways French Properties: The Green, Morcombelake, nr Bridport, Dorset DT6 6EA; tel/fax 01297-489366.

The French Property Shop: The Clergyhouse, Churchyard, Ashford, Kent TN23 1QG; ☎ 01233-666902; fax 01233-666903; e-mail sales@frenchpropertyshop.com; www.frenchpropertyshop.com. Southwest.

Francophiles Ltd: Barker Chambers, Barker Rd, Maidstone, Kent ME16 8SF; ☎ 01622-688165; fax 01622-671840; e-mail Fphiles@aol.com; www.francophiles.co.uk. Property searches in Normandy, Brittany, Pas de Calais, Southwest.

Gascony Property: 12 Royal Terrace, Southend-on-Sea, Essex SS1 1DY; ☎ 01702-390382; fax 01702-390415; www.gascony-property.com.

Hamptons International: 168 Brompton Rd, Knightsbridge, London SW3 1HW; ☎ 020-7589 8844; e-mail international@hamptons-int.com; www.hamptons-int.com. Côte d'Azur. Branch in Nice.

Hexagone France Ltd: Webster House, 24 Jesmond Street, Folkestone, Kent CT19 5QW; ☎ 01303-221077; fax 01303-244409; e-mail gwen@hexagonefrance.com; www.hexagonefrance.com. Normandy, Picardy, Brittany.

A House in France Ltd: John Hart, 11 Mountview, Mill Hill, London
NW7 3HT; ☎ 020-8959 5182; fax 020-8906 8749; e-mail
john.hart@virgin.net; www.ahouseinfrance.co.uk. Residential and
commercial property.

Jacwood Estates French Properties: 2 Warwick New Road, Leamington Spa,
Warwickshire CV32 5JP; ☎ 01926-883714; fax 01926-883714; e-mail
jacwood@compuserve.com. Gite complexes and holiday rental properties, mainly in the south-west.

La Résidence: St Martin's House, 17 St Martin's St, Wallingford,
Oxon OX10 0EA; ☎ 01491-838485; fax 01491-839977; e-mail
sales@laresidence.co.uk; www.laresidence.co.uk.

Latitudes: Penny Zoldan, Grosvenor House, 1 High St, Edgware, Middx HA8 7TA; ☎ 020-8951 5155; fax 020-8951 5156;
www.latitudes.co.uk.

Leisure & Land: Grosvenor House, 1 High St, Edgware, Middx HA8
7TA; ☎ 020-8951 5152; fax 020-8951 5156; e-mail sales@leisureandl
and.co.uk; www.leisureandland.co.uk. Specialises in income-producing
properties.

Maison France: Lincolnshire; ☎ 01427-628537; fax 01427-628855; e-
mail info@maisonfrance.com; www.agence-maisonfrance.com.

North & West France Properties: Park Lodge, Park Rd, East Twickenham,
Middx TW1 2PT; ☎ 020-8891 1750; fax 020-8891 1760; e-mail
sales@all-france-properties.com; www.all-france-properties.com.

A Place in France Ltd: The Old Workshop, 34 Middle St, Southsea, Hants
PO5 4BP; ☎ 023-9283 2949; fax 023-9285 1988; e-mail pfevrier@pla
ceinfrance.co.uk. Newly-built properties.

Propriétés Roussillon: Roussillon House, 29 Aversley Rd, Kings Norton,
Birmingham B38 8PD; ☎ 021-459 9058; fax 021-608 8884; e-mail Pr
ops.Rouss@btinternet.com; www.proprietes-roussillon.com. All areas.

La Residence: St Martin's House: St Martin's House, 17 St Martin's Street,
Wallingford, Oxfordshire OX10 OEA; ☎ 01491-838485; fax 01491-

839977; e-mail sales @laresidence.co.uk; www.laresidence.co.uk.

Sifex Ltd: 1 Doneraile St, Fulham, London SW6 6EL; ☎ 020-7384 1200; fax 020-7384 2001; e-mail info@sifex.co.uk; www.sifex.co.uk. Exclusive properties in Southern France. Châteaux in all regions of France.

Sinclair Overseas Property Network: The Business Centre, P.O. Box 492, Leighton Buzzard, Beds LU7 7WG; ☎ 01525-375319; fax 01525-851418. Associate offices throughout France.

Spratley & Co Ltd, International Property Consultants: 60 St Martin's Lane, London WC2N 4JS; ☎ 020-7240 2445; fax 020-7240 2469.

VEF (Vivre en France) UK: 4 Raleigh House, Admirals Way, London E14 9SN; e-mail www.vefuk.com. New-build.

Villas Abroad Ltd: Lacey House, St Clare Business Park, Holly Rd, Hampton Hill, Middx TW12 1QQ; ☎ 020-8941 4499; fax 020-8941 0202; e-mail villas abroad@fopdac.com; www.villasabroadproperties.com. Côte d'Azur. Mostly new-build.

Waterside Properties: ☎ 01892-750011; fax 01892-750033. Properties with waterside locations.

G.A.K. Williamson & Assoc.: 28 Broad St, Alresford, Hampshire SO24 9AQ; ☎ 01862-734633; fax 01862-734929; e-mail gakwfrance@aol.com. Residential and agricultural.

World Class Homes Ltd: 22 High St, Wheathampstead, Herts AL4 8AA; ☎ 01582-832001; fax 01582-831071; e-mail info@worldclasshomes.co .uk; www.worldclasshomes.co.uk. Languedoc Roussillon. New-build.

France-based Estate Agents

ABC Immobilier: 41 ave Clémenceau, 34500 Béziers; 04 67 93 51 66; fax 04 67 49 26 92; e-mail abc-immobilier3@wanadoo.fr; www.abc-immo.fr. Béziers.

Agence Hamilton: 30 rue Armagnac, 11000 Carcassonne; ☎ 04 68 72 48 38; fax 04 68 72 62 26; e-mail info@agence-hamilton.com; www.agence-hamilton.com. Languedoc, Midi-Pyrénées.

Agence Hermann de Graaf: Le Bourg, 24800 St Jean de Côle; ☎ 05 53 62 38 03; fax 05 53 55 08 03; e-mail agence@immobilier-dordogne.com; www.immobilier-dordogne.com. Dordogne.

Agence L'Union: Charles Smallwood, Place de la Halle, 82140 St Antonin-Noble-Val; ☎ 05 63 30 60 24; fax 05 63 68 24 67; e-mail info@agencelunion.com; www.agencelunion.com. Tarn, Tarn-et-Garonne, Lot, Aveyron.

Agence Tredinnick: 12 rue Dupuy, 16100 Cognac; tel/fax 05 45 82 42 93; e-mail props@charente-properties.com; www.charente-properties.com. Charente.

Coast & Country: 'La Palombière', 71 ave de Tournamy, 06250 Mougins;

☎ 04 92 92 47 50; fax 04 93 90 02 36; e-mail info@coast-country.com; http://coast-country.com.

Conseil Patrimoine: 52 bvd Victor Hugo, 06600 Nice; ☎ 04 97 03 03 33; fax 04 97 03 03 34. Paris, Riviera.

Janssens Immobilier: 2 rue de la République, Bonnieux; ☎ 04 90 75 96 98; e-mail janssens.immobilier@wanadoo.fr. Luberon.

France Limousin Immobilier: 1 rue Fosse du Trech, 1900 Tulle; ☎ 05 55 20 01 97; fax 05 55 26 16 17. Limousin.

L'Affaire Française: 25 Grand Rue, Jarnac 16200; ☎ 05 45 81 76 79; fax 05 45 35 09 52; e-mail FrenchProperties@aol.com; www.French-Property-Net.com. Charente, Dordogne, Limousin.

Langlois Gordon Hay: 234 rue de Périgueux, 16000 Angoulême; ☎ 05 45 95 08 51; fax 05 45 69 77 12; e-mail agence.lgh@laposte.net; www.lghfrance.com. Charente.

Privilège Immobilier: Gestion Privée et Patrimoine, 13 rue du Maréchal Clauzel, 09500 Mirepoix; ☎ 05 61 69 79 56; fax 05 61 69 79 76; e-mail gp.p@net-up.com. Ariège.

Properties in France Sarl PIF: 6 allée de la Croix de Noël, 49390 Mouliherne; 02 41 52 02 18; fax 02 41 52 02 47; e-mail pif@compuserve.com. Loire Valley.

Snow and Sea: Kingsland House, 1st Floor, 122-124 Regent St, London W1B 5SA; ☎ 020 7494 0706; fax 020-7734 9462; e-mail pascal@snowandsea.com; www.snowandsea.com. PACA.

Property Consultants

While it is sometimes difficult to separate them from property agents, there are some consultants who offer wide-ranging services covering all aspects of property purchase:

A Home in France: The Old Anchor, Moat Lane, Wingrave, Bucks HP22 4PQ; ☎ 01296-688727; fax 01296-681433; e-mail info@ahomeinfrance.com. Contact Danielle Seabrook.

Anglo-French Homes: 9 rue 14 juin 1944, 61120 Vimoutiers; ☎ 02 33 39 80 55; http://anglo-french-homes.co.uk. Calvados, Orne.

Sam Crabb: ☎ 01935-851155; www.samcrabb.com. Independent consultant since 1993.

ADVERTS

The first place one might consider looking would be British newspapers: the *Daily Telegraph* has regular adverts for French property. *The Times* also carries some adverts; these are generally in a high price bracket; some are from private advertisers. There are generally fewer adverts for property in

French newspapers than in the UK; the national newspapers advertise very little. *Le Figaro* has a section for Paris. French magazines with an international readership, such as *L'Express* and *Nouvel Observateur* have adverts for expensive properties, mainly in the south of France, on their inside back pages in some issues.

The main French property magazines distributed in the UK carry some adverts for individual properties, and a lot of ads for agents: these are *France, Living France* and *French Property News.* The websites are a good source for advertisements. British agents' websites are a fertile source of properties; they will also send you lists. French *immobiliers* are not that keen to send lists of properties to anyone based outside France; they prefer to deal with people who are on the spot. If you are travelling around France, it is easy to pick up lists of property that are left outside the *immobiliers* all the year round.

There is a wealth of French websites with property adverts, and there are numerous French magazines with adverts sorted by department. The main national magazine for second homes is *Résidences Sécondaires* which also has interesting articles about the property market. The main publisher for holiday properties and rentals is Indicateur Bertrand, and they have specialised magazines for Paris, Rhône-Alpes and the South. For more downmarket properties, it is best to try to get hold of local estate agents' lists. The cheapest properties are often in the hands of notaires, who advertise on the internet. There are separate magazines for new property developments, mainly apartments, such as *Immobilier Neuf.*

The Internet

Thousands of properties are advertised on the internet in French and English. The estate agents' websites given below, and above under Estate Agents, are one starting point. Notaires' websites (see below) often have a section on property and carry some very general information about legal issues. General websites on property carry a wealth of useful information (in French), and offer the possibility of advertising your own requests. Newspapers have *immobilier* sections on their websites (given below); reading the local news can help you to know more about an area. Property magazines have their own specialised websites. There are also government websites with information on regulations and changes in the law.

Property Websites in English

www.efmag.co.uk.   www.french-property-news.com.
www.frenchconnections.co.uk   www.green-acre.com.
www.french-property.com.   www.homesoverseas.co.uk.
www.frenchproperty.co.uk.   www.livingfrance.com

Private Advertisers

www.appelimmo.fr.
www.bonjour.fr.
www.entreparticuliers.fr.
www.explorimmo.com.
www.journaldesparticuliers.fr.
www.kitrouve.com.
www.lacentrale.fr.
www.lesiteimmobilier.com.
www.pap.fr.

National Property Websites

www.123immo.fr.
www.abonim.com
www.century21.fr.
www.eurofoncier.com.
www.europropertysearch.com.
www.fnaim.fr. National estate
agents organisation.
www.immoneuf.com. New property.
www.lesiteimmobilier.com.
www.letuc.com.
www.logic-immo.com.
www.nexdom.com.
www.orpi.com.
www.panorimmo.com.
www.partenaire-europeen.fr.
www.p-e.fr.
www.proprietesdefrance.com. Up-
market properties.
www.seloger.com

Golf Sites

www.backspin.com.
www.europegolftravel.com.
www.golfagora.com.
www.doucefrance.com/golf.
www.golflounge.com

French Property Magazines

www.ibneuf.com.

www.immobilierenfrance.com.
www.immoneuf.com.
www.indicateurbertrand.com.
www.residencessecondaires.com.

General Information Sites

www.ademe.fr. Agency promoting
environmentally friendly building.
www.anah.fr. National association
for housing improvement.
www.anil.org. State agency for
housing information.
www.fnaim.fr. Estate agents organisation.
www.ideesmaison.com. Information on building new property.
www.immoprix.com. Prices of
property and land by areas.
www.immostreet.com. General
information.
www.infologement.fr. Mortgage
advice.
www.juri-logement.org. Legal
information.
www.logement.equipment.gouv.fr.
Ministry of Housing and Urban
Planning.
www.logement.org. General information.
ww.mon-immeuble.com. General
information.
www.panoranet.com. Information
on mortgages and insurance.
www.seloger.com. General information.
www.snpi.fr. Estate agents organisation.
www.uncmi.org. National union of
residential property builders.
www.unpi.org. Proprietors' union.

Newspapers

Alsace: *L'Alsace* (www.alsapresse.com); *Dernières Nouvelles d'Alsace* (www.dna.fr/dna).

Aquitaine: *Sud Ouest* (www.sudouest.com); *Nouvelle République des Pyrénées* (www.nrpyrenees.com).

Auvergne: *Centre France-La Montagne* (www.centrefrance.com).

Brittany: *France Ouest* (www.france-ouest.tm.fr; www.ouestfrance-immobilier.com); *Télégramme de Brest* (www.letelegramme.com).

Burgundy: *Bien Public* (www.bienpublic.com); *Journal du Saône-et-Loire* (www.lejsl.com); *Journal du Centre* (www.centre-france.com).

Centre: *Berry Républicain* (www.centrefrance.com); *La Nouvelle République* (www.lanouvellerepublique.fr); *La République du Centre* (www.larep.com).

Champagne-Ardennes: *L'Union Reims* (http://lunion/presse.fr); *L'Ardennais* (http://lunion/presse.fr); *Journal de la Haute Marne* (www.journaldelahautemarne.com); *Libération Champagne*.

Corsica: *Corse Matin* (www.corse.info); *Journal de Corse* (www.jdcorse.com).

Franche-Comté: *Progrès de Lyon* (www.leprogres.fr); *Voix du Jura* (www.voixdujura.fr); *L'Est*.

Languedoc-Roussillon: *Midi Libre* (www.midilibre.fr); *Dépêche du Midi* (www.ladepeche.com); *L'Indépendant* (www/lindependant.com); *Lozère Nouvelle* (www.lozere-nouvelle.com).

Limousin: *Centre France-Le Populaire du Centre* (www.centrefrance.com).

Lorraine: *Est Républicain* (www.estrepublicain.fr); *Liberté de l'Est* (www.lalibertedelest.fr).

Midi-Pyrénées: *Nouvelle République des Pyrénées* (www.nrpyrenees.com); *Journal de Millau* (www.journaldemillau.com); *La Dépêche* (www.ladepeche.fr).

Nord-Pas de Calais: *La Voix du Nord* (www.lavoixdunord.fr).

Normandy: *France Ouest* (www.france-ouest.tm.fr); *Informations Dieppoises* (http://infos-dieppoises.fr); *La Manche Libre* (www.normandiepa.com).

Paris-Ile-de-France: *Le Parisien* (www.leparisien.fr); *Nouvel Observateur Paris-Ile-de-France* (www.parisobs.com).

Pays de la Loire: *France Ouest* (www.france-ouest.tm.fr); *Presse Océan*.

Picardie: *Courrier Picard* (www.courrier-picard.fr); *Voix de l'Aisne* (www.nordnet.fr/voixdelaisne).

Poitou-Charente: *Charente Libre* (www.charente.com); *Sud Ouest* (www.sudouest.com); *Courrier de l'Ouest* (www.district-parthenay.fr/courrierdelouest.htm).

Provence-Alpes-Côte d'Azur: *La Provence* (www.laprovence-presse.fr); *Nice Matin* (www.nicematin.fr); *Var Matin* (www.varmatin.com); *La Marseillaise* (www.lamarseillaise.tm.fr).

Rhône-Alpes: *Progrès de Lyon* (www.leprogres.fr); *Le Dauphiné Libéré* (www.ledauphine.com)

Notaires' Websites

General sites: www.notaire.fr; www.immonot.com; www.min-immo.com. Some *départements* have websites. For others, try www.immonot.com or chambre+des+notaires+[name of *département*].

Regional sites

Aquitaine: www.chambre-dordogne.notaires.fr; www.chambre-gironde.notaires.fr; www.cr-bordeaux.notaires.fr; www.cr-agen.notaires.fr; www.cr-pau.notaires.fr.

Basse Normandie: www.cr-bassenormandie.notaires.fr www.chambre-manche.notaires.fr; www.chambre-calvados.notaires.fr; www.chambre-orne.notaires.fr.

Brittany: www.chambre-cotes-armor.notaires.fr; www.chambre-finistere.notaires.fr; www.chambre-ille-et-vilaine.notaires.fr; www.chambre-morbihan.notaires.fr; www.cr-rennes.notaires.fr.

Burgundy: www.chambre-yonne.notaires.fr; www.chambre-nievre.notaires.fr.

Champagne-Ardenne: www.chambre-aube.notaires.fr; www.chambre-ardennes.notaires.fr; www.chambre-marne.notaires.fr; www.cr-reims.notaires.fr.

Haute Normandie: www.cr-rouen.notaires.fr.

Languedoc-Roussillon: www.chambre-lozere.notaires.fr; www.chambre-montpellier.notaires.fr; www.chambre-nimes.notaires.fr.

Loire Valley: www.chambre-eureetloir.notaires.fr; www.chambre-indre.notaires.fr; www.chambre-indreetloire.notaires.fr; www.chambre-loiretcher.notaires.fr; www.chambre-loiret.notaires.fr; www.cr-orleans.notaires.fr.

Lorraine: www.chambre-meurthe-moselle.notaires.fr; www.chambre-meuse.notaires.fr; www.chambre-vosges.notaires.fr; weww.cr-lorraine.notaires.fr.

Nord-Pas de Calais: www.cr-nord-pas-de-calais.notaires.fr.

Midi-Pyrenees: www.chambre-hautegaronne.notaires.fr.

Paris-Ile-de-France: www.paris.notaires.fr; www.cr-paris2.notaires.fr; www.chambre-versailles.notaires.fr; www.chambre-seineetmarne.notaires.fr.

Pays de la Loire: www.chambre-loire-atlantique.notaires.fr;
www.chambre-maine-et-loire.notaires.fr; www.chambre-
sarthe.notaires.fr; www.chambre-vendee.notaires.fr.
Picardie: www.chambre-aisne.notaires.fr; www.cr-picardie.notaires.fr.
Poitou et Charente: www.charente-notaires.fr.
Provence-Alpes-Côte-d'Azur: www.chambre-alpesdehauteprovence.n
otaires.fr; www.chambre-alpesmaritimes.notaires.fr; www.chambre-
bouchesdurhone.notaires.fr; www.chambre-var.notaires.fr;
www.chambre-vaucluse.notaires.fr; www.cr-aixenprovence.notaires
.fr.
Rhône-Alpes: www.chambre-drome.notaires.fr; www.chambre-
loire.notaires.fr; www.chambre-rhone.notaires.fr.
Savoie-Dauphiné: www.chambre-isere.notaires.fr;
www.www.chambre-hautesavoie.notaires.fr; www.chambre-
savoie.notaires.fr.

Interpreting Property Advertisements

Property advertisements in French are not always that informative and
can be hard to interpret. Estate agents do not give the kinds of detailed
measurements of rooms that you would expect from a UK estate agent. By
law, the advertised price must include the estate agent's commission. Some
agents still advertise *net vendeur* (i.e. the price the seller gets), which will be
indicated by the abbreviation *HNC* or *n.c.*

The price given in an advert is only the starting point for your
negotiations. It is normal to offer 10%-20% less than the price stated;
French sellers do not expect you to offer the asking price, although you
may not get that much of a discount in the very competitive markets of
the Dordogne and Lot.

Some aspects of property terms are baffling: the terms T1, F1, Formule
1, and Type 1 all mean exactly the same thing: one room plus a kitchen
and bathroom (which may be very small). The word English people take
to mean a room – *une chambre* – actually means a bedroom; a room is *une
pièce*. Some words can give rise to odd misunderstandings. If the advert says
there is a *verger* included, you shouldn't imagine that you are taking over
a vicarage; it means an orchard. Ads also use the English word *standing*
meaning quality, rather than parking. The term *haut standing* implies a
high-quality development, while *moyen standing* might be a warning that
this is not such a good area. There is no such thing as *bas standing.* Some
adverts have *hors lotissement,* 'non-estate' in English estate-agent parlance;
the implications of being on an estate are not necessarily as dire as they
would be in England. Houses on *lotissements* are modern and uniform in
style, but not necessarily in a bad area. Properties can be said to be in a

quartier difficile or *quartier à problèmes* – an area with social problems. The absolute pits is a *quartier sinistré* – a seriously rundown area.

The term *maison de bourg* is used for a town centre house; the original meaning was a house within a fortified hilltop village. Nowadays, *bourg* implies that there are some shops in the vicinity; *bourgade* means much the same. The term *bungalow* is not the same as in English as it implies a holiday home which is unsuitable for year-round occupation. A *plain-pied* is on one storey. A *pavillon* originally meant a hunting lodge, but now refers to a 2-3 bed holiday villa.

It is normal, but not obligatory, to give the habitable surface area of the property in the advert. Ads for apartments should always give the surface area; there is a law that requires the surface area of an apartment in a *copropriété* to be given in the contract. Ads for newly built houses will always give the habitable surface area. The following glossary should guide you through the idiosyncracies of property ads:

GLOSSARY OF PROPERTY TERMS

à débattre	negotiable
à rénover	to be renovated
aménageable	can be put to use
appentis	lean-to
attenant	adjoining
bien(s)	goods, property, estate, assets
bornage	boundary marking
bornes	boundary markers
buanderie	washhouse
carrelage	tiling
carrelé	tiled
cave	cellar
cellier	storeroom, pantry
chai	wine/spirit storehouse
chauffage fuel	oil heating
clôture	fencing, paling, hedge or other enclosure
combles aménageables	loft conversion possible
CC/commission comprise	estate agent's commission included
débarras	junk-room
dépendances	outhouses
double séjour	large living room
écurie	stables
en exclusivité	only one estate agent is handling the sale
F1	one room + kitchen/bathroom

FAC/frais agence compris	agency's commission included
grenier	attic
HNC/honoraires agence	
non compris	agent's commission not included
HT/hors taxes	not including taxes
immeuble	apartment block, or commercial property
maison de caractère	dilapidated or unusual
maison mitoyenne	semi-detached/terrace house
n.c./non compris	not included
plain pied	one storey
prestations	features
ravalement	rendering
refait à neuf	completely renovated
rez	ground floor
salle	living room
sans mitoyenneté	no commonly owned boundary walls or structures
sans vis-à-vis	no houses opposite
SdB/salle de bain	bathroom
SdE/salle d'eau	washroom
séj/séjour	living room
séjour cathédrale	open-plan living room on two floors
sous-sol	below ground-level
T1	Type 1; same as F1
TBE/très bon état	very good condition
TTC/toutes taxes comprises	all taxes included
verger	orchard
vue imprenable	unrestricted view

WHAT TYPE OF PROPERTY TO BUY

CHAPTER SUMMARY

- ⊙ The secret of a happy house purchase is to choose the right location and to stick within your budget.
- ⊙ The French generally prefer new properties, while the foreigners go for the old ones.
- ⊙ In France it is common to buy an unbuilt or unfinished property on the basis of its plans.
- ⊙ Building land is cheap in France and many French people build their own homes.
- ⊙ Sometimes property is sold by auction: this is fairly unusual, but there are real bargains to be found by buying this way.

THE RIGHT PROPERTY FOR YOU

Buying your French property should be the experience of a lifetime, if it is approached in the right way. It would be disingenuous to say that no one has ever regretted buying property in France. The main causes of disappointment are buying in the wrong location, and not setting a realistic limit on the budget. By going through a list of simple questions it is easy enough to see whether a property is the right one for you:

- ⊙ What is my budget?
- ⊙ Do I need to rent it out to make it affordable?
- ⊙ How much work does it need doing, and what will it cost?
- ⊙ How easy is the property to get to?
- ⊙ Are there any airports nearby?
- ⊙ Do I want to live there all the year round?
- ⊙ Is the climate bearable in the winter?
- ⊙ How close is it to tourist attractions?
- ⊙ Will I or my partner be able to pursue our hobbies there?
- ⊙ Will we or our family still want to use it in 20 years' time?

As a general rule, it is wise to decide on your budget and stick to it, no matter how tempted you might be to spend an extra €20,000 or whatever. If the property needs renovating, ask for some quotations beforehand. You should have outline planning permission – a *certificat d'urbanisme* – before buying, if you are planning a change of use or large-scale renovations. Your notaire will advise you on whether you need this.

It is risky to buy a property if you can only finance it by renting it out or running *gîtes*. More and more foreigners are buying in France with the same idea, while the tourist market is actually contracting. It is far more realistic to have a profession that you can carry on in France which leaves you financially secure, rather than struggling.

Unless you know exactly what you are doing, buying in the hope of selling at a profit is a very risky proposition. In the last ten years, the French stock market has been a much better investment than property, which in many places has only just returned to prices seen in 1991.

Old versus New

It is an oddity of the French property scene that the French consistently prefer new-build, or completely renovated property, leaving the decrepit character farmhouses to the foreigners. Perhaps until 30 years ago the average Frenchman didn't mind living in a damp, crumbling farmhouse, with broken chairs and tables, and water coming through the roof. French women have, however, voted with their feet, and moved to the comfort of the towns, forcing the male of the species to follow suit.

The French have seen what the British and other foreigners can do with old properties, but not that many are interested in imitating them. On the whole, foreign buyers and the French are looking for quite different types of property. The incomers look for a beautiful location and authenticity, while what the French really want is elegance and convenience. The most telling statistic is the fact that the average new property is worth 40% more than an old one. It is therefore important to understand that it may be very difficult to recoup the investment that you make in renovating an old property in a remote area, unless you are lucky enough to find another foreigner who happens to like it.

Even though you may know what you are looking for, it is useful to consider a checklist of the pros and cons of old versus new:

Advantages of the Old

- The property has an authentic feel and rustic charm.
- There will probably be more land attached to it.
- The garden will be well-established.
- You know from the outset what you are buying.

○ The view will probably be better than with new property.

○ There will be more craftsmanship in the construction.

○ You are more likely to be able to rent it out to holiday-makers.

Advantages of the New

○ There will be a garage or parking spaces already built.

○ The kitchen will be more modern.

○ The wiring and plumbing won't need replacing.

○ The building is guaranteed for 10 years from construction.

○ You can design the property yourself.

○ The heating will be more efficient.

○ There should be insulation.

○ On some developments, there are shared sports facilities.[endbp]

The great majority of foreigners would prefer to buy an old property, even if it has some defects, and needs more maintenance than the new. The average first-time buyer in France will buy an apartment in a *copropriété*. The crucial point for foreign buyers is: Do I want to rent it out? If you plan to make a living from bed-and-breakfast the property will have to be substantial, and even more so for *gîtes*. If you only intend to live there for part of the year, and rent it out the rest of the time, there is more leeway. Holidaymakers will be quite satisfied with an apartment or a standard French holiday bungalow, as long as it is near the sea or the ski fields.

BUYING UNCOMPLETED PROPERTY

It is common in France to buy property on the basis of plans – *achat sur plan* – or which has not yet been completed – *vente en l'état futur d'achèvement* (VEFA). A developer – *promoteur constructeur* – buys a piece of land, arranges for planning permission, and then looks for potential buyers before the property is built, or when it is partially built. The VEFA is defined in the Code Civil as:

> *a contract by which a seller immediately transfers his rights to a piece of land, as well as the ownership of any existing construction. The building that is to be done becomes the property of the buyer as the work is completed. The buyer is required to pay the cost as the work progresses. The seller is in charge of the building until the handover [to the buyer].*

The dwelling can be an apartment, or an individual house, as in the case of a *lotissement* or estate.

The first step in the process is to sign a preliminary contract, or *contrat de réservation*, with a developer. The contract must contain certain information, as well as any get-out clauses in the sale:

- The habitable surface area.
- The number of main rooms.
- A list of any attached rooms, or spaces.
- The location of the building in the estate.
- The technical quality of the construction, with a list of the materials to be used.
- The provisional price of the building, and any conditions that allow for the price to change.
- The date by which the final contract can be signed.
- Where relevant, any loans that the developer intends to obtain for the buyer.
- The conditions for paying the deposit.

The buyer has the right to ask for changes to the contract. Once the contract has been received by registered post, there is a 7-day cooling-off period during which the buyer can change their mind.

The deposit – *dépôt de garantie* – depends on the length of time before the completion of the project: 5% if within one year, under 2% if between one and two years, and no deposit if beyond two years. The deposit will be returned if:

- The sale does not go through.
- The sale price exceeds the provisional price by 5%.
- The buyer fails to obtain a mortgage.
- Equipment that has been promised is not installed.
- The property falls 10% in value.

The developer is legally required to present a guarantee that the project will be finished, or a guarantee of full reimbursement if it is not completed. In most cases the developer will have their own guarantor, a bank or co-operative society, as a backer.

Final Signing of Contract

The second, final, contract is signed once the building programme has been decided on, and construction can commence. A draft of the *contrat définitif de vente* is sent to the buyer at least a month before the signing date. The final contract must contain certain information:

- The description of the building or the part of the building to be sold.

- ○ The price, the method of payment, and any possible revisions in the payment.
- ○ The completion date.
- ○ Details of the developer's financial guarantees.

There are two categories of faults that can appear in new constructions: the *défaut de conformité* and the *vice de construction*. The first is where an incorrect piece of equipment has been installed, e.g. a shower instead of a bath. Payment for the item can be withheld until the fault has been rectified. *Vice de construction* covers bad workmanship or mistakes in installing equipment. A new building comes with a guarantee that the construction is satisfactory. The guarantee covers any faults that the buyer may find within the first year of occupation, and ensures that all faults are corrected.

Payment
Under normal circumstances, the buyer pays in four instalments, which include the deposit:

- ○ 35% when the foundations are completed
- ○ 70% when the roof has been built and the terraces are no longer exposed to water
- ○ 95% when the building has been completed
- ○ the final 5% is payable at the handing-over stage, unless there is a dispute.

When the property is ready to be handed over, there has to be a formal *réception des travaux* between you (or your representative) – the *maître d'ouvrage* – and the developer – the *maître d'œuvre*. The *réception des travaux* (acceptance of the work), can take place with or without reservations. The final 5% of the payment is known as the *retenue de garantie* and this can be withheld until any defects have been put right, or to cover your own expenses in putting them right if the builder fails to do the work. If the 5% is withheld, it should be deposited in an escrow account held by a notaire.

Before the handing-over the buyer should inspect the building, with the help of an expert if necessary, to determine if there are any faults that need correcting. You – or your representative – will need to have plans and lists of all the equipment that is supposed to be installed. Electrics and heating should be tested. At the *réception des travaux* you will sign a document – a *procès-verbal* – accepting the handover. You can only refuse to take over the building if there are serious defects or equipment is missing. At the handing-over the developer has to show that they have the necessary insurance policy to cover their *responsabilité décennale* – the compulsory

10-year guarantee against major construction faults. There is also a 2-year guarantee – *garantie biennale* – against faults in the equipment, such as the fitted kitchen, heating and double glazing.

The developer also has to present the electricity safety board's certificate of approval, the *Attestation de Consuel*. In order to guarantee the quality of the construction and equipment, it is possible to engage an organisation such as Qualitel, based in Paris, who will oversee the whole process of design and construction. See the website: www.qualitel.org. Another agency, Promotelec, is involved in promoting efficient energy: see www.promotelec.fr. You can also check whether your developer is a member of the *Fédération Nationale des Promoteurs Constructeurs:* 106 rue de l'Université, 75007 Paris; www.fnpc.fr.

Penalties

There are, naturally, penalties where either the buyer or the seller fails to meet their obligations. If the buyer fails to make stage payments on time, the developer can add on 1% for each month in arrears. There will be a clause in the contract imposing a penalty of up to 10% of the purchase price if the buyer does not meet their payment schedule, and other clauses which allow the developer to find another buyer if necessary.

From the side of the developer, the contract must give the period of time within which the stages of construction are to be completed, in the case of an individual house. Penalties are payable by the developer once the date has been exceeded by 30 days, unless there this is due to forces outside his control. The penalty is set at a maximum of 0.033% of the total price per day of delay. The buyer is in a stronger position if they can set an actual deadline, rather than a period of time in which the work has to be done.

Taxation

There are both advantages and disadvantages to buying a new property, as far as taxes go. The downside is that 19.6% TVA is payable, although this can be avoided in some circumstances. The costs associated with the purchase, to be paid to the notaire, are reduced to about 2%-3% of the price, before TVA. There is a 20% reduction if you buy a unit in a development of more than 10 units. In addition there is the *taxe de publicité foncière* – at 0.615% of the price before TVA – and another €900 in charges.

TVA is also payable if you buy a property within 5 years of its completion. TVA can be avoided if:

- ⭘ You buy property under a leaseback scheme;
- ⭘ You run a hotel or similar TVA-registered business from the property;

- You let the property to someone running a hotel;
- You sell the property at a loss within five years of purchase;
- You are a *marchand de biens* – dealer in property.

TVA is only payable the first time the property changes hands within the first five years after construction, unless this was through a *marchand de biens*. There are strict rules about the avoidance of TVA; professional advice is essential if you are looking for ways of avoiding TVA.

LEASEBACK

Leaseback, or *le leaseback,* is a useful scheme, somewhat like 'buy-to-let', but within a formal structure that guarantees your investment is safe. It was originally promoted by the French government as a way of encouraging private investors to fund new tourist accommodation. The idea is quite ingenious: you agree to buy a new or completely rebuilt property in a tourist complex, and then lease it back to the developer for a period of between nine and 20 years. The developer's management company runs it for you, and guarantees a rental income which goes towards paying off any mortgage that you have taken out to buy the property. You can also expect to have the use of the property during the off-season for a number of weeks each year. At the end of the fixed leaseback period, you are the owner of the property, and you can do with it what you wish; hopefully you will be sitting on a substantial profit.

Leaseback schemes will only be found in tourist areas on the coast, in Paris, and in the Alps. They are more like hotel complexes than anything else. Everything is managed for you; the developer takes all the risk. The major attraction of the leaseback scheme is that no TVA is payable on the purchase, unless you end the lease and use the property yourself, in which case TVA has to be reimbursed.

The following are some companies that deal in leaseback properties. Others can be found through the organisation FOPDAC – the Federation of Overseas Property developers and Agents – see www.fopdac.com:

Overseas Properties: ☎ 01803-290004; fax 01803-290084; www.overseas-properties.com. Côte d'Azur.

Villas Abroad (Properties) Ltd: ☎ 020-8941 4499; fax 020-8941 0202; e-mail villasabroad@fopdac.com; www.villasabroadproperties.com. Côte d'Azur.

Vivre en France: ☎ 020-7515 8660; www.vefuk.com. La Rochelle, Charente.

BUYING LAND FOR BUILDING

It is not unusual for the French to buy a piece of land with the intention of building a property on it themselves. There are, naturally, a lot of formalities involved; this is not something you could do while sitting at home in England. In many ways, it could be an ideal solution. Building land is cheap in the countryside, and you will have complete control over the design of your property.

A lot of land cannot be built on, especially on the coast. Agricultural land is also protected. Many *communes* have a PLU – *Plan Local d'Urbanisme* – which states which pieces of land may be built on; the PLU is still popularly referred by its old name: POS or *Plan d'Occupation des Sols*. Linked to this is the COS – *Coéfficient d'Occupation des Sols* – a figure giving the maximum amount of square metres of surface area that can built on each square metre of land. The implication is that if you want to build a property with more than a certain number of storeys then you will have to pay a further charge, if permission is granted at all. If the *commune* has no PLU, then the use of the land is decided by central government. Planning permission – the *certificat d'urbanisme* – will only be granted where there are adequate access roads, drains, water and electricity supplies, and so on.

A usual way to buy land for building is to buy a plot in a *lotissement* or new estate; otherwise you may find a single plot or *parcelle* by looking in the usual property magazines. If you are thinking of buying land for building, it is vital to be aware of any plans on the part of the local authorities to construct new roads, industrial parks, etc. Look in the local *Plan Cadastral* or Land Registry, to see what the precise measurements of your piece of land should be, and whether there are new developments planned near to your property. If the boundaries are not clearly defined then you will need the services of a *géomètre-expert* – see yellow pages – to carry out the *bornage,* that is put in markers to show the boundaries. Only a *géomètre-expert* is allowed to change boundaries. For companies selling land see the following websites:

www.allobat.fr.
http://frenchland.com.
www.terrain.fr.
www.terrain-a-batir.com.
www.terrains.com.
www.villesetvillages.fr.

Pre-emptive Rights/Droit de Préemption

In many areas, the state, or state organisations can have pre-emptive rights on land purchase. Even after you buy a piece of land, the state can make a compulsory purchase order; you will receive a 10% compensation. It is also conceivable that a private person has a pre-emptive right, or some other right, such as the use of the land for a fixed period, or rights of passage. In order to avoid pointlessly acquiring land, it is essential to conduct a search of all the possible *servitudes* or obligations attaching to a piece of land.

In agricultural areas, the main organisation to watch for is the SAFER – *Société d'Aménagement Foncier et d'Établissement Rural* – which exists to ensure that agricultural land, forests and fields are put to appropriate use, and in particular to try to bring small parcels of land under one ownership. The notaire handling the sale is legally obliged to inform SAFER of the impending transfer. Where it appears that there is going to be a change in the use of land, the SAFER can intervene and negotiate with the seller to find a more suitable use for the land, or they can buy the land themselves and sell it on. Where the land is being sold to family members, or co-heirs, the SAFER will not intervene.

While some 10,000 owners voluntarily sell some 80,000 hectares to SAFER each year, the right to pre-emptive purchase is not often exercised. In many regions, the local SAFER is a fairly toothless organisation, without the means to buy more land, but it is still necessary to inform SAFER if you are selling land.

BUILDING YOUR OWN PROPERTY

There are a number of ways one can go about building one's own property. You can either hire an architect to design the building, or design it yourself, if it is fairly small, or go to a builder and ask them to supply you with a ready-made plan. If you choose to take a ready-made plan, then the contract you sign is a *contrat de construction d'une maison individuelle avec fourniture de plan*. The terms of the contract are strictly regulated by law. The builder must have financial guarantees and insurance. Payments are made according to a well-defined schedule:

15%	on starting the work
25%	on completion of foundations
40%	on completion of walls
60%	when the roof is put on (*mise hors d'eau*)
75%	on completion of walls (*mise hors d'air*)
95%	when the heating, plumbing and carpentry are completed
100%	at the hand-over

Not many foreigners go for this type of arrangement, since they would rather have a design of their own.

The more usual procedure is to hire an architect to draw the plans. The contract is not regulated in law. Evidently, it should include details of estimates of the cost, and stage payments. The actual building work is usually handled by a *maître d'œuvre,* who oversees the whole process, and engages various specialist tradesmen. A *maître d'œuvre* is not usually as highly qualified as an architect, but will have more time to spend on-site. Note that the person who engages a *maître d'œuvre* is called the *maître d'ouvrage.* The contract you sign with him is the *contrat de maîtrise d'œuvre* which is again not regulated by law. The *maître d'œuvre* will normally hire tradesmen that he has worked with in the past, or he may give the job to a local co-operative. In other respects, many of the details of having your house constructed are similar to those described under VEFA above.

One final possibility is to act as your own *maître d'œuvre* and to conclude contracts – *contrats d'entreprise* – with the various builders and tradesmen that you need. Such contracts are regulated. They are more used for commercial property, and it is unlikely that a foreigner would want to go about building in this way.

Planning Permission

Further information about planning permission, and building procedures, is given in chapter 11, *Building or Renovating.*

BUYING AT AUCTION

The idea of buying at auction may not occur to many foreigners, but there are real bargains to be found if you are prepared to take a risk, and the process itself holds some excitement. Fewer than 1% of property transactions in France take place through auctions; in an average year only 500 properties are sold in Paris by this method, and perhaps only 250 in the rest of the country. About 25 buyers attend an auction on average; the prices realised depend very much on the current climate of the property market. Auctions (*ventes aux enchères*) can be divided into three types: *vente judiciaire, vente de notaires,* and *vente des domaines.*

Ventes Judiciaires. This type of sale occurs when the owner of a property has gone bankrupt or defaulted on their mortgage payments. It is a forced sale by the creditors, i.e. mortgage lender. They take place less and less and are really a last resort for creditors. Sales are advertised in the local press, in *Le Journal des Enchères* (every two months), *Les Affiches Parisiennes,* and in the *Programme des Ventes* given out by the clerk of the lower court (*greffier du tribunal*). To bid at the sale, you hire a lawyer (*avocat*) registered at the court where the sale is going to take place. You give him/her a *mandat* (authorisation) to bid up to a certain limit, and a certified cheque for 20%

of the sum you are prepared to go up to. Your lawyer will not exceed the amount you have stated unless you are standing next to him at the sale and give your permission for him to bid higher.

If your bid is successful, you have 30 days to pay in full in the case where a property has been seized by the creditor (*saisie immobilière*) and three months in the case of bankruptcy proceedings (*mise en liquidation*). Properties with sitting tenants or squatters are best avoided, otherwise you will be involved in a long legal fight to evict them.

Ventes de Notaires. In this case properties and goods are voluntarily submitted for auction by their owners at a *séance d'adjudication* or auction. Sales are publicised in a national bulletin (*Les Ventes aux Enchères des Notaires*). Information about notarial auctions can be found on the website: www.min-immo.com/Encheres. Again, you cannot bid directly yourself, rather you are represented by your notaire. Owners use this type of auction in the hope of gaining a higher price than through the usual channels. If you are looking for prestigious older properties you may get a good deal here.

In order to take part you will have to deposit a certified cheque for 20% of the estimated price to the notaire carrying out the sale. You have 45 days after the sale to pay the remainder. There are hefty costs involved, between 10% and 20% of the sale price.

Ventes des Domaines. The state sometimes sells properties at auction: these are announced in the *Bulletin Officiel d'Annonces des Domaines*. You are required to deposit a certified cheque for 5% of the estimated price in order to bid.

Vente à la Chandelle. The 'auction by candle' is a relic going back to the 15th century. The idea is that three tapers are placed on a board: the first two are lit simultaneously, and burn down within tens of seconds, while bids are made. The third taper is then lit, and if no higher bid is made then the property is sold. Nowadays, the tapers are being replaced with electric lights. This is not the end of the matter: if a bid of 10% more than the successful bid is made then the property has to be auctioned all over again, but this rarely happens. The latter condition does not apply to the *ventes des domaines*.

Points to Watch For

It goes without saying that you should view the property in question, and try to get an estimate of the likely costs of renovation. You are required to take the property as seen; there is no comeback in case of structural faults, and there is no *condition suspensive* (get-out clause) making the sale dependent on getting a mortgage. If you fail to pay for the property in full, it will be auctioned again without a reserve price (*folle enchère*) and you will be liable to pay the difference between what you bid and the price that is finally realised.

Before you get carried away by the idea of an auction, you need to consider the total costs of the transaction, and whether you can afford to do a place up. There is no margin for error; you will need a lawyer or notary in any case to handle the process. It is essential to contact the seller's notary or the tax office or local court to find out the costs associated with the purchase, property taxes, whether any third parties have any rights of way (*droits de passage*) or other claims on the property (*servitudes*), whether you can obtain permits to make alterations or extensions to the property, and if the local municipality has any plans that could affect the property.

Make a tour of the area and find out the local prices of property; talk to neighbours and anyone who might know the history of the property. On the day of the sale be there right from the beginning. Try to attend other auctions before you bid yourself.

Finding Out About Auctions

The trickiest part of French auctions is finding out when and where they are happening if you are not in France. Notaries' offices and estate agents are kept informed of auctions, and can help you to find one in a suitable area. Anyone who is interested in auctions should look at the magazine *Journal des Enchères* which covers every kind of auction, including furniture, antiques, etc. The following are useful websites: www.licitor.com; www.ventes-judiciaires.com; www.encheres-paris.com; www.min-immo.com/Encheres; www.ilf.fr (for PACA).

OTHER WAYS OF BUYING

Rent-to-Buy/Location Accession

It is possible to enter into an agreement with an owner whereby you rent the property for a number of years before buying it. The seller incorporates a clause in the contract promising to sell you the property. The clause is only activated when the prospective buyer pays a 5% deposit into a blocked account. From then on, the tenant/buyer makes further payments towards the eventual purchase price, on top of their rent. After an agreed time – usually two or three years – the buyer then has the option of paying the remainder of the purchase price. If the potential buyer changes their mind there is a small penalty to be paid to the seller. If the seller breaks the contract there is a heavier penalty of up to 3% of the value of the property.

Rente Viagère

This is a system that is rather alien to the British, although it does have something in common with an annuity taken out on the value of your house. The idea of the *rente viagère* (literally meaning 'income for life') is that you come to an agreement with the owner of a property that you will pay them a certain monthly sum and in exchange the property will revert to you on the owner's death. The buyer also pays out an initial sum known as a *bouquet* equivalent to 20% to 30% of the total price. The person who pays out the money is the *débirentier* and the one who receives money is the *crédirentier*. There are two types of *viager:* one where the *crédirentier* continues to live in the house, and the other where they live elsewhere.

Properties are sometimes sold with the elderly person included, so to speak. Thus one may see ads giving the cost of the property, the age and sex of the occupant, and how much you have to go on paying them. If you want to sell your property *en viager,* you can try looking at the website: www.viager.fr.

The popularity of this kind of scheme has been on the decline as people live longer and longer, since you are gambling that someone is going to die quite soon. On average, you will pay less for a property this way than by purchasing outright.

> The classic example of where the *rente viagère* turned out badly for a buyer is the case of Jeanne Calment who died in 1997 at the age of 122. A notary, André-François Raffray, age 47, made a deal with Calment, who was then 90, that he would pay her £300 a month for the rest of her life on condition that he inherited her house in Arles, Provence (where Van Gogh once lived). Thirty years later, Raffray died, having paid out £120,000 or twice the value of the property, and his heirs were obliged to shell out for another two years. Calment joked to Raffray on her 120th birthday: 'We all make bad deals in life.' Calment was a famous wit, and even inspired a sect of followers.

Anyone thinking of entering into this arrangement would be well advised to look at the projected lifespans of the French.

TIMESHARE/CO-OWNERSHIP

Timeshare has as bad a reputation in France as anywhere else. The European Union issues brochures warning about the dire consequences of signing a timeshare agreement and leaves them in French railway stations. Unfortunately, the paranoia about timeshare is entirely justified. The French legal system leaves less scope for timeshare crooks than other countries, however, and there is far less timeshare property available than in Spain or Portugal. Many French people have bought timeshare themselves in other countries and lived to regret it.

The idea behind timeshare seems sensible enough at first sight. Instead of renting a room in an expensive hotel on the French Riviera, or a chalet in the Alps, you buy a share in a timeshare company that gives you the right to use a property for a certain number of weeks for the rest of your life, and to pass it on to your heirs. A timeshare can cost from £2000 to £10,000 or more. The catch is that you never actually own any part of the property: you just have a right to use it for a fixed period each year. The French often call timeshare *'multipropriété'* which is entirely misleading: you never own the property. It should really be called *multilocation* (i.e. multiple rental) or *multi-jouissance* or *jouissance en temps partagé*. Under the French system, you are buying shares in a timeshare company, which you can then sell on if you want or leave to your heirs. If the timeshare company goes out of business you will lose the right to use the property, and you may even be held liable for some of the company's debts. You can take out a loan to buy the timeshare (if you can find a lender), and there can be a get-out clause in the timeshare contract if you fail to get a loan. You are allowed to rent out the property for the weeks that you have bought, which could make you a profit. The contract does not have to be signed in the presence of a notary; usually it is done *sous seing privé*, or 'under hand' in British parlance.

The first disadvantage of timeshare is that other people will be using the property for most of the year, so it will never feel like it is yours. If you decide that you don't like the property it is difficult to sell your share without making a substantial loss. In addition there are still costs involved with timeshare: you can expect to pay between £200 and £500 a year in management fees.

How Timeshare is Sold

Most potential buyers do not look for timeshares themselves. The usual procedure is for a timeshare company to employ young, good-looking students who are on the lookout for likely targets in tourist locations. You are taken to a presentation where you are plied with drink and shown glossy brochures of the holiday properties. The sales techniques are highly sophisticated: you may be kept at the presentation for several hours and subjected to all kinds of high-pressure sales talk; it will be suggested that you pay a deposit on the spot, to make sure that the opportunity you are offered doesn't slip away. This is a clear sign that the sellers are crooks; you should never pay any cash up front. Under French law you cannot sign a timeshare contract on the spot; it has to be sent to you and returned by recorded delivery.

The risks involved in timeshare are considerable: the property may not even be built yet, or the photos may be misleading. You will be shown an apartment or building and promised that you will have access to it if you sign up. One scam is to sign up far more customers than there are properties, and then to wind up the company once the customers start to complain. Timeshare touts try to find tourists who have just arrived in, say, the Riviera, in the hope of clinching a deal before they leave again. It is a wise precaution to ask for the contract to be sent to your address in England so that you have sufficient time to look at the details. This may be enough to put off dishonest sellers.

Under French law the timeshare contract must include a 10-day cooling-off period after you have sent off the signed contract, during which you can change your mind. The seller is not allowed to ask for or receive any money until the end of the 10-day cooling-off period. The contract should give the identity and address of the sellers, and all the costs involved, the location and description of the property, and the weeks you can use it for.

Because of the low resale value, a timeshare can be bought for less than half the original asking price, so there is little purpose in buying a new one. They are sometimes advertised in *Dalton's Weekly* and *Exchange & Mart*. You can look at the Timeshare Consumers' Association (TCA) website (www.tcaforum.com) to see if there have been any complaints about the timeshare company. There are also professional dealers who take timeshares off your hands at a low price to resell, sometimes to the company you originally bought the timeshare from. You should not agree to pay any fees to such dealers up-front: they will be thousands of miles away by the time you try to catch up with them. Dealers that resell timeshares should be members of the OTE – Organisation for Timeshare in Europe (see www.ote-info.com). French timeshare companies have their own federation – Syndicat des Professionnels en Temps Partagé, 3 square Malherbe, 75016 Paris – who can advise you on timeshare purchase.

Offers of shares in *multipropriétés* can be found in some small ad magazines. These are timeshares rather than genuine offers of part ownership. The weekly *De Particulier à Particulier* and its website – www.pap.fr – always has some offers. *Le Journal des Particuliers* (www.jo urnaldesparticuliers.fr) has many of the same offers. Weeks at peak times of the year are hard to find. The fact that the week on offer falls during a school holiday is a key selling point.

Holiday Property Bonds and Holiday Clubs
Given the bad reputation of timeshare, other similar schemes have been thought up, which can claim to be 'not timeshare'. One of these is HPBs – Holiday Property Bonds. You pay a sum of money, the majority (around 75%) is invested in a portfolio of properties, and the rest goes into manage-

ment fees. In return for your investment you are allocated points. Provided you have enough points you can stay in one of the properties offered by the bond company, if it is available. The positive side of the HPB is that you will be staying in well-managed properties but you still have to pay a user's fee for cleaning and maintenance. The downside is much the same as with timeshare: the property is never yours and you may make a loss if you decide to sell your HPB. These are suitable schemes if you take several short holidays a year and are prepared to take pot luck about where you go.

More downmarket are Holiday Clubs or Travel Clubs, which promise holidays for life for a lump sum payment, with even bigger risks than timeshare. The most common scam is to tell thousands of people that they have won a free holiday, and charge them to attend a presentation. There are endless horror stories about holiday clubs and no one should touch them with a barge pole.

French-Style Co-ownership: Multipropriété

Instead of getting involved with timeshare, it is more sensible to buy a property jointly with some other like-minded people, and agree on who will use it at what time of the year. This is not a cheap option, but you will at least be the owner of part of the property. The important thing is to draw up the deed of sale correctly, and this can only be done with a lawyer who is familiar with French property law. The law companies mentioned in the section on Inheritance Tax in chapter 4 can advise. The most suitable form is a *Société Civile Immobilière*, as long as it is constituted correctly. The SCI allows one to get around French inheritance laws, which would automatically favour children over spouses. It is particularly useful where several unrelated people own shares in a property, and wish to be free to pass their share on to others. The SCI is a company but is not subject to corporation tax. It is treated as 'fiscally transparent'; the directors are taxed as individuals. If you hold property through a company you could also be liable to UK tax on directors' benefits in kind, and the tax bill would have to be shared out between the owners. Owners pay for the running costs of the property in proportion to the number of weeks they use the place.

Selling your French property to a group of owners while keeping a part for yourself, is an ideal way to retain the use of your property for some weeks of the year, while at the same time regaining the money you invested in it. There is also an agency in the UK – OwnerGroups Company – that specialises in finding, and handling the purchase of property for the purpose of co-ownership. Their fee is 6.5% of the value of the property. In 2002 they had a share in a six-bedroom château in Charente-Maritime on offer for £100,000. They can be contacted on 01628-486350; www.ownergroups.com.

Copropriété

This is also a type of co-ownership, normally applicable to apartments, although it can be used for any kind of building split into several units. As there is no such thing as leasehold in France, *copropriétés*, in which a group of owners run a building themselves, are extremely common and many foreigners find themselves involved with one. It should be said that, while there is no leasehold, the land on which a building stands could be owned by someone else. A property company can buy parts of a *copropriété*, and has the right to be represented at meetings.

Any building or buildings divided between several owners with private and common areas automatically comes under the 1965 law on *copropriétés*. The group of owners, or *copropriétaires*, automatically constitutes a *syndicat de copropriété*. The owners are legally obliged to appoint a *syndic* or manager responsible for the day-to-day running of the building; they are also required to elect a *conseil syndical* (council of the syndicate) for a three-year term, and to hold annual general meetings.

There is a basic text that defines the conditions under which a *copropriété* functions, known as the *règlement de copropriété*. This includes:

- A list of the common and private areas.
- The uses to which the property may be put: e.g. whether you can run a business from it.
- The administration of the common areas.
- The division of the charges.

A general assembly of the *copropriétaires* can be called at any time by the *conseil syndical*, or by the *copropriétaires* holding at least 25% of the votes. There has to be at least one assembly per year. If you rent out your part of the *copropriété* the tenant can also take part in an assembly, but they cannot vote on the same motions as you. The *syndic* will notify you at least 15 days before the meeting that it is happening. Any of the *copropriétaires* can ask for an amendment to the order of the meeting. You can appoint a representative to attend the meeting in your place.

Motions concerning the day-to-day running of the *copropriété* are passed by simple majority. Matters affecting the basic running of the *copropriété* must be approved by two-thirds majority. Some other matters, such as changing the division of the charges, can only be approved by unanimous vote. All the *copropriétaires* should receive a notification within two months of the decisions taken at the meeting. Strictly speaking, only those who opposed a decision, or were absent from the meeting, have to be informed, but it is normal to inform all the *copropriétaires*. Decisions can be challenged in a court of law, unless you have already voted in favour of them.

The general assembly is required to elect a board of management – *conseil syndical* – whose term of office runs for three years. *Copropriétaires,* their partners, and their representatives are all allowed to sit on the board. The board chooses a president who stays in contact with the manager of the property.

The *Syndic*. The *syndic* – the manager of the property – deals with the day-to-day running of the property. A part of their job is to keep a logbook of all the maintenance of the building, and to give advice to the owners. They are expected to present a provisional budget for the year at the AGM, and to keep accounts of the running of the property. The *syndic* maintains a bank account in the name of the syndicate. As a rule, the *syndic* does not need to go to the *conseil syndical* to carry out urgent repairs. There is generally an agreed figure which the *syndic* may spend for necessary repairs without calling a general meeting.

The *syndic* can be appointed by the general assembly of the *copropriété,* by the board of management, or they may be named in the constitution of the *copropriété.* Since their task requires specialised knowledge in accounting and law, the *syndic* usually holds a professional qualification, the *carte professionnelle de gestion immobilière.* It is virtually a requirement to have a professional *syndic* if there are more than five or so *copropriétaires.* Although any of the *copropriétaires* or their partners can act as the *syndic* they will not be able to obtain the professional indemnity insurance that is available to a professionally qualified person.

> **Peter owned a two-bedroom apartment in St Malo, Brittany, for 10 years in a *copropriété.* This was in an old building which required some renovation.**
>
> *I rarely went to the meetings of the copropriété. The syndic was generally very slow to do repairs; at one point I did some work on the plaster myself and all the other people thanked me effusively. Another time a woman who had water running into her flat had already waited four months to have something done; when I went to the manager and told him firmly that I wanted it fixed before I left he did it within a week. Straight talking is generally the best way to get things done in this situation.*

The terms of the *syndic's* remuneration are negotiable. There is no legal obligation to pay the *syndic;* the job could, in theory, be done on a voluntary basis. Their term of office is for three years. If it can be proved that they have made a serious mistake, the *syndic* can be dismissed by a simple majority vote at a general meeting.

The *copropriétaires* are entitled to look at the accounts of the *copropriété* in between notification of a general meeting and the meeting itself. The accounts of the *copropriété* are separate from the *syndic*'s own personal accounts. If the *syndic* is suspected of taking bribes from suppliers you would need a court order to look at his accounts. The *copropriétaires* have a right to instruct the *syndic* to use, or not to use the services of a particular company. **Alterations to the Property.** There are strict rules about what you can change in your part of the *copropriété*, since any changes to the property affect all the owners. You need the permission of the *syndic* for any redecoration, new shutters, plastering and so on. Anything that alters the external appearance of the *copropriété* is of concern to all the members.

Needless to say, any work that is to be done to the common areas is the responsibility of the *syndic*.

Charges. You will receive a regular bill for insurance, cleaning, maintenance and so on in the communal area. The cost of heating the common areas is also shared. There may also be a charge for the television aerial. The *syndic*'s remuneration is paid by all the owners.

The percentage of the charges that you are due to pay depends on the value of your part of the *copropriété*. You will have to pay for your share of a service, even if you do not make use of it, unless there is some good reason. For example, if you live on the ground floor, you do not pay for the lift. The list of charges and their distribution is included in the regulations of the *copropriété*. There is a time limit if you want to object to the amount you have to pay: either five years from the publication of the regulations, or within two years if you buy a share in a *copropriété*, but only if this is the first time it has been sold. Since the beginning of 2003, the percentages of charges and the way these are calculated have to be included in the regulations of the *copropriété*.

If you are thinking of buying into a *copropriété* be sure to look at the minutes of the last three years' AGMs at the very least.

Other Types of Common Ownership

When a piece of land is divided up into parcels and an estate – *lotissement* – is constructed, the owners of the dwellings can set up an *Association Syndicale Libre* to manage the shared spaces and equipment. The creation of an ASL is not obligatory. A *copropriété* can only be set up where the land has not been divided up.

An *indivision*, where more than one person owns a share in a property – usually through inheritance – does not come under the *copropriété* regime. For legal purposes it is considered an indivisible entity. A property company – *Société Civile Immobilière* – is not a *copropriété* either, but it can own parts of a *copropriété* and send representatives to general meetings.

FARMS AND VINEYARDS

The French government is keen to encourage foreigners to take over farms since so many French farmers are giving up and moving to the cities. Local governments in central France are particularly interested in attracting new farmers. The land and buildings are far cheaper than in the UK, but newcomers may not get a very friendly welcome from the long-established locals. There are grants available for setting up farms. The first port of call is the departmental ADASEA or *Agence Déparatementale pour l'Aménagement des Structures des Exploitations Agricoles.* See the websites www.cte.fnsea.fr/adasea/adasea.htm and www.safer-fr.com. Also see www.eurofarms.com.

It is also possible to buy a vineyard: it takes a brave person to try and beat the French at their own game, but it has been done. You should watch out for potentially useless vineyards. One Englishman was on the point of buying one in Provence when a local informed him that all the vines would have to be replanted and he wouldn't harvest a single grape for seven years.

RENTING A HOME

CHAPTER SUMMARY

○ There are plenty of hotels, *gîtes* and bed and breakfasts to stay at while looking for property.

○ It is less common to rent out properties for short periods of time than in the UK, but you may be able to find another foreigner who will let you rent their property with a minimum of formalities.

○ Estate agents – *agents immobiliers* – and specialised agents – *marchands de liste* – also have rented property available.

○ It is essential to draw up an *état des lieux*, or description, of the property on entry and on leaving, to ensure that you recover your deposit in full.

THE RENTAL SCENE

Renting rather than buying has until recently been the favoured choice of many French people. With some steep rises in the price of property, and plenty of cheap loans, the idea of buying is now becoming more popular, although there are still fewer owner-occupiers than in the UK. The most significant feature of the French rental scene, is that while there are more properties for rent than in the UK, the percentage of social housing is smaller. The previous socialist government passed a law which would require *communes* in towns with more than 50,000 inhabitants to ensure that at least 20% of principal residences are social housing. The right-wing government that came to power in 2002 is likely to shelve this proposal, which was always quite unrealistic.

Foreigners looking for property to buy are not going to remain in France long enough to qualify for subsidised rentals, and are forced to look on the open market. Rents vary enormously around the country. The highest prices are in Paris, Strasbourg, Lyon, western coastal resorts, and the Riviera. The lowest can be found in the economically depressed areas of the northwest, central and eastern France. The typical rental property is an unfurnished apartment, often in a *copropriété*. Large apartment blocks are often owned by banks or insurance companies. The main thing to look for is a *digicode* – a digital entry system, or *vidéophone*. The presence of a *concierge* or *gardien* is a great advantage. The kinds of problems found in large apartment blocks in the UK also exist on certain estates in France – the HLM. Apart from these estates with social problems, privately-run apartment blocks are acceptable places to live. In addition to paying rent, one has to expect to pay one's share of the communal *charges*. Whether you rent an apartment or a house, you will be required to take out a minimum amount of insurance: the *assurance multirisques habitation*.

For legal reasons property must be either fully furnished or not at all. A property that lacks essential equipment such as a cooker or fridge is not considered furnished. It is also illegal to rent out an apartment where the principal room has a surface area of less than 9 square metres. There are plenty of studios or *studettes* with 10 sq.m. living rooms. There should also be cooking facilities and running water. The lessor will require evidence that you can pay the rent, such as recent pay slips and bank statements. They may not agree to rent a property to you if the rent exceeds one-third of your monthly income. You will require the usual identification documents. The lessor will have a standard rental agreement for you to sign. There is a deposit to pay – the *dépôt de garantie*. Further details of property rentals will be found in chapter 12, *Making Money out of Your Property*.

Rental deposit (dépôt de garantie)

The deposit is often referred to by the French as *la caution*, but the official term is *dépôt de garantie*. The amount of the rental deposit can vary: Where a property is rented out by the month, the maximum is two months' rent. Where rented out by the year, the maximum is three months. For some dwellings, known as *logements conventionnés,* the maximum is one month's rent. Owners are required to refund the deposit within two months of the tenant leaving the property, minus any deductions for damage. Where the owner fails to restore the deposit in time, the tenant can obtain a summary judgment from a lower court obliging the owner to pay up, by filling in a simple form called a *déclaration au greffe*; should the sum be over €3,800 a hearing has to take place before a *juge d'instance* (civil magistrate). If the tenant is aware that they owe money to the owner, then they can have this taken into account by the court.

Unlike in some countries, the owner can invest the deposit as they please; the tenant does not receive any interest on the money.

Advertising

The basic term for rental is *location:* every local newspaper has a section. If you are simply looking around shops or houses, you will come across adverts *A Louer* (For Rent). Some advertisements are put up by professional agents, called *marchands de listes,* who look for tenants on behalf of owners. They are subject to the same regulations as *agents immobiliers,* who also have rental property. Many of the property websites that are given in the previous chapter under 'Advertising' have rental sections. A few are more specialised:

www.alouer.fr.
www.appelimmo.fr.
www.bonjour.fr.
www.colocataire.fr. For those looking for a shared house or apartment.
www.entreparticuliers.fr.
www.foncia.fr.
www.journaldesparticuliers.fr.
www.kitrouve.com.
www.lacentrale.fr.
www.lesiteimmobilier.com.
www.locat.com.
www.pap.fr.
www.seloger.com.

WHERE TO STAY WHILE HOUSE-HUNTING

Fortunately, France has plentiful and cheap hotel accommodation which puts the UK to shame. Starting at the top end, you could check out the website www.chateauhotels.com, or order their brochure. Naturally, the prices are fairly steep, but the locations are superb. The next step down is the organisation Logis de France (www.logis-de-france.fr), which covers hotel-restaurants in the two- to four-star category; many Brits swear by it.

If you are looking for *chambres d'hôtes* or *gîtes,* Gîtes de France dominates the market: their annual catalogue will give you places to stay anywhere in the country; see www.gitesdefrance.com. You can get in touch with owners for longer-term rentals through www.cheznous.com or www.abritel.fr (in French). For Paris try the very useful website www.paris-exchange.com. If you want to be guaranteed a personal and welcoming service, the best book is Alastair Sawday's *Special Places to Stay in France.* In spite of the over-the-top style, the places recommended are exceptional and not that expensive.

Longer stays in France can be more difficult to arrange than holiday lets. Because the French tend to stay put for years thanks to the letting regulations, it is less common to rent a place for three or six months than it would be in the UK. One way around this is to advertise on a website such as www.french-property-news.com or www.french-news.com to see if another foreign property owner will rent you their property (usually out of season) for a lengthy period, or you could offer to be a caretaker and live rent-free. You can also look around in your favoured location for a French owner who is willing to rent out for a few months. The British company French Locations specialises in lettings over three months: see www.french.locations.freeserve.co.uk.

Finally, there are youth hostels. The more remote ones are virtually empty out of season, and some managers are quite happy to rent you a room (which you will not have to share) for months at a time. The main drawback is that the buildings are not very well heated.

FORMALITIES OF RENTING

Househunters will be looking for short-term rented accommodation, but not at an exorbitant price. While long-term unfurnished rentals are covered by the 1989 laws, which give tenants wide-ranging rights and make eviction very difficult, furnished seasonal rentals, holiday homes and sub-lets are governed only by the *Code Civil*, the handbook of civil law. Such rentals are termed *location libre*. The landlord (*bailleur*) and tenant (*locataire*) can come to any agreement they wish – unless it is illegal – regarding the length of the tenancy and the conditions of payment. This can be a verbal or written agreement. The duration of the rental agreement can be fixed or indeterminate.

The main obligations on the landlord are:
- To make the property available to the tenant;
- To carry out major repairs;
- Not to interfere with the lessee's use of the property.

The lessee engages himself to:
- Use the premises in a reasonable way;
- Pay for minor repairs;
- Pay the rent and charges on time.

Tenants are liable for some repairs – the *réparations locatives*. Anything that is not a *réparation locative* is the responsibility of the landlord. One also needs to be aware of the *charges récupérables* – the costs the landlord can require the tenant to pay. These are fixed by law. These items are listed in great detail in the relevant books, e.g. *Propriétaires et Locataires: Qui Paie Quoi?* published by PRAT, and *Letting French Property Successfully*, published by PKF Guernsey.

L'État des Lieux
Drawing up a description of 'the state of the premises' is an important step

to be undertaken before actually moving into a new home. It is meant to safeguard the tenant from being accused of damage that is not of their doing, and thus unfairly being made to pay for repairs before they can recover their rental deposit (*dépôt de garantie*). It also protects the owner from having to pay for damage caused by the tenant.

Under ideal circumstances, both the lessor and lessee agree to the *état des lieux* and are both present when it is carried out. An *état des lieux* which is signed by both parties is always valid. Where one party refuses to co-operate, the other may have the *état des lieux* carried out by a *huissier* (bailiff). Where one party decides to call in a bailiff to carry out the *état*, the other party must be informed by registered letter (*recommandée avec AR*) at least seven days in advance. The costs are then split between owner and tenant. Where the *état des lieux* is carried out by an agent of the owner, e.g. an estate agent, the tenant is not required to pay any of the owner's costs.

When the tenant leaves the premises, an *état des lieux de sortie* will be carried out to determine any damage for which the tenant could be liable. In cases where a tenant leaves suddenly and cannot be traced, the owner is required to draw up an *état des lieux* immediately, using a bailiff. Otherwise, the owner should make this description on the day the tenant leaves. Where the owner has not taken sufficient trouble to carry out the *état des lieux de sortie* as soon as possible, any claims against the former tenant or their agents are inadmissible.

Model forms for *états des lieux* can be found at town halls and in some publications, such as *Propriétaires et Locataires: Qui Paie Quoi?*. Needless to say, the same form should be used for both the first and final *état*. Taking photos of the premises (conventional rather than digital, which could be tampered with) will make the job easier, if neither party objects.

The whole business of the *état des lieux* may seem an unnecessary bother, but it does have advantages for both parties. Without this description of the premises, it is assumed that they were in good condition when the tenant moved in. The tenant will not then easily be able to contest the owner's demand that the premises be restored to their original condition (*remise en état*). On the other hand, if the owner refuses to have an *état des lieux* carried out at the beginning, then the tenant cannot be held responsible for any supposed defects in the premises on their departure.

RENTAL CONTRACTS

Models of rental contracts can be found on some websites: e.g. the national information site www.anil.org, and also in *Letting Your French Property Successfully* (PKF).

Fees, Contracts and Costs

CHAPTER SUMMARY

○ It is rare for French buyers to have a survey done.
○ It is worth having the survey done by a qualified British surveyor, of whom there are several in France.
○ Reports on the presence of termites, asbestos and lead are compulsory in many areas.
○ The notaire handles conveyancing and should ensure that you have good title to your property.
○ It is simplest if all moneys payable go through the notaire's blocked account or *séquestre*.
○ Pre-contracts are binding and difficult to get out of, so think very carefully before signing.
○ There are various types of pre-contract but you may not be given the choice of which one you are asked to sign.
○ If possible have your contract checked for you by a lawyer.
○ Make sure that you understand everything in the contract; if it is in French take someone to translate for you.
○ When you move in, check that everything that is mentioned in the contract is still there.

INSPECTIONS AND SURVEYS

Having a property surveyed before you buy it is more or less a matter of course in the UK, but not so in France. Fewer than 3% of buyers have a survey done, against 95% in the UK.

The reasons for the lack of interest in surveys are cultural. In the countryside people assume that if a house looks solid it is not likely to fall down within their lifetime. French property sellers are not likely to accept a clause such as 'subject to survey' in the preliminary contract. Any general survey should be done before signing the preliminary contract. If you want to secure the property by signing a preliminary contract, but you have a concern about a specific aspect of the property, then it may be possible to insert a clause requiring further checks to be done.

There is also the fact that there is no such profession as 'chartered surveyor' in France. There is the *géomètre-expert* whose job is to calculate the surface area of buildings and land, and then there are architects who do some surveying as well. Specialised firms of surveyors are hard to find, and their services are expensive since they have to keep a whole group of different professionals working together under one roof.

The national organisation of *géomètres-experts* is promoting the idea of more widely qualified surveyors. Information can be found on www.geometre-expert.fr, or contact: Ordre des Géomètres-Experts, 40 ave Hoche, 75008 Paris; ☎ 01 53 83 88 00; fax 01 45 61 14 07; ordre@geometre-expert.fr.

Compulsory Surveys

In some respects, there is protection for buyers from '*vices cachés*' – hidden faults – in that in many areas of France an inspection has to be done for the presence of:

- termites
- asbestos
- lead paint

The inspection is done at the expense of the seller of the property, who has to present the expert's report when the pre-sale agreement is signed. The expert who carries out the work is not allowed to have any links with firms who carry out treatment for termites, asbestos or lead paint. The inspection must be carried out by a qualified surveyor, not by a salesman. There is a national organisation of experts in these three areas, grouped under www.ex pertimmobilier.com, or one can look under *expert* in the yellow pages. Note that the term *expertise immobilière* refers to valuations; people who them carry out are often notaires, not surveyors. Technical surveys come under *expertises techniques*. Some notaires have surveyors working for them.

Termites. The original law intended to protect house-buyers from insect infestations dates from 1999; it was originally intended to cover not only '*termites*' but also other kinds of insect infestations, such as death watch beetle (*grosse vrillette*) and woodworm (*petite vrillette*), as well as dry rot, wet rot and other fungi. The subsequent decree from 2000, only mentions '*termites*'. Other wood-eating insects are not covered; nor are dry-rot and wet-rot. Inspections only have to be done where a prefectural decree has been issued requiring one; much of the southwestern quarter of France comes under this category. The expert will draw up an *état parasitaire*. If the expert notices other signs of wood-eating insects apart from termites, he will mention them, but the search is basically only for termites. The report is valid for three months and must be presented at the signing of the *acte de vente*.

The worst infestations of termites are in the Landes, followed by Gironde, Charente Maritime, and Lot-et-Garonne, where over half the *communes* are affected. The Dordogne is also quite badly affected, as are parts of the Loire Valley. For maps of infested areas and those where there is a prefectural decree in force requiring a report, look at the CBTA website: www.termites.com. If treatment has to be carried out for termites, etc., check that the company is a member of the CBTA in France, or the BWPDA in the UK. The cost of the work is tax-deductible.

Asbestos/*amiante*. Under current French law the owners of *copropriétés* built before 1 July 1997 have until the end of 2005 to prepare a report on the possible presence of asbestos in their buildings. Out of the three types of asbestos, blue and brown asbestos are known to be dangerous; white asbestos is apparently harmless. Asbestos can be found mixed with cement, plaster and paint, and has been used for pipes, wall panels, floor tiles, corrugated sheeting and slates. It has also been used a lot in industrial and commercial buildings. In itself, asbestos does not present a risk unless it starts to flake and release dust.

Sellers of apartments in *copropriétés* are required to provide a report – the *constat de recherche d'amiante* – on the presence of asbestos before the *compromis de vente* is signed. They can be fined €1,500 if they do not. The technical expert who prepares the report will tell you what action needs to be taken. You should not try to remove or cut through asbestos-containing materials yourself. Enquire about asbestos before you sign any contract, whatever the property.

Lead/*plomb*. Paint containing lead was widely used until recently. It presents a danger to human health where it flakes off or turns to dust. This can cause the syndrome known as *saturnisme* in French, a retarding of the brain functions, hence one will see notices about *la lutte contre le saturnisme*, 'the struggle against saturnism'. The main victims are immigrants living in damp old houses in the big cities. One way of dealing with lead paint is to cover it up with wallpaper or wood panels; the other, far more expensive, is to have it removed entirely.

The seller of a property is required to call in an expert to prepare a report – a *diagnostic plomb* – in an areas where there is a prefectural decree in force. The report is valid for one year and is to be presented before the signing of the pre-sale agreement. Where there is no prefectural decree in force requiring an inspection, you need to be on your guard that there is no lead paint in the basement of the property you want to buy, or elsewhere; once you sign a contract you have little chance of negotiating a reduction because of the existence of lead paint, termites, or any other fault, without a specific clause to this effect.

Radon Gas. This is a colourless, odourless gas, released by the breakdown of uranium, which increases the risk of lung cancer. Unhealthy concentrations can be found in houses built on granite, such as one might find in some parts of Brittany. There is as yet no law requiring a seller to have the air tested for radon.

Boundaries. When buying a property, you need to know where the boundaries lie, otherwise you may find that you have less land than you expected. It is quite common for there to be no precise boundaries between properties. The *géomètre-expert's* job is to establish *bornes* or boundary markers. See www.geometre-expert.fr.

UK Surveyors

Since there is a gap in the market not filled by French surveyors, a number of British chartered surveyors have started business in France, mainly in the southwest where there is a lot of old property to be bought for renovation. Some are based in the UK and France, and will travel out to France for you. There are also British architects who carry out surveys, prepare applications for building permits, etc. French surveyors should belong to the Ordre des Architectes. Names and co-ordinates are given in property magazines and English-language newspapers.

Qualified Surveyors:

Nick Adams: 06 74 87 93 51; e-mail nick.adams@adamsgautier.com; www.adamsgautier.com. Mid-SW France.

Burrows Hutchison: tel/fax 02 97 39 45 53; e-mail burrowhutch@aol.com; www.surveyors-en-france.com. Brittany, Loire Valley, Vendée, Charente.

Ian Graham: 07970-923048; e-mail r-psurveys@orange.net; www.riviera-propertysurveys.com. Riviera.

Mary Hall: ☎ 05 65 24 66 46; maisonminders@aol.com; www.French-property-news.com/fpn/minders.htm. SW France.

James Latter: ☎ 02 31 90 17 70; fax 02 31 90 98 50; e-mail james.latter@wanadoo.fr; www.surveyors-en-france.com. Normandy, Pays de Loire, Ile de France.

Ian Morris: ☎ 01684-576775 (UK); tel/fax 04 67 89 43 46 (FR); e-

mail French-Surveys@ianmorris.co.uk; www.surveyors-en-france.com.
Languedoc-Roussillon, Midi-Pyrénées, Aquitaine.
Nick Norrie: 07979-771166/01869-346973; e-mail surveysfrance@subjec
t2survey.fsnet.co.uk; www.subject2survey.com.
Pierre Weingaertner: 06 60 55 29 74; e-mail expert-surveyor@wanadoo.fr.
PACA.

CONVEYANCING

Transferring the title of a property is the job of the notaire. Monsieur le
Notaire is a stock figure in French folklore; there are still very few Madame
le Notaires. The institution of notary dates back to a time when few people
could read or write and the state needed someone to certify documents as
genuine. There are a few notaries public in the UK; on the whole this is a
purely continental institution. These days the notaire is a public official,
appointed by the state, whose main function, as far as property transfers
are concerned, is to ensure that everything is done correctly, and that all
taxes have been paid. Notaries do not have a good reputation in France; as
a foreigner you are not in a strong position to obtain redress if they make
a mistake.

It is normal for the notaire appointed by the seller to handle the
transaction. They may have handled the sale of the property in the past.
The buyer is entitled to appoint their own notaire without paying any
additional costs; the two notaires share the fees between them. Although a
notaire may know a great deal about the property being sold, they are not
likely to tell you anything more than they have to. A notaire can advise
you not to buy a property, but they will rarely do so. The most important
thing to understand is that the notaire does not look out for your interests.
One of the biggest mistakes that Britons make in France is to imagine that
a notaire is the equivalent of a solicitor. If you want impartial legal advice
it is best to approach a bilingual lawyer or *avocat*, most likely one based in
the UK; some are listed below. Few notaires speak good English, and they
will be doubly cautious about giving advice in a foreign language.

The notaire's main concern is to ensure that they do not make an error
and leave themselves open to being sued. The chances of a foreigner
successfully suing a French notaire are slim. Since they also act as tax
collectors, you should be on your guard about what you tell them. A notaire
has professional liability insurance. In addition, his (or her) activities are
supervised by the departmental *chambre des notaires*. Websites of *chambres
de notaires* are given in chapter 5.

Functions of a Notary. You may be told that 'We don't use notaires for
property transactions in France.' There is some truth in this. A property

transaction can be carried out through private treaty – *sous seing privé* – but such an agreement is only binding on the parties who have entered into it: it is legally inferior to an *acte authentique* signed by a notaire. If you want a deed of sale that is binding on third parties, then the intervention of a notaire is legally necessary at the signing of the *acte de vente*. The notaire will deposit a copy of the *acte* with the deed and mortgage registry (*bureau des hypothèques*) and that is it. As a foreigner buying property in France, it would be foolish not to use a notaire, otherwise you leave yourself at risk of all sorts of unpleasant surprises later on after you have taken possession of your property.

Amongst other things the notaire will:

- Conduct a search in the land registry to see whether any third parties have any claim on the property, or the right to use the land for any purpose.
- Transfer your money via an escrow or blocked account to the seller, while ensuring that all fees and taxes have been paid in full.
- Ensure that any pre-emptive rights on the property are 'purged'.
- Witness the *acte de vente* or other agreement to sell the property to you.

PRE-CONTRACTS

Once you find a property that you like, the next step is to make an offer. Private sellers will ask for rather more than the property is worth, and you can reasonably offer 10-20% less than the asking price. In the areas where there is a lot of foreign interest and prices are rising, there is rather less scope for bargaining. Knowing how long a property has been on the market is a useful guide to bidding. The offer is made to the estate agent, or the vendor if it is a private sale. You can make a formal written offer, an *offre d'achat*, or *promesse d'achat* – promise to buy – which the seller can consider. It only becomes legally binding on the seller if he or she accepts it. You are not allowed to make any deposits accompanying an *offre d'achat*. On the whole, it is simpler to make a verbal offer, and then ask for a preliminary contract to be drawn up.

If your offer is accepted, a preliminary contract – an *avant-contrat* – will be drawn up. Although there is no legal obligation to use a preliminary contract, it is universally used. There are two main types of contract in use in France: the *compromis de vente* which is binding on both parties, and, less commonly, the *promesse de vente* (promise to sell), which is binding on the seller. The latter is commonly used north of the River Loire, including Paris. It is normal to pay 5-10% of the sale price as a deposit.

BEFORE SIGNING THE PRE-SALE CONTRACT

○ Because of the binding nature of pre-contracts, it is vital to go through the following points before you sign anything:

○ Are you sure that you can use the property for your intended purpose?

○ Have you obtained preliminary planning permission for any work you want to do?

○ Does the sale include all the outbuildings and attached land, without reservation?

○ Are the boundaries of the property clearly marked out?

○ Are there any rights of way over the land?

○ Do any third parties have any rights relating to the property?

○ Will you share property rights over boundary walls with neighbours?

○ If the property is recent, have you seen the handing-over report: the *procès verbal réception des travaux*?

○ Has planning permission been obtained in the past for any work?

○ Has the contract been checked by a qualified person?

You have the right to obtain an extract from the land registry (*extrait de matrice cadastrale*) from the *mairie* to verify the above points.

The Promesse de Vente

With the 'promise to sell' the seller commits himself to selling within at least one month, or more usually within two to three months. In return the potential buyer will pay an *indemnité d'immobilisation*, a sum that compensates the seller for temporarily taking his property off the market. The usual amount is 10% of the sale price. The *promesse de vente* can be signed in front of a notaire, or can be signed privately. The seller pays a charge of €300-€400 to the notaire. If the *promesse* is signed privately, it is to be signed in triplicate, and one copy is deposited with the *recette des impôts*. It is in the buyer's interests to sign the *promesse* in front of a notaire. The notaire will not witness a contract unless they have drawn it up themselves, or they are satisfied that it is free of flaws.

It is strongly recommended that the *indemnité d'immobilisation* be paid into a blocked account held by a *notaire,* and not directly to the seller. If you exercise your option to purchase – *lever l'option* – the *indemnité* will be deducted from the sale price. If the deal falls through the *indemnité* will be returned to you if one of the get-out clauses can be invoked within the allotted time; otherwise you will lose it outright.

Pacte de Préférence. This is a variation on a *promesse de vente*, whereby the seller promises to sell the property to the potential buyer if they choose to exercise their option on it. Essentially, it is a right of first refusal. This type of contract is becoming less popular, as it is difficult to enforce penalties in a court of law if it is broken by the seller. It is still used a lot for rental properties.

The Compromis de Vente

The more common type of pre-contract, or *avant-contrat*, also goes under the name of *promesse synallagmatique*, since it binds both seller and buyer. It is usual to pay 5-10% of the sale price as a deposit or *indemnité;* this is not the same as the *indemnité d'immobilisation* mentioned above. The deposit should be paid into a blocked account – *compte séquestre* – held by a notaire or by the estate agent.

The nature of the deposit is vitally important. If it is an *arrhes*, then the buyer can withdraw from the agreement but will forfeit the deposit. If the seller decides not to sell, then they are required to pay the buyer twice the amount of the *arrhes* as compensation. A variation on this type of deposit is a *dédit*, a specified sum that is forfeited if the buyer pulls out of the deal.

The other type of deposit, the *acompte* – which can be translated as 'down-payment' or 'instalment' – has more serious implications. In this case the sale is legally enforceable on both buyer and seller. There is no way to prevent the sale from going ahead.

The *compromis de vente* can be signed in front of a notaire, for which there is a charge. It can also be done privately – *sous seing privé* – in duplicate, and no copy has to be registered. In the former case, you have a week's cooling-off period after receiving the draft *compromis de vente* by registered post, during which you can decide not to go ahead with the deal. With the private contract, you have a week after signing during which you can withdraw without penalties.

All payments should be made by bank transfer through the estate agent or notaire's blocked account. The days when Brits paid with suitcases full of cash are long gone; there are serious risks involved in carrying a lot of cash around. On top of this, cash sales of properties will not be registered in some parts of the south of France, as a measure against money laundering.

The Contents of the Compromis de Vente

It is important to understand that signing the *compromis de vente* virtually makes you the owner of the property you are promising to buy. If you sign a *promesse de vente* the seller remains the owner of the property. Getting out of a *compromis de vente* will be expensive and difficult, so you must be entirely satisfied that the contract is worded the way that you want.

You may be asked to sign a standard printed contract by the estate agent, which will not contain the get-out clauses that you need. While there are no standardised requirements as to the content, the contract should at least contain the following:

- The *état civil* (entry in the population register) of the buyer(s) if they are already living in France.
- Details of passports, birth certificates, marriage certificates, divorce certificates.
- Official declaration as to the marriage regime, or civil partnership contract (PACS).
- A description of the property, including outbuildings.
- The address.
- The surface area of the land.
- The habitable surface area of the property (compulsory in the case of *copropriétés*).
- Proof that the seller is the rightful owner of the property, i.e. an authentic copy of the previous *acte de vente*.
- The agreed selling price of the property.
- Name of the notaire handling the sale.
- Who is to pay the notary's fees and other costs.
- Who is to pay the estate agent's commission.
- The property's unique number in the *Plan Cadastral* – land registry.
- Any equipment or fixtures included in the sale: e.g. fitted kitchens, burglar alarms.
- Results of reports on termites, lead and asbestos.
- Details of guarantees with newer properties.
- Date by which the *acte de vente* is to be signed.
- Receipt for any deposit.
- Date on which you will have the use of the property.
- Penalties if one of the parties withdraws from the deal.
- Get-out clauses: *conditions suspensives*.
- Who will be responsible for dealing with *vices cachés* or 'hidden defects'.

The last point is very important. It is necessary to determine who will pay the costs of repairs if hidden defects are later discovered. Any clause that frees the seller from having to make good hidden defects can be challenged if they have not followed the proper procedures in relation to termites, asbestos and lead. If the property is less than 10 years old, it will be covered by a *garantie décennale* – a 10-year insurance policy against major construction defects. Evidently, once a buyer agrees to take responsibility for hidden defects, then there is no further room for negotiation if any are found.

Another solution is for either the seller or the buyer to take out an insurance policy against the discovery or appearance of major faults in the building. The policy will cover you against faults in the walls and foundations for five years, in the secondary construction (e.g. roof) for three years, and in the heavy equipment (e.g. lifts and heating) for one year.

Get-Out Clauses

The negotiation of *conditions suspensives* is an area where expert legal help can be very useful. The most usual one is that the signature of the final deed is dependent on obtaining mortgage finance. This get-out clause should not be treated lightly. If you do not make reasonable efforts to obtain mortgage finance, and you are shown to be acting in bad faith, then you could lose your deposit. If you require a loan to complete the purchase, you can benefit from the provisions of the Loi Scrivener as regards get-out clauses: see under 'Mortgages' in chapter 4, *Finance.*

Other clauses can be inserted, e.g. you can make the purchase dependent on being able to sell your existing property. For example, you can put in get-out clauses such as:

- The owner has to carry out necessary repairs.
- There are no works planned by the local government that would interfere with your use of the property.
- Building permits can be obtained.
- A report on the presence of 'termites' has to be produced.
- No one is going to exercise pre-emptive rights on the property.
- The property will have no sitting tenants.
- There are no legal constraints on the owner selling the property.
- The dimensions of the property correspond to what is in the contract.

A variation on the term *condition suspensive* is the *condition résolutoire:* a clause that nullifies the contract automatically if its conditions are met.

It is easy enough to find out if the local municipality is planning to construct a main road or do some other works near your property in the near future, by asking the local *Division Départementale de l'Équipement,* the town-planning office.

Rights and Obligations/Servitudes

In between the signing of the *compromis de vente* and the *acte de vente,* the notaire has some time in which to make enquiries about the status of the property. Between one and three months can elapse between the preliminary and final contract signings; two months is a normal interval.

During this time he will be able to obtain clearance from any bodies – such as SAFER – that might have pre-emptive rights over the property that they do not intend to exercise them. He should establish that there are no mortgages still applying to the property. The seller should have made the necessary arrangements for the purging of the mortgage from the mortgage register. In the case of property that has been completed recently the seller will have to supply a *certificat de conformité* from the *mairie* certifying that all the necessary building permits were obtained when the property was constructed, and no regulations regarding urban planning have been broken. There are cases where older properties have been constructed without planning permission, so it pays to be on your guard.

The matter of *servitudes,* that is rights and obligations, is particularly important. The most common type of *servitude* is where a farmer has the right to use part of your land, or allow animals to roam on it, or to draw water from your well. Your neighbour may have obtained the right to make windows in a wall overlooking your property, a *servitude de vue.* The biggest headache can be rights of passage – *droits de passage* – which allow hunters to walk over your grounds on their way to a designated hunting area. One Brit in Provence was shocked to see a carload of men with shotguns drawing up to his house soon after he moved in, and found himself in a long legal battle to get them to take another route. No one had warned him about the existing right of way for hunters. If you see notices saying *chasse gardée* or *chasse privée* you know that there will be hunters in the vicinity. It is quite possible that your notaire will ask everyone in a village to sign a document agreeing that they have no right of way over your land.

Any *servitudes* that the previous owner of a property has entered into will have been drawn up in an *acte authentique,* signed by a notaire, and registered with the land registry. *Servitudes* can be registered for a limited number of years, or for as long as the property exists. They come with a property, and are not attached to the owner. They can work in your favour if they give you the right to use someone else's land. The seller of the property should inform you of *servitudes;* the notaire will find the details in previous title deeds and the land registry.

If you are worried about *servitudes* and other claims by third parties, it is possible to take out an insurance policy guaranteeing good title to the property for a small sum.

The Acte *Final*

After a period stated in the preliminary contract the parties will proceed to signing the final deed of sale, known as the *acte authentique de vente.* Only *actes* witnessed by a notaire are considered *actes authentiques,* legally binding on third parties.

The *acte de vente* is signed by the buyer, the seller and one notaire. If there are two notaires involved, one acting for the buyer and one for the seller, only one of them will witness the *acte de vente*. Which one depends on local custom.

You will be sent a *projet de l'acte* – a draft of the *acte de vente* – well in advance; a month is normal. This will contain much the same information as the original *compromis de vente*. You will be asked to produce originals of your birth/marriage/divorce certificates, and they may have to be translated and notarised; ask well in advance. At this point you should have made arrangements for payment of all the sums involved in the purchase, including the taxes and notary's fees. The notaire will in any case require advance payments to cover his expenses. If a mortgage is involved, the notaire will draw down the money from your bank account.

Power of Attorney

A date will be fixed for the signing. Very often there are last-minute hitches and the date may be put off. For this reason it is highly desirable to arrange to give a trusted person a power of attorney – a *mandat* – to act on your behalf if you are unable to attend the actual signing.

For practical reasons, the power of attorney is best made up in the French form. It should be witnessed by a notary, or at a French consulate. If it is witnessed by a British notary public, it will have to be legalised by the Foreign and Commonwealth Office (www.fco.gov.uk) to make it valid in France. The document should state what powers you are giving to your representative. The power of attorney allows your representative to do virtually anything you wish, and should only be given to a reliable person; preferably a close relative.

The Actual Signing

Assuming that all the loose ends are tied up, you will be invited to the signing of the *acte de vente*. This will be an interesting experience, or perhaps nerve-wracking if there are last-minute hitches. Apart from yourself, the seller and the notaire, and their clerk, there may be other interested parties present. By this point, all the necessary funds should have been transferred to your notaire's blocked bank account. There are various taxes and fees to be paid at the last minute, and you should be prepared for this. It is highly embarrassing to find that the sale cannot go ahead because you haven't left any money in your French bank account. You should also have paid the first insurance premium on the property, *before* signing the *acte de vente*. Subsequent payment dates are based on the date of the signing.

Certain items will often be mentioned in or attached to the *acte de vente* that will not have appeared in the *compromis de vente,* such as:

○ Details of mortgage loans.
○ Full description of the property, with details of previous sales.
○ Details of the insurance policy on the property.
○ The amount of Capital Gains Tax payable by the seller; or exemption.
○ Reports on the presence of termites/lead/asbestos (required in some areas).

You will be asked to confirm that all the information you have given is truthful: the *affirmation de sincerité*.

COSTS ASSOCIATED WITH PROPERTY PURCHASE

The high level of costs involved with property purchase is one of the main reasons that property prices do not go up very fast in France. The fees and taxes that have to be paid to the notaire and to the state are inaccurately referred to as *frais de notaire*, when only a part of them go to the notaire. The notaire's own emoluments are based on a sliding scale between 5% and 0.825% + TVA at 19.6%, depending on the value of the property. Some properties, so-called Group 2 and Group 3, attract smaller notaire fees, but most fall into Group 1. The notaire's fees are fixed by the state, and are not negotiable. It is normal practice for the notaire to ask in advance for more than the final bill, to cover for all eventualities, so you will probably receive a small repayment.

NOTARY'S FEES	
up to €3,049	5%
€3,049–€6,098	3.3%
€6,098-16,769	1.65%
€16,769 and above	0.825%

It follows from the above, that the notaire's fees will come to about 1% of the sale price, except for very cheap properties, where it will be slightly more.

In addition there are the *droits de mutation* – transfer taxes – that add up to 4.89% on old property, made up of:

taxe départementale	3.60%
frais de recouvrement	0.09% (2.5% of the above)
taxe communale	1.20%
	– – – – – – – –
	4.89%

The *frais de recouvrement* are the expenses involved in collecting the *taxe départementale*. TVA (Valued Added Tax) is levied at 19.6% on new properties. The same rate is applied to extensions, garages and outbuildings added on by the seller in the last 10 years, which could come to a substantial amount.

There are some other fees to be paid, namely:

- The salary of the keeper of the land registry: 0.10% of the sale price;
- costs of registering a mortgage, at about 2% (see chapter 4, *Finance*);
- costs of paper, official forms, stamps, extracts from the land register, etc. paid by the notaire.

Finally, there is the commission payable to the estate agent or *immobilier*, which can range from 3% to 10% or even more with very cheap properties.

Before signing the *acte de vente*, it is advisable for you or your representative to check again on what is included in the sale price. The contract will state whether you will have vacant possession – *possession libre* – or if there are any tenants present. In the UK it is assumed that once the final contract is signed the property is available to move into, but this does not always happen in France. If the sellers wish to remain for a few weeks, you can expect them to pay you something as compensation. The date by which the property is ready to move into should be stated in the *acte de vente*.

After the Sale

Once the *acte de vente* has been signed, the notaire has to pay all the taxes and commissions (unless you are paying the *immobilier* directly) out of the sums that you have passed over to him. The title is registered with the *bureau des hypothèques* – the register of deeds and mortgages, as well as the mortgage, if any. Eventually you will receive a certificate informing you that the title has been registered. The whole process will take some months. The original title deed – *la minute* – remains with the notaire. He is authorised to make authentic copies if necessary.

Under-Declaring the Sale Price

It was once common practice to under-declare the sale price so as to save on taxes and fees, while paying a part 'under the table', or *sous la table*. There is no advantage in the long run to the buyer, since they will be penalised with higher Capital Gains Tax in the future when they resell. The penalties for under-declaring are serious. The one way around this is for the seller to leave some furniture or other moveable goods in the property which can then be given a slightly inflated value, thus reducing taxes payable. This is acceptable to the authorities, as long as you do not go too far.

Special Procedures in Relation to Copropriétés

The subject of *copropriétés* or multiple ownership, has been covered in chapter 6, *Which Type of Property to Buy*. Apart from the asbestos report, there is also a requirement for the *copropriété* to draw up a report on the solidity of the structure, and many other aspects – the *diagnostic technique* – at the time of setting-up the *copropriété* where the property is more than 15 years old. This is a measure to prevent unsound blocks of flats being turned into *copropriétés* without proper repairs. You should also ask to see the *carnet d'entretien*, or log-book of the building, to see what kind of repairs have been carried out in recent years.

The manager of the *copropriété* will most likely be present at the signing of the *acte de vente*. This should contain details of what percentage of the communal areas belong to you – your *quote part* – and what percentage of the communal charges you will be required to pay.

Notaires as Estate Agents

It might come as a surprise to Brits that notaires also act as estate agents, especially in western France and in country areas. Many French wouldn't dream of using an *agent immobilier* to find property. Notaires keep lists of properties; they often have the best deals around. They make very good estate agents: they have the best database on property prices, they are keen to make a quick sale to get their clients out of difficulty, and they are more likely to give an honest description of the property, compared with an *immobilier*, who will try to embellish on its merits. The notaire will require a commission on the sale, but not as much as an *immobilier;* the commission is on a sliding of scale of 5% on the first €50,000 and then 2.5% above, plus TVA. One can reckon on paying 3% of the sale price.

Some properties held by notaires have 'problems' associated with them. This mainly happens when legatees find themselves in a situation known as *indivision* after someone has died, when two or more people have rights to the proceeds of a sale, and neither can sell without the other's agreement. There are also properties which have *servitudes* or obligations attached to them, e.g. someone has the right to live in the property for the rest of their life, or someone has a right to use the land or rights of way.

Few Brits deal directly with notaires: it takes a long time to set up appointments and viewings, and the notary will probably not speak much English. For this reason, English-speaking *immobiliers* and agents can seize the opportunity to act as middlemen in deals and make a handsome

profit. The only way to deal directly with the notary is to stay in the area for a few months, and have a French-speaker on hand to translate if you can't manage yourself.

Law Firms Dealing with French Property

Ideally, one will want to use the services of a UK law firm, with lawyers qualified in both UK and French law. Some firms have French lawyers working for them in the UK, or have offices in France. Such lawyers can advise one on whose name to put the property in, and what measures to take to minimise inheritance taxes. The *acte de vente* still has to be signed in front of a French notary and registered in France.

A Home in France: The Old Anchor, Moat Lane, Wingrave, Bucks HP22 4PQ; ☎ 01296-688727; fax 01296-681433; www.ahomeinfrance.com. Run by Danielle Seabrook, this company offers complete bilingual legal assistance to British residents to manage their risk in buying in a foreign jurisdiction.

Bennett & Co Solicitors: 144 Knutsford Rd, Wilmslow, Cheshire SK9 6JP; ☎ 01625-586937; fax 01625-585362; e-mail: internationallawyers@bennett-and-co.com; www.bennett-and-co.com.

Blake Lapthorn Solicitors: Holbrook House, 14 Great Queen St, London WC2B 5DG; ☎ 020-7430 1709; fax 020-7430 1709; www.blakelapthorn.co.uk. Has an in-house team of three French lawyers.

Henry Dyson, ☎ 00 33 04 93 62 70 70; fax 00 39 0184 67 24 79. International legal consultant who can advise on inheritance and SCIs.

Fox Hayes Solicitors: Bank House, 150 Rounday Rd, Leeds LS8 5LD; ☎ 0113-249 6496; www.foxhayes.co.uk. Contact Graham Platt: qualified both in Britain as a solicitor, and admitted to practise as an Avocat in France. Deals with property, company, litigation and probate.

John Howell & Co: 17 Maiden Lane, Covent Garden, London WC2E 7NL;

☎ 020-7420 0400; fax 020-7836 3626; e-mail info@europelaw.com; www.europelaw.com. Law firm specialising entirely in foreign property purchase.

Howard Kennedy Solicitors: ☎ 020-7636 1616; www.howard-kennedy.com. Large London firm dealing with the top end of the market. Ask for Anthony Slingsby.

Kingsfords Solicitors: 5/7 Bank St, Ashford, Kent TN23 1BZ; ☎ 01233-665544; fax 01233-645836; e-mail jdc@kingsfords-solicitors.com; www.kingsfords-solicitors.com. British lawyers with expertise in French conveyancing. Fixed-price property buyer's package and other services.

Liliane Levasseur-Hills: 69 Pullman Lane, Godalming, Surrey GU7 1YB. Fully qualified French notaire offering assistance with buying and selling French property, French inheritance law, and French wills.

Pannone & Partners: 123 Deansgate, Manchester M3 2BU; ☎ 0161-909 3000; fax 0161-909 4444; www.pannone.com. Contact: Lindsay Kennealy.

Penningtons Solicitors: Bucklersbury House, 83 Cannon St, London EC4N 8PE; ☎ 020-7457 3000; fax 020-7457 3240; www.penningtons.co.uk. Paris office: 23 rue d'Anjou, 75008 Paris; ☎ 01 44 51 59 70; fax 01 44 51 59 71.

Prettys Solicitors: Elm House, 25 Elm St, Ipswich, Suffolk IP1 2AD; ☎ 01473-232121; fax 01473-230002; www.prettys.co.uk.

Riddell Croft & Co Solicitors: 27 St Helen's St, Ipswich, Suffolk IP14 1HH; ☎ 01473-384870; fax 01473-384878; www.riddellcroft.com. Experienced, bilingual practitioners offer help with buying and selling property in France, rentals, tax and estate planning and wills. Can also help with property search. Contact: sue.busby@riddellcroft.com.

Russell-Cooke: 2 Putney Hill, Putney, London SW15 6AB; ☎ 020-8789 9111; fax 020-8780 1679; e-mail aldersond@russell-cooke.co.uk; www.russell-cooke.co.uk. Large firm with French law and property department, headed by Dawn Alderson, qualified in both English and French law and member of the Bordeaux bar. Bordeaux office: 42 place Gambetta, 33000 Bordeaux; 05 56 90 83 10; fax 05 56 90 83 11.

Sean O'Connor & Co: Bilingual Solicitors, 2 River Walk, Tonbridge, Kent TN9 1DT; ☎ 01732-365378; fax 01732-360144; e-mail seanoconnorco@aol.com.

Stephen Smith (France) Ltd: 161 Cemetery Rd, Ipswich, Suffolk IP4 2HL; ☎ 01473-437186; fax 01473-436573; e-mail stephen@stephensmithfranceltd.com; www.stephensmithfranceltd.com. Stephen Smith is the author of *Letting Your French Property Successfully,* published by PKF Guernsey.

Taylors Solicitors and Notaries Public: The Red Brick House, 28-32 Trippet Lane, Sheffield S1 4EL; ☎ 0114-276 67 67; fax 0114-273 1287; www.taylorsolicitors.co.uk.

Turner and Co Solicitors: 94 New Hall St, Birmingham B3 1PB; 0121-200 1612; fax 0121-200 1613; e-mail turneranco@aol.com; www.french-property-news.com/turnerandco.htm.

Thrings and Townsend Solicitors: Midland Bridge, Bath BA1 2HQ; ☎ 01225-340165 (Tony Wilkin); fax 01225-319735; twilkin@ttuk.com; www.ttuk.com. French property purchase, setting up a French business. Offices in Newbury, Swindon and Frome.

Part IV

WHAT HAPPENS NEXT

SERVICES

MAKING THE MOVE

BUILDING OR RENOVATING

MAKING MONEY FROM YOUR PROPERTY

SERVICES

CHAPTER SUMMARY

○ Gas and electricity are the monopoly of EDF-GDF, for the moment at least.

○ Mains gas is only found in built-up areas, so you will need to rely on bottled gas.

○ Wiring in older French properties is often unsafe, and is best replaced.

○ Particular attention needs to be paid to the earthing of appliances.

○ Winters can be cold in the south of France, as well as the north, so think about how you are going to heat your property.

○ If you employ domestic staff, you have to pay their social security contributions.

○ Think about security when buying properties in remote areas.

UTILITIES

Gas

In urban areas you may have access to *gaz de ville* – mains gas. Elsewhere it is usual to rely on bottled gas; it is easy to have it delivered to your home, or you can fetch it yourself. There is a choice between propane and butane. Propane is reckoned to be more suitable for properties where the temperature goes below freezing in winter; you may find yourself unable to cook in the winter if you rely on butane. Alternatively you can have a *citerne* or metal container of about two cubic metres installed on your property which is periodically filled by a tanker with liquefied gas. The *citerne* should have a meter to show how much gas is left.

Mains gas is supplied by the monopoly Gaz de France (GDF), which shares offices with Électricité de France. There is a similar payment system in place to electricity, with four different tariffs depending on how much gas you use. Bills are sent every two months. For more information see the website www.gazdefrance.com/particuliers.

Electricity

The supply of domestic electricity is a monopoly of Électricité de France (EDF), a 55% state-owned enterprise. Where your house has no electricity supply, EDF will connect you to the grid, but the price could be steep. There is a basic charge of €600 for a new connection, plus €1,500 for every new electricity pole that has to be erected. If you cannot see an electricity pylon nearby then your connection could cost more than the property itself.

EDF supplies electricity at different KvA or kilovolt amperes (colloquially kilowatts or kW) depending on customer requirements. The following will give you an idea of how many kilowatts you might require:

3kW	lighting, fridge, TV, computer, vacuum cleaner
6kW	washing machine, dishwasher, electric cooker, water heater
9kW	allows you to run two of the above simultaneously, along with the lighter appliances
12kW-36kW	makes it possible to run heavy equipment simultaneously, and electric heating as well.

The above are charged at different monthly rates. If you use very little electricity and only require 3kW then you can get a very low monthly standing charge. If you can remember not to run more than one heavy amperage appliance at a time then you may manage with 6kW; 9kW will give you more of a margin for error. If you increase the kilowattage higher than 12kW you may have to install heavier wiring to the electricity meter.

Electricity tariffs. Up until the time of writing EDF had three different tariffs for electricity: the *Tarif de Base,* the *Tarif Heures Creuses,* and the *Tarif Tempo.* Which one is suitable for you depends on how much electricity you use:

- ○ *Base:* basic tariff for 3-18 kW use.
- ○ *Heures Creuses/Heures Pleines:* allows you to benefit from cheaper electricity at periods of low demand. For 6-36 kW.
- ○ *Tempo:* for heavy users, above 9 kW. The price varies according to three tariffs, with 300 white days, 43 blue days, and 22 red days, when the price is very high. This requires installation of a system to let you know what tariff is in force at any particular time.

The *Tempo* tariff is likely to be changed as an EU court has declared it illegal. If you have a *Bi-Énergie* heating system, *Tempo* allows you to run the system on cheap electricity for much of the time, and then switch over to oil when a 'red day' is signalled. See the EDF website for current information: www.edf.fr.

Electricity meters are read every six months; bills are sent every two months, the intervening readings are estimated. If you are never in when the meter reader calls you can arrange to send readings yourself, at a stipulated time. For further information see the websites: http://monagence.edf.fr and www.mamaison.edf.fr, which has helpful tips on saving on electricity and all the tariffs.

Foreign appliances. The electricity supply is 220 volts, 50 AC, which is fine for British-made equipment, but do remember to bring enough adapters for your three-pin plugs. Otherwise you can remove the British plugs and attach French plugs. American-made equipment designed to run on 110 volts will work satisfactorily with a transformer, as long as you can adjust it to 50 AC (look on it for a label with 50/60). The transformer must be able to handle the wattage of the equipment. Clocks and other devices with timing mechanisms may not work properly. You should never try to plug an American-made appliance directly into the mains in France without a suitable transformer.

French Wiring. Brits tend to be contemptuous about French wiring, perhaps with good reason, because the British system is probably the safest in the world. One survey of French housing built before 1974 estimated that 46% of units had some deficiencies in the wiring; another survey put the figure at 96%. The main problems are lack of, or insufficient, earthing, corroded wiring, and unsuitable circuit-breakers. Because of the higher risk of electrocution, if you are taking over an older property it is a good idea to strip out the old wiring and start again. For one thing the wiring may not be able to handle heavy-amperage equipment such as washing machines and electric cookers.

The basic system of wiring in French houses is what is known as a 'spur' system rather than the ring main system used in the UK. A ring main is a way of connecting a series of power sockets. The cabling starts and ends at the fuse box, having gone through each socket on the circuit so creating a 'ring'. The 'spur' system used in France, starts at the fuse box and can either daisy chain on from one socket to the next or can branch out from a junction box. Consequently there may be more fuses that can blow if you overload the system. You may find that there are two types of socket in your house: two-pin sockets for low-amperage equipment, and two-pin sockets with an earth pin (*prise de terre*) for heavier appliances. With the latter there is a socket in the plug itself to take the earth pin.

You are best advised to employ a registered French-trained electrician (*électricien*) to do a rewiring job. It is allowable to do rewiring yourself, but the results must be approved by the electricity safety organisation, Consuel, who will issue a *Certificat de Conformité*. A professionally trained electrician's work may only be checked by Consuel one time out of ten, while a DIY job will always be checked. If the power has been cut off for work to be done, then the EDF will not reconnect your property to the grid without the *Certificat de Conformité*. If the power was not cut off, then it is up to the electrician to apply for the *Certificat*. However, EDF has the power to inspect any property where it considers the wiring suspect, at your expense. For more information about rewiring see David Everett's *Buying and Restoring Old Property in France*.

EARTH TO EARTH

David Evans, an electrician working in France, gives the following advice about earthing appliances:

Earthing electrical appliances & electrical installations is very important for the safety of all users.

The 'earth bonding' connects the earth in the main consumer box (fuse box) to the main water, gas, and/or oil inlets to the house and the main earth rod. In the bathroom all metal work (copper pipes, metal framed windows etc.) MUST be earthed and connected to the earth wire in both the power circuit and the lighting circuit. In old buildings this has not always been done and so these installations are not very safe. It is a good idea for anyone having the electrical circuits replaced in an old property they have bought to make sure that the electrician they use provides them with a Certificat de Conformité to guarantee that the electrical work complies with the French regulations. This certificate is issued by an independent body called Consuel, after they have inspected the installation and if anything is not up to the standards laid down it has to be rectified before a certificate is issued.

Types of earthing system. There are three types of earthing system in France. The earthing, or *prise de terre,* is a metal electrode running from the distribution box via a sensor to the earth. The *prise de terre* must be protected from moisture or corrosive chemicals. Electrical circuits as well as electrical appliances and conductive surfaces such as pipes should be earthed:

- ○ In the case of new-build a 100m² steel mesh (*feuillard en acier*) or cable of 95mm² can be buried in the foundations.
- ○ Where practical, a cable of copper or galvanised steel may be buried in the ground encircling the building (*boucle à fond de fouilles*).
- ○ With older buildings, one or more earth spurs (*piquet vertical*) are buried in the ground at a depth of at least 2 metres. The spur is made

of 15mm diameter copper or steel.

As part of a satisfactory system, you will need a *disjoncteur différentiel* or circuit-breaker to cut off the current in case of an incident.

Note for tenants. By all means enquire first about the wiring and electricity tariff before you move into a new home. In some buildings it may not be possible to increase the amperage of your supply. If you overload the system with heavy-amperage equipment and cause a fire or explosion, then you are liable for the cost of repairs, not the owner.

Water

The mains water supply is safe to drink, if not always that tasty. The French consume a lot of bottled mineral water, on average 100 litres per person per year.

Mains water is supplied by Générale des Eaux and other local companies around France. Lyonnaise des Eaux is well-known and owns some UK water suppliers. There have been water shortages in central and southern France in recent years during hot weather. The water supply is metered and can cost twice as much as in the UK. There will be a meter outside the property. It is essential to check the reliability of the supply if you are buying property. Water leaks should be reported quickly.

If there is no water supply to a property, one can either arrange for a connection to be made, or try to sink a well – *puits* – on the land or tap into an underground spring. The quality of the water has to be analysed first before you can use it. Water with a high nitrate content – where there is intensive agriculture – presents a real health risk. Although it is legal to sell a property without running water, it is not legal to rent one out without a proper water supply. In the case of an apartment without a water supply the situation can be even more difficult, since the local water company will only make one connection to a property.

On average, mains water costs €2.8 per cubic metre. The average person in the north of France uses 43 cubic metres a year, while on the Côte d'Azur the figure is 74 cubic metres. In Paris it is 66 cubic metres. Evidently, it is worth investing in water saving measures if possible. To find out the local price of water, and the nearest supplier look at the website www.generale-des-eaux.com.

Heating

The subject of heating is often overlooked by Brits looking at a property when the weather is sunny. Northern France is as cold as southern England in winter. You may get away without central heating – *chauffage central* – in the south of France, but you will still need some kind of heating. Upland areas, such as the Massif Central, can be bitterly cold in winter. You also need to consider whether your property is in a 'frost-hollow', which can lower the temperature by up to 5 degrees in winter.

Gas central heating is not common outside the cities; in much of France there is no mains gas supply. Although one can run gas central heating from a *citerne* in one's garden, the experience of foreign property owners has been that this is not a good solution. You are then left with a choice between using cheap rate electricity or heating oil – *mazout* or *fioul* (which is the English word *fuel*). The downside of oil is that the price can fluctuate a lot. One solution is to combine electricity and oil in a system called Bi-Énergie, which you can switch over to oil when electricity is at peak rate.

If the property is to be left unoccupied during the winter then central heating may be unnecessary. Wood-burning stoves are a good solution, with some portable heaters or oil-filled radiators as a back-up. If you are interested in using solar panels or heat exchangers, contact the energy efficiency organisation ADEME: see www.ademe.fr.

Water Heaters

One will find the same kinds of water heaters in many houses France as are found in the UK. One type that is not found in the UK is the *chauffe-eau* (short for *chauffe-eau à accumulation*) a tank with a double skin that heats water using cheap tariff electricity or gas. The advantage of the *chauffe-eau* is not only the good insulation, but also the fact that it can be located anywhere in a building as it works from mains pressure. The main consideration is to make sure that the capacity is large enough to fill a bath. A *chauffe-eau direct/à faible capacité* heats water at the point of delivery, i.e. by gas.

Septic Tanks/Fosses Septiques

The state of one's septic tank is a favourite subject of conversation with foreign residents in France. Septic tanks exist in the UK, but they are more common in France, where many properties are far from the local sewage system. There is a trend in France to connect more properties to the main sewage system, known as *tout à l'égout;* there are some costs involved for the owner. Cess pits – *puisards* – where all the waste simply goes into a hole in the ground are being phased out, and it is no longer legal to build one. All *fosses septiques* are supposed to meet a new government standard by the year 2005.

The septic tank was supposedly invented by a Frenchman, Jean-Louis Mouras in 1871, at Vesoul, although the first system was patented in the USA. The idea of the septic tank is to process the waste from toilets, and other used water, through the natural action of bacteria, so that eventually only fairly harmless water is left. All the waste runs into the first settling tank, or septic tank, where the solid matter sinks to the bottom, while scum forms on the surface. The naturally present bacteria break the waste matter down, releasing methane; so no naked flames! The remainder goes into a second settling tank, which should be half the length of the first tank, and then into a 'drain field' or system of soakaways, with a series of drain pipes or drain tiles laid on gravel. The drain pipes or tiles are perforated so that the effluent filters away into the ground. Before the effluent reaches the soakaways, there has to be an inspection chamber, or *regard de visite*. The solid matter in the septic tank has to be emptied once in a while, the so-called *vidange.* The interval depends very much on how well the tank is maintained. The local municipality will recommend at what intervals the tank should be emptied, but there are no hard and fast rules. Anywhere between two and 10 years is possible.

The soil has to be tested for percolation properties before the *fosse septique* is built. Too much clay or too much sand will have a detrimental effect on the percolation. The system must not be built within 100 feet of a well, or within 50 feet of a watercourse. It also needs to slope downwards away from the property to help the throughput. One is not obliged to use commercial preparations to maintain the bacteria level, since waste water is already full of bacteria. Bleach and other chemicals will tend to reduce the amount of helpful bacteria, but only temporarily. Cooking oil and grease are particularly noxious to a *fosse septique.*

If you are looking at country properties, make sure to find out whether there is a *fosse septique.* If there is none you will be required to install one. Since the whole contraption extends at least 70 feet from the house, it is essential to have enough land to build one. The larger your *fosse septique* the less trouble it will give you. You cannot construct anything over the *fosse septique,* and there should be a minimum of trees around it. You should also look at the slope of the land, and make sure that the water table is not too close to the surface. Generally, *fosses septiques* work better in hotter climates, which favour the breakdown of the wastes. The price of new *fosses septiques* is going up rapidly because of ever more stringent regulations. A new one, including the cost of installation, can cost €5000. For suppliers look at French property magazines, or the website www.profosse.com.

SECURITY AND HOUSESITTERS

For second home-owners, burglary is a major concern. If a property is left empty for long periods of time then there is a likelihood that professional burglars will notice. These will generally be outsiders rather than local people, who cruise around looking to see whether properties are empty. The classic tactic is to come along in a white van and remove the entire contents of the house, down to the fitted cupboards.

Your insurers will advise you on what measures to take; they may not insure you unless you have added more locks, bars and shutters to the property. The most effective method is to fit heavy shutters to all doors and windows. Even then burglars have been known to smash down doors. You are much safer if you have close neighbours, or if your property is in a terrace. Otherwise you could consider using housesitters, or professional watchmen.

Housesitters

There is considerable scope for looking after properties as a house sitter; one of the main problems for an owner whose property is in a remote area is burglary, others being possible damage from blocked gutters, burst pipes or fire, which can be avoided or at least dealt with if there is someone on the spot to deal with it.

Prospective housesitters advertise their services in the local English-language magazines, such as *The News, FUSAC* or *Riviera Times*. It would be advisable to insist on references. Your housesitter should have their own transport. From the housesitter's point of view the main drawback is isolation – this is something best done in pairs – and also the lack of income. Having a place to live is not enough: you need to be able to feed yourself, but with a bit of ingenuity you should be able to get by. Very often there will be work to do in the garden, or maintenance work, but payment is not likely to be all that generous. According to French regulations, housesitters are entitled to payment, so there is a case for asking.

There are also agencies who deal with all aspects of looking after properties. With very expensive properties, a caretaker is essential. One agency that arranges this is AzurAssistance: see www.azurassistance.com. For regular security inspections and other services, try Coastal Couriers: www.coastalcouriers.co.uk.

Employing Staff

As with most things in France there are complex regulations governing the employment of domestic staff, gardeners, handymen etc. The rules require domestic employees to enjoy the same rights as other workers. You are expected to draw up a written contract, specifying the number of hours and nature of the worker's duties. The minimum level of remuneration is determined by a *Convention Collective Nationale* for all workers employed in the home, covering cooks, cleaners, nurses, handymen/women, nannies, babysitters, governesses, butlers and chauffeurs, amongst others, but not gardeners and caretakers.

Often the person working for you will be working for other people as well, but this makes no difference to the amount of social security charges you have to pay. To take a simple example: if you pay a babysitter €100, you may pay €70 in social security charges. For anyone on an average income, half the charges, the employer's part, are refunded by the Caisse d'Allocations Familiales. Half the rest is refunded as tax credits: effectively you pay €17.50 of the total. The employer is not liable for payroll tax if they pay no more than €10,000 to domestic employees in total (this sum may change in the future).

Domestic workers enjoy the same protection as every other worker: they cannot be dismissed without a good reason. The law regarding workers who are paid in kind or partly in kind is less specific. In principle the remuneration should reflect the value of the work, but cannot fall below the minimum wage. If you take someone into your house and they do work in exchange for board and lodging then the total value has to reflect the minimum wage. If you help out your neighbour or a relative then this is not regarded as paid employment and there is no obligation to declare the work to the taxman. You should not underestimate the zealousness of the tax inspectors in tracking down cash-in-hand workers; there is a general culture of informing on your neighbours in France, and the person you employ may inform the authorities if you do not pay their social security contributions.

In order to ensure that domestic employees are correctly paid, town halls will provide a ready-made cheque-book, the *Chèque Emploi-Service,* specifically for domestic employees. The cheques have two parts: one section is to pay the employee; the other is a declaration to send to the URSSAF, the authority that collects social security contributions. By using the cheques you can meet your obligations as regards social security payments and avoid breaking any laws.

As a rule, one should be cautious about whom one employs to do work around one's property. References should be taken up. It is not easy to judge the trustworthiness of domestic staff in a foreign country. There are Britons and other English-speaking foreigners who will take advantage of the fact that they speak the same language as you to try to gain entry into your property for nefarious purposes. There was a case in the 1990s of a Dutch couple living in the Charente, who were murdered by a handyman.

MAKING THE MOVE

CHAPTER SUMMARY

- There are few formalities involved in moving household effects from the UK to France.
- If you use a removal firm, make sure that they are bonded.
- Taking your car is relatively straightforward.
- Pets can be taken from the UK into France with just a health check.
- If you want to return with your pet, you need to make your plans nine months before you leave.
- France declared itself rabies-free in 2002 but rabies will probably return.

IMPORT PROCEDURES

Import Procedures for EU citizens

As far as citizens from other EU countries are concerned, there are few restrictions on the importation of household goods and tools required for your work. Thanks to the provisions of the Single Market, which have been in force since 1993, moving from the UK to France should not be a lot different from moving from Scotland to England. If you are an EU citizen entering France with your household effects you should have your *carte de séjour* with you, and a notarised certificate of ownership of your French property. The French authorities can also ask for an official statement that you have left your town or village in your country of origin (you would have to ask your local town council for one). There are restrictions on the importation of firearms, alcohol, tobacco and medicines. The British Customs and Excise has a Helpline on 0845-010 9000 to advise you, or look at the website: www.hmce.gov.uk.

Many Brits would like to save money by transporting their furniture and other goods with a trailer to their new home in France. One should sound a note of caution here. French customs at ferry ports have the right to inspect your goods and may ask questions about where you got them from. It is best to be as polite and co-operative as possible. If the douane want to be awkward they can ask you for proof that the goods are really yours, and this does happen to a small number of Brits every year. Producing receipts for your household goods is likely to be difficult. If you are moving very valuable goods you need to have some explanation as to why, and receipts. You should on no account carry large sums of cash with you: there are regulations in force requiring you to account for movements of money over £5,000 (to prevent money-laundering).

Another difficulty can arise if the French customs think that you are carrying a large amount of one particular item, which might lead them to believe that you are actually going to France to sell the goods you have with you.

Import Procedures For Non-EU citizens

Assuming that you have registered with your commune and are planning to move your residence to France, you are entitled to import household goods, your car and tools needed for your work without paying import duty, as long as you can show that you have owned these items for over six months or if there is some wear and tear on them. Importation must take place within 12 months of your registration as resident in France. Subsequently you are not allowed to sell or otherwise dispose of your goods for a period of 12 months, unless you have the permission of French Customs. Contact your local French embassy for details.

Importing a Car

Under EU regulations, you can bring in one car for your personal use, as long as you can show that you are going to be permanently resident in France. There are few conditions attached to importing a car: you need to have the original registration papers, invoice and proof that you have paid VAT in your home country.

Once you have your *carte de séjour* you need to register your car with the local authorities. The local *préfecture* will send you a leaflet explaining how to obtain your French registration document, the *carte grise*. Generally you will need to make modifications to the headlights and the exhaust for your car to pass the required norms. France is the only country in Europe that insists on yellow headlights. Once you are resident in France you will need to change your number plates. Ask at the nearest *préfecture de police*. For further information see *Live & Work in France* (Vacation Work; www.vacationwork.co.uk).

There are very good reasons for buying a left-hand drive vehicle once you are in France.

○ The roads here are dangerous enough without having the added handicap of having the steering wheel on the wrong side.

- Having a foreign-registered car in front of your house attracts the attention of burglars.
- You run a higher risk of car-jacking if your car looks foreign.
- Spare parts for British-made cars can be very expensive or impossible to obtain.
- Most cars are cheaper in France than in the UK.

An alternative to buying a new car in France is to buy one in another EU country where prices are low, and then pay the VAT in France. There are dealers in Belgium who specialise in this kind of arrangement and who will do all the paperwork. One could also try Luxembourg or Portugal. New car dealers are under pressure from manufacturers not to sell to foreign buyers, thus, while Denmark has the cheapest ex-VAT cars in Europe, the dealers will put a lot of obstacles in your way if you try to buy your car there. You may not get the model you want, and you may have to wait a long time. You can buy through a *mandataire* or person appointed to act on your behalf.

Once your car has been delivered in France you have 15 days to pay the VAT to the *recette des impôts du département d'immatriculation* and you will then have a provisional *immatriculation*. The downside of getting a new car abroad are potential problems with the warranty in France. A Peugeot in Belgium is considerably cheaper than in France; legally, French garages are required to carry out service checks on French models. A better plan could be to buy a second-hand up-market car in Belgium, where they are very cheap, to import into France.

Insurance. If you are going to France as a visitor, you only require third-party insurance. Your UK insurance policy should provide a basic level of cover when you go abroad, but be sure to check first before you go. It makes good sense to take out additional cover, given the risks that you run in France with a right-hand drive vehicle. It is not compulsory to carry the Green Card, which simply confirms that you have third-party cover, but it may be useful.

With French car insurance it is the car rather than the driver which is insured, so you can give anyone permission to drive your car. Well-known insurers include AXA, AGF, CNP, Generali France, Matmut and Groupama. You may get a good deal if you are moving from the UK if you can convince your French insurer to take over your no-claims bonus from the UK. In France it takes up to 13 years before you get the maximum no-claims reduction of 50%, and any claims you make are heavily penalised with higher premiums. Much depends on your degree of responsibility if you have an accident. If you were breaking the law when the accident happened you may lose the no-claims bonus entirely. If you have records from the UK showing you have made no claims in the last 13 years then you should bring these with you to show the French car insurer.

REMOVALS

The first principle is to consider what the bare minimum is that you will actually need, and then try to cut it down. Using a removal firm will cost you a minimum of £600 for the areas of France close to England, and much more if you are further away from the ferry ports. Electrical equipment should function satisfactorily in France with adapters, bearing in mind the generally dubious nature of older French wiring. Household appliances are generally more expensive in France than in the UK (and far more than in the USA), but it may be simpler to buy some new items in France than to ship over old equipment which you may not be able to have repaired if it goes wrong.

With furniture, and larger items, it is worth considering whether the contents of your English semi are going to fit into a cottage in the Dordogne, or whether British-style armchairs would look good in Provence. If you plan to rent out your property in France, then it is far better to furnish it locally.

There are numerous removals firms; many advertise in the French property magazines. It is important to check that they have the necessary experience, and whether you are covered if things go wrong. Membership of the BAR (the British Association of Removers) provides a guarantee that you are dealing with a reputable company which is not likely suddenly to go bankrupt. Individuals normally have to pay the removal company up front for the removal so if you are worried about the removal company going bust or what will happen if your most precious items are damaged or lost, BAR has set up International Movers Mutual Insurance so that clients of any of the companies belonging to BAR will be compensated for loss or damage, or in the case of bankruptcy the removal will be taken over by another member company.

Companies with offices in France as well as in the UK are generally the safest bet, although they will be more expensive. The BAR can provide a list of international removers in your area and other information in return for an SAE (BAR, 3 Churchill Court, 58 Station Road, North Harrow, Middlesex HA2 7SA; ☎ 020-8861 3331; fax 020-8861 3332; e-mail info@bar.co.uk; www.barmovers.com). Removals can be done door-to-door or your possessions can be put into a warehouse in France. Charges start around £600 for three cubic metres, but the exact price depends very much on the total distance involved at both ends, and whether you are flexible about the delivery time.

Removers dealing with France include:
Allied Pickfords: Heritage House, 345 Southbury Road, Enfield, Middlesex EN1 1UP; ☎ 0800-289 229; www.allied-pickfords.co.uk (UK) www.alliedintl.com (USA).

Crown Worldwide Movers: Security House, Abbey Wharf Industrial Estate, Kingsbridge Road, Barking, Essex IG11 0BT; ☎ 020-8591 3388; fax 020-8594 4571; www.crownww.com.

Robinsons International Moving Services: Nuffield Way, Abingdon, Oxfordshire OX14 1TN: ☎ 0800-833 638; fax 01235-553573; e-mail international@robinsons-intl.com; www.robinsons-intl.com.

EXPORTING PETS TO FRANCE

Many expatriates would like to have their four-legged friends – *animaux de compagnie* – with them abroad, and in some ways this has become a routine procedure. France declared itself rabies-free in 2002 – there were no cases of rabies in the previous year – but since it borders on countries with rabies, there is the risk that the disease will return, especially from Switzerland. Before 2001 the French authorities required owners of dogs and cats coming from the UK to have their pets vaccinated against rabies if they were going to remain in one of 18 rabies-infected departments.

When you bring the animal into France, you will need a certificate of good health from a vet in the UK, acquired five days or less before you leave for France. You are limited to three dogs, of which one may be a puppy. If the animal passes through a rabies-infected country then rabies vaccination is required. If you plan to export your pet to a country outside the EU, the French authorities are likely to insist on a translation of the import documents into French, which could cost several hundred pounds. Do check on the current regulations before you plan your journey.

If you are planning to bring the pet back to the UK, it is advisable to obtain a PETS Certificate 1, together with a PETS Certificate 5, which can only be issued by a licensed veterinary inspector. The French do not require any further export health certificates.

If you want to bring in pets other than cats and dogs, there are other rules. There are no particular formalities for importing rabbits, guinea pigs and hamsters. If you want to bring in a parrot or similar you will have to swear that you are not going to resell it in France, and agree to a veterinary inspection. The local French consulate will advise you on other types of animals. The UK Department of Food, Environment and Rural Affairs (DEFRA) can provide forms for France. If you are thinking of

exporting animals other than cats and dogs the PETS Helpline will give
you the number of the section you need to call.

Planning ahead

An American couple decided that they wanted to take a St Bernard, a Yorkshire
terrier and a cat with them when they went to live in England. The regulations
make it easier to import animals into the UK if they have stayed in an EU country
first for three months, so the animals were shipped over to Paris. They hired an
English couple from the Dordogne to go to Charles de Gaulle airport to pick them
up in a van. Unfortunately, the vet in the US had given the animals their rabies
shots on the wrong day, so they could not be handed over. The officials at the
airport apologised profusely, but insisted that the animals had to remain in the
airport for another week.

Non-EU Pets

The situation for dogs coming from outside the EU changed in late
2002. From now on a blood sample taken from your pet has to be sent
in advance to a laboratory in Nancy for testing. The animal also has to
fulfil the conditions given above for UK animals. It should be stressed that
regulations change, and the best people to ask for up-do-date information
are vets or specialised pet-carriers (see below). The French government does
not make much effort to publicise the rules on the internet, and you should
not rely on what you find there. Rules frequently change in France so it is
best to make thorough enquiries before you plan to bring your pet here.

Returning to the UK

You can bring your pet back into the UK without entering quarantine as
long as you follow the rules laid down by the UK Department of Food,
Environment and Rural Affairs (DEFRA) in the Pets Travel Scheme
(PETS). Six months have to elapse after a successful blood test following
vaccination against rabies before you can get a re-entry certificate from
your vet, so you need to plan ahead. When in France you must have your
pet vaccinated against rabies annually, otherwise the British authorities will
consider it as having originated from France, and you would need to apply
for a new PETS Certificate in France. Call the PETS Helpline on 0870-
241 1710 or the Export of Cats and Dogs Section on 020-704 6347 or
look at the Website www.defra.gov.uk for further information.

If you are coming from France, take your pet to a government-authorised
vet for the necessary certificates. The animal has to be treated against ticks
and tapeworm between 24 and 48 hours before leaving France.

Useful Addresses

Dogs Away: ☎ 020-8441 9311; www.dogsaway.co.uk.

Independent Pet and Animal Transport Association: fax 00 1 903 769 2867; e-mail ipata@aol.com; www.ipata.com.

Par Air Services: ☎ 01206-330332; www.parair.com.

Pets Travel Scheme: 1 Page St, London SW1P 4PQ; ☎ 0870-241 1710; fax 020-7904 6834; e-mail pets.helpline@defra.gsi.gov.uk; www.defra.gov.uk.

Pets originating from France require a globally standardised tattoo (*tatouage*) or microchip (*micropuce*), as well as other vaccinations, if you intend to take them abroad. If you buy a dog or cat in France, there is no legal requirement to have a tattoo or microchip implanted unless you are taking them abroad. There is, however, an odd tradition in France that pedigree dogs are given a name beginning with the same letter depending on the year; if your dog was born in 1999 then the name had to begin with P. A similar tradition applies to horses.

BUILDING OR RENOVATING

CHAPTER SUMMARY

- **Local or Not?** Not using local tradesmen may make you unpopular.
- **British or Not?** There are a lot of advantages to using French tradesmen, as long as you can communicate with them.
- **Trying it On.** French tradesmen are usually honest, but will take advantage if you are not on the spot to supervise them.
- **Finding Tradesmen.** The best tradesmen are booked up for months in advance.
- **Permits.** Nothing can be done without a permit, or an exemption from a permit.
- **Outline Planning Permission.** It is necessary to obtain outline planning permission before applying for a permit.
- **Grants.** There are grants for renovating older properties, which the local mayor will know about.
- **Town Planning.** There is a limit to how much new building is possible on a given plot of land.
- **Swimming Pools.** These are a necessity if you want to make a good income from your property.

LOCAL OR NOT?

Most Britons will tell you that, while most French builders are good at their job, they are also in great demand and booked up for months in advance. In addition, many French tradesmen are used to a two- or three-hour lunch-break; they may well knock back a bottle of wine with lunch, and you will probably end up joining them. There is naturally a great temptation to bring over your own British or Irish builders who are ready and willing to get on with the job. Not using the local tradesmen, however, may create resentment and put you on bad terms with the village. You also need to consider that British builders may be quite unqualified to make repairs to traditional French buildings, and will probably only have rudimentary French. A Brit faced with repairing Norman pugging may well give up and go home.

The mayor of one Normandy village regularly organises a 'meet-the-tradesmen' day for newcomers. The local artisans line up and shake the Brits' hands one by one, as a hint that they should use their services. There are great risks involved in employing someone just because they speak English; many Brits have been the victims of incompetent or dishonest builders brought over from the UK, whose work carried no guarantees. Work done by builders registered in France has to be insured for 10 years – the *garantie décennale*. Registered French builders have gone through a long apprenticeship. You should beware of using unregistered British builders, unless you know them well, because of the insurance implications. You are 100% liable if the builder is injured, and you will not have the usual guarantee against bad workmanship. In addition you will not qualify for grants towards doing the work, and the cost may not be taken into account in reducing your Capital Gains Tax liability.

Keeping the locals happy

Two English builders set up a thriving business in Castelnau-de-Montmiral in the Tarn, working all hours of the day for British newcomers. They went off for a well-deserved week's holiday, leaving their hired cement mixer, hoist and generator in the garden while they were in England. Imagine their surprise when they returned to find their equipment at the bottom of a gorge…

All tradesmen in France should be registered with the local *chambre des métiers* and have an official business number: the SIRET. This is shown on advertisements. One will find numerous British and other English-speaking tradesmen advertising in French property magazines, many with a SIRET number, the others in the process of applying for one: SIRET *en cours*. The normal procedure is to ask for an estimate – a *devis* – from several tradesmen; the *devis* is then binding. It is essential to obtain references from builders, and ask to see photos of their previous work if possible. TVA is levied at only 5.5% on work done to restore or maintain properties more than two years old. The reduction in TVA will be reviewed at the end of 2003.

If you are having a substantial job done, involving several tradesmen, you may wish to appoint a *maître d'œuvre* to supervise the whole operation. You will need to draw up a written contract with the *maître d'œuvre*. For more information see 'New Buildings' in the chapter *What Type of Property to Buy*.

> **Dr Richard Coman, who had a property in the Vendée at one time, has the following observations on French tradespersons:**
>
> *In the beginning I made the mistake of engaging a roofer from a neighbouring village and a builder over from the UK, but the only reason I did this was because I couldn't find anyone in the village who was willing to start work. The locals want you to use local tradesmen, preferably engaging the local consortium with the chief honcho as well so there is a bit of work for everyone. Tradesmen will not do someone else's job: an electrician will not remove a piece of skirting board, because that is the carpenter's job.*
>
> *The roofer did the work while I was away. He threw down broken tiles, insulating materials and pallets all around the house and I had to clear it up. Of course the next time I saw him he had a broad beaming smile, so what could I do? If you ask them to do work while you are away they will take advantage.*

Before building work begins, you can draw up an *état des lieux*, a description of the property, in the presence of the builder so that you have some evidence if they damage trees or verges. They may not, of course, agree to this. Every foreign property-owner who has had work done by French tradesmen will tell you that they need to be supervised. They are generally very honest, but they may have assistants who are not.

There are plenty of English and other foreign builders, carpenters etc. who take advantage of the French tradesmen's lack of ambition to take work off them. English-speaking tradesmen advertise in the French property magazines, such as *French Property News, France* and *Living France.* The local English-language press also carries adverts: see *Riviera Times, Riviera News,* and *The News.* Their websites have some classified adverts: see chapter 5 for addresses.

RESTORING A PROPERTY

For many Brits, the whole point of buying in France is to find a derelict building and turn it into a des-res they can hopefully sell on. Some properties in remoter areas are put on the market by the French in the full knowledge that only a foreigner would buy them. One should be wary of getting sucked into a project which could eat up huge sums of money for little return. Doing up a derelict property can cost as much as building a house from scratch. The French admire the Brits' determination, but one should be carefully not to let them 'take you for an Englishman' or 'for a *pigeon*', another expression for taking someone for a ride. The fact that Brits tend to pay over the odds for building work might have something to do with it.

Before you buy a property for renovation, you need to have some estimates from builders as to the likely cost. It can be difficult to obtain mortgage finance if most of the money is for renovation. There is also the risk of over-extending oneself, being tempted to spend more and more on expensive features which one had not thought of at the start. This is a labour of love; if you are lucky you may sell the property for a profit to another foreigner, if you are in an area with rising property prices, but you are not likely to make the same returns you could on a similar project in the UK.

The details of property renovation are beyond the scope of this book. There are few books on the market that deal with renovation; the best is David Everett's *Buying and Restoring Old Property in France,* which is mainly concerned with restoring rather than buying. If you read French, it is worth getting *Architecture Rurale et Bourgeoise en France,* by Georges Doyon and Robert Hubrecht, a fascinating survey of traditional building techniques and terminology covering the whole of France, through www.amazon.fr. This also gives advice on how to restore properties in an authentic style.

Grants

It is worth enquiring about grants – *subventions* – for restoration. The ANAH – *Association Nationale pour l'Amélioration de l'Habitat* – has offices in every DDE – *Division Départementale de l'Équipement.* There are more generous grants available for listed buildings and buildings considered to be noteworthy because some famous person lived there. See the website: www.anah.fr. There are more possibilities if you are planning to start a business or run *gîtes,* which are listed in the following chapter, *Making Money from your Property.* Some *communes* may offer grants towards the cost of being connected up to the electricity or water supply. The *mairie* will let you know what is available.

Glossary of French Building Terms

Building has its own terminology which is generally ignored in the big French-English dictionaries. Unfortunately, there is no readily available French-English glossary of building terms on the internet. The more basic terminology is explained in the Canadian *Grande Dictionnaire de Terminologie,* available free on www.granddictionnaire.com. The best, and very extensive, work is Don Montague's *Dictionary of Building and Civil Engineering,* published by Spon, which is both French-English and English-French. Hadley Pager Info (Surrey House, 114 Tilt Rd, Cobham, Surrey KT11 3JH; ☎01372-458550) publish a range of French/English technical glossaries, including *Glossary of House Purchase and Renovation Terms* (56 pages), and *Concise Dictionary of House Building, Arranged by Trades* (256 pages).

GLOSSARY

abri	shelter
accès	access
accotement	roadside verge
adossé	backing onto
affaissement	subsidence, collapse, sinking
affaisser	subside
aggloméré	agglomerate, chipboard
agrafe	staple, wall tie, retaining clip
aiguisoir	sharpener, whetstone
aménagement	conversion, fitting out
antigel	frost protection, anti-freeze
appui	abutment, support, window sill
are	100 square metres
argile	clay
arpent	4221 sq.m.; 1.043 acres
ardoise	slate tile used in Anjou, Brittany, Ardennes, parts of Alps and Auvergne, etc.
arrhes	non-returnable deposit (pron. 'aarr')
âtre	fireplace, hearth
badigeon blanc (de chaux)	(lime) whitewash
badigeonner	to whitewash
bande de calfeutrement	draught excluder strip
bauge	clay and straw daub
béton armé	reinforced concrete
béton préparé	ready-mixed concrete
bloc à poncer	sandpaper block
boulon	threaded bolt, pin
branchement	connection, electrical lead, junction
cailloutage	pebbledash
canalisation	ducting, pipework
caniveau	road drain
chaux hydratée/éteinte	slaked lime
chaux vive	quicklime
cintré/cinglé	arched, vaulted (also slang for bonkers)
cloqué	blistered (paint)
cloquer	to set (e.g. of glue), to blister
coffrage	casing, formwork, shuttering
couvreur	roofer
crépi	roughcast rendering

cuvette	toilet basin, bowl
débit	discharge, yield, debit
déblayage	excavation
disjoncteur	circuit-breaker
écrou	nut
écrou à oreilles	wing nut
encastré	embedded, flush, built-in (e.g. cupboard)
enduit	rendering, coating
entretien	maintenance
équerre	set-square, angle-bracket
espagnolette	shutter bar; shutter bolt
essente	wooden shingle, used in Alps, Vosges
étagère	shelving
éverit	Everite; white asbestos
fibre de verre	fibreglass
flotteur	ballcock
foreuse	electric drill
fossé	ditch
galet	pebble, cobble
gazon	turf
gond	hinge
gouttière	gutter
gravier concassé	gravel
haie	hedge
hectare	2.471 acres; 10,000 sq. metres
isolation	insulation
installateur	fitter
lambrissage	wainscoting, pannelling
latte	batten, lath
lauze/lave/platin	thick stone slate, used in Auvergne, Alps, Burgundy, Manche, Anjou
lavabo	wash basin
lime	file
lucarne	dormer window
madrier	massive beam
mastic	mastic
mazout	heating oil
menuisier	joiner, carpenter
moellon	quarried stone
moellon brut	rough stone
moquette	fitted carpet

moulure	moulding
nappe phréatique	water table
nivelle	spirit level
nivellement	levelling
norme française	French standard
ossature	framework
panne	pantile; also mechanical breakdown
panneau de plâtre	plasterboard
parpaing	breeze block; block exposed at both faces of a wall
pignon	gable
pignon à gradins	Flemish-style stepped gable
placoplâtre	plasterboard
plafond suspendu	suspended ceiling
plafonneur	plasterer
plâtrier	plasterer
plombier	plumber
ponceuse	sander
poteau	post
poutre	roof beam
poutre apparente	exposed beam
poutrelle	smaller roof beam
rabot	plane
ramoner	to sweep a chimney
ravalé	resurfaced, newly rendered
ravalement	resurfacing, rendering
remblai	embankment, hardcore
remise	storeroom
rive	edge of roof or panel, riverbank
sable	sand
scie	saw
serrure	lock
souche	chimney stack (visible part)
stère	One cubic metre
tamis	sieve
tapisser	to wallpaper, upholster
tapisserie	wallpaper, wall-covering, tapestry, upholstery
tôle ondulée	corrugated steel sheet
tôle zinguée	galvanised steel sheet
tondeuse	lawnmower
torchis	cob, wattle and daub

tournevis	screwdriver
trappe de visite	inspection hatch
trop-plein	overflow pipe
tuile	flat tile in baked clay, used in Burgundy, Ile-de-France, Normandy, Nièvre, Dordogne, Champagne, Loiret
tuile canal	Spanish-style pipe tile
tuile faîtière	ridge tile
tuile flamande (panne du nord)	S-shaped Flemish pantile
tuyau	pipe, tube
vanne	valve
vernis	varnish
vilebrequin	brace and bit
voyant	inspection window
zingué(e)	galvanised

Builder's Suppliers

There are plenty of do-it-yourself shops, just as in Britain. The best-known are Castorama, Leroy-Merlin and Mr Bricolage. The main drawback is the terminology, which can make it a laborious task getting what you want. Islay Currie, of Currie French Property Services, has the following story:

> *I was fairly new to building in France. I went into a builder's shop and spent an hour and a half explaining all the different stuff I needed, like left- and right-threaded joins and so on. The assistant patiently went back and forth showing me everything they had. As I was leaving, he said 'Have a nice day.' 'So you speak English, then', I said. 'Of course', came the reply, 'I lived in New York for 14 years. But, you know, this is France, so you have to learn to ask for things in French.'*

BUILDING PERMITS

Planning permission – the *permis de construire* – is needed for most altera-tions to property; even if you do not require a PC, you will need to enter a declaration that you are exempt. A change of use, or any work that will alter the external appearance of the property first requires a *certificat d'urbanisme*, or outline planning permission, which is treated below.

The first rule to remember is that if your restoration or building work cover more than 170 square metres – this is the total floor area, whether one or more storeys – you have to have architect's plans drawn up. It is not unheard of for owners to try to bribe architects to sign plans that they have made themselves. The second rule is that you cannot build anything within 3 metres (10 feet) of a neighbouring property, or half the height of a neighbouring wall if it exceeds 6 metres. Another thing to remember is that water from your house cannot run on to your neighbours' land.

It is not necessary to enter the application for the PC yourself; your architect or *maître d'œuvre* or your representative (*mandataire*) can do this for you, but you are ultimately responsible if the right PC has not been acquired first. The forms you need are held by the *mairie*; they are exactly the same throughout France.

Calculating the surface area of the works is a complicated process. A distinction is made between the *surface hors œuvre brute* or *SHOB* (the total surface area including cellars and roofspaces and the thickness of the walls, but not including inaccessible flat roofs or terraces at ground level), and *surface hors œuvre nette* or *SHON,* the surface area used for deciding whether you need a PC or not, which allows you to subtract some surfaces according to complicated formulae. If you are unsure about the surface area concerned you can consult an *architecte conseiller* working for the municipality or other state body, free of charge.

It is not always necessary to get a PC for minor work to the house, nor for some smaller external constructions, but it is necessary to enter a *déclaration de travaux exemptés de permis* for any building work that is exempt from a PC. The authorities have one month to respond with any objections, otherwise you are free to proceed. You can ask for an *attestation* that no negative decision has been given if you want to be on the safe side. Any work which involves a change of use or increases the number of rooms in the house (e.g. making a workshop or converting a loft into a bedroom) and thus affects the taxable value of the property, does require a PC. Changing windows or installing double-glazing will require a PC. Knocking out walls always requires one; putting in new internal walls does not.

Items that are exempt from the PC include covered swimming pools, terraces and walls under 2 metres, or any structure with a surface area of less than 20 sq.m. Some work requires another form, the *déclaration préalable de construction,* a statement that you are beginning work. This includes greenhouses, uncovered swimming pools, rendering, and minor alterations to your house. You will in any case still have to submit plans.

It is easy enough to go to the local office or *Sub-Division de la Direction d'Équipement* (there are several in every *département*) to get an opinion about what type of PC you need. The opinion of a local builder is not always reliable: the owner of the building is liable not the builder. The authorities are tougher about PCs in some *communes* than in others.

Troubles with the *tout à l'égout* (Richard Coman):

For about 10 years we were fine with our fosse septique *but then we were told by the commune that we had to be on the main drainage system, the* tout a l'égout. *The contractors had to use dynamite because the ground was solid granite under three inches of soil. Then the next-door neighbour found cracks in his walls and accused us of having planted trees too close to his house. I had got a* pépiniériste *(nurseryman) to plant some trees along our boundary 14 years earlier, but he had failed to observe the regulation that says you can't plant trees within three metres of an adjoining property so I had to ask him to come and dig the trees up. On top of all that the contractors who dug the sewage trenches left a huge mound of granite chippings on my land. I went to see the* maire *and got a London firm of translators to write a business letter in French, at great expense, but to no effect. Finally I had the notaire threaten legal action, which did the trick, but of course I had to pay the legal fees.*

The request for the PC is sent to the *mairie* by registered letter (*recommandée avec demande d'avis de réception* (colloquially *accusé de réception* or AR)*, or it can be delivered by hand, and you will receive a receipt (*décharge*). Your request has to be dealt with within two months from the date on your *avis de réception* or *décharge*, a period known as the *delai d'instruction,* unless the authorities get a court order giving them more time. The authorities are required to send you a *lettre de notification* with your application number. If the authorities fail to give a decision within two months then it is assumed that the PC has been granted automatically, a PC *tacite.* The *mairie* will handle the application in urban areas, or pass it onto the relevant intercommunal authority. A printed version of your application will be posted on the wall in the *mairie* with your name and address, so that anyone can raise objections if they wish.

Several bodies are involved in granting the PC. Apart from the *maire,* the *conseil municipal* and the *Direction Départementale de l'Équipement* have to give their approval. If you are carrying out work in an area subject to flooding, namely the Loire Valley or near the Rhine, a state-appointed engineer has to assess the application. If you are building within 100 metres of a cemetery the *maire* has to be consulted. The *Direction Départementale des Affaires Sanitaires et Sociales* and the *Sous-Commission Départementale d'Accessibilité des Personnes Handicapées* also have to give their approval if you are building or converting property for holiday complexes. The number of bodies that have to give their approval depends on the nature of the work.

Special rules apply if you are carrying out work on or next to or within view of a listed building or site. The authorities have four months after acknowledging receipt of your application to consider the case. You should never assume that you have tacit approval where listed buildings are concerned, even if you hear nothing from the authorities. If the application is passed to the national ministry of public works they are not necessarily required to give you any response. If you are working within 500 metres of a listed site, you may be told to use only certain kinds of building material, which can make the work far more expensive.

Documentation for PCs

The documents and plans that are required are listed on the PC application form. These will include:

- A plan of the piece of land.
- A site plan with the proposed work with a scale of between 1/100 and 1/500, showing the orientation and the property.
- The *volet paysager*, two photographs of the property, from close up and distance.
- Plans of different floors of the property.
- Decisions regarding rights and obligations (*servitudes*).
- Documents concerning grants.

Don't forget the *Permis de Construire*
The seriousness with which PCs are viewed is illustrated by the case of Christian Pellerin, a property developer who built a villa with a surface area of 1600 sq.m. on the Cap d'Antibes without ever applying for planning permission; he even went as far as to build some of his villa underground to fool the authorities. Ten years later (in 2002) he was required to demolish the whole thing and pay the costs, although he had already sold it on to someone else.

As in the UK, it is possible to begin your building work before obtaining a PC, on the understanding that a PC is generally granted for the type of work you are undertaking, but as an outsider it pays to be doubly careful about following the rules, even if you risk making life more difficult for yourself.

Types of building permits

- *demande de permis de construire* request for a general-purpose PC.
- *demande de permis de construire une maison individuelle* request to construct or modify a private dwelling, where works are not exempted from PC.
- *demande de permis de construire modificatif* request for minor

modification to an existing PC; for major modifications an entirely
new request for a PC must be entered.

○ *demande de permis de démolir* request for permission to demolish.

○ *demande d'autorisation de coupe ou d'abbatage d'arbres*   r e q u e s t
to cut back or cut down trees.

When the work starts you enter a *déclaration d'ouverture de chantier* (declaration the work has begun). The authorities have the right to inspect the
building site to ensure that you are respecting the terms of the PC. The PC
has to be displayed on a *panonceau* or panel at the entrance to the building site so that third parties can enter objections if you have failed to take
their interests into account when you applied for the PC. After building
work is completed you have 30 days to enter a declaration that you have
done the work according to the terms of the PC *(déclaration d'achèvement
des travaux)*. The authorities can inspect the work; they will then send a
certificat de conformité within three months. No *certificat* needs to be issued
if the work has not created any new surface outside the *surface hors œuvre
brute* or SHOB (see above).

Constructions requiring a PC may be liable to local taxes, the *taxe locale
d'équipement* and the *taxe d'urbanisme*. The amount will be entered on the
PC; if no amount is given you are not required to pay.

The Certificat d'Urbanisme

Prior to applying for a PC, you need outline planning permission, or the
certificat d'urbanisme (CU), which guarantees you a PC if you choose to
apply for one within one year of a positive response. Anyone can apply
for a CU, even before they have bought a property or piece of land. The
application for the CU – *demande de certificat d'urbanisme* – requires plans
and maps of the property, in four copies, and a description and drawings
or photos of the work you propose to do. You can expect a decision within
two months.

Minor work that does not affect the external appearance of the building,
and does not constitute change of use, or a change in taxable value, will
only require you to obtain a *note de renseignements d'urbanisme*. The
notaire who holds your title deeds should have a copy. Otherwise you can
apply for one at the *mairie* and you should get it very quickly.

NEW BUILDINGS

Most *communes* have a *Plan Locale d'Urbanisme (PLU)*, formerly called a
Plan d'Occupations des Sols (POS), which states how many buildings with
how much floor area can be put up on a certain piece of land. Each area of
the *commune* has a coefficient – the *Coefficient d'Occupation du Sol (COS)*,

a number used to calculate the maximum SHON or floor area (defined above) that can be constructed. If the COS is 0.40, then it allows you to build 200 sq. metres of SHON on a 500 sq. metre piece of land. In some cases you will be allowed to build more, but you will then have to pay financial penalties.

Assuming that your land is close to existing water mains, electricity supplies and access roads, you can apply to the local *mairie* for a specific permission to build on it, the *Certificat d'Urbanisme* or CU. This gives you permission to put up a certain type of building with a maximum surface area, and other specifications. The CU is delivered within two months of the application, if it is not turned down. You then have one year during which you are guaranteed a *Permis de Construire* for your project. Even then this may not be enough. If you are planning to construct something close to a listed building, then a departmental official, the Architecte des Bâtiments de France has to be involved. They may add more conditions to the permit, such as the type of building materials you can use, which will make the job far more expensive.

For further information on new houses, see chapter 6.

SWIMMING POOLS

A swimming pool (*piscine*) is not just a luxury in France: if you are buying a property of a substantial size to rent out to an up-market clientele then it is virtually a necessity, whether you are on the French Riviera or in Normandy. The presence of a swimming pool is the most crucial factor in determining the pulling-power of your property, and installing one is an investment well worth making. It is important to bear in mind that a swimming pool entails substantial running costs; £1,000 annually for a minimum £10,000 pool is a fair average.

Deciding on what kind of swimming pool to install is not an easy decision. The three main possibilities are the pre-fabricated fibre-glass pool, a galvanised steel construction with a vinyl liner, or reinforced concrete. The first crucial point is to determine the water table of the land. If the pool bottom is below the water table then you will first have to install pumps to drain the land before you can install the pool. Should it rain heavily you will need to pump out again, otherwise your pool could literally float away, or, if it is made of concrete, it could break up. In any case, it would be unwise to empty your pool in this kind of situation without expert assistance, since the weight of the water could be keeping it anchored to the ground.

> **At first sight it might seem simple to go to a French contractor to build you a pool. Lynda Durr, of Anglo-French Homes, who has had several pools installed in the Orne and Calvados, has the following cautionary tale:**
>
> *We went to one of France's best-known swimming-pool companies, and paid 70% of the price up-front when we signed the contract. In October the materials were delivered and the contractors came in, dug the hole and reduced the garden to a bog. But then the hole filled up with water. During the following five months, we telephoned weekly, eventually got them to pump in the concrete, but due to the water table it just broke up. The company delivered the materials and had a sub-contractor do the cement work, but then it cracked and they just left it. They had not reckoned with the fact that there was a spring on our land, and that the water table is very high in Normandy in any case, so we were left with a hole in the ground rapidly filling up with water. In the end we had to employ a local engineer to sort out the mess. The original contractor churned up the land with their tractor and there is still a huge pile of earth. It is not a good idea to pay up front; they will cash your cheque the day the equipment arrives. The sub-contractor we dealt with actually came and took back the coping stones* (margelles) *after they had abandoned the job. Rule number one is to ask around local swimming pool contractors and find out who has a bad reputation!*

A concrete construction consists of a double layer of blocks with steel reinforced concrete inside. Another possibility is a prefabricated fibre-glass pool which is then back-filled with pea-shingle. The Oxford-based company, Bakewell Pools, can arrange for the pools to be delivered anywhere in France (they are manufactured in Dijon), for a uniform price; the installation is then DIY or with the help of local contractors. Another possibility is to bring over a pool from the UK, in the form of metal sheets with a vinyl liner. The pool can be flat-packed and loaded onto a trailer. The advantage in this case is that the pool can be erected above ground, or even on top of a building, avoiding the water table problem. There is also the possibility of a smaller plastic pool of which there are plenty available in France.

France has numerous swimming pool manufacturers; it is a matter of whether you feel comfortable dealing with French contractors, or would rather deal with a British-based company. If you want to know more about French pools, there is a dedicated magazine: *Techniques Piscines* (www.techniques-piscines.fr).

Construction of swimming pools up to 20 sq.m. does not require a *permis de construire* but you must apply for an exemption from the PC, on form PC156. The local mayor or town planning authority may raise objections, so it is essential to find out first what you can do. In principle, the authorities are not allowed to stop you from building your pool. An experienced swimming pool contractor will be able to advise you on the procedures.

You are not allowed to build a swimming pool within view of a road, as the sight of scantily clad swimmers could cause a traffic accident. There is also a rule that you cannot build anything closer than 3 metres to someone else's property or boundary, or half the height of the adjoining wall if this exceeds 6 metres.

Useful Addresses

Bakewell Pools: 38 Bagley Wood Rd, Kennington, Oxford OX1 5LY; ☎ 01865 735205; fax 01865 327003; e-mail bob@bakewellpools.co.uk; www.bakewellpools.co.uk.

Christal Pools: 139 Enville St, Stourbridge, W. Midlands DY8 3TD; ☎ 01384-440990; fax 01384-441887; e-mail sales@christalpools.com; www.christalpools.com.

Dominipech: Prayssas 47360; tel/fax 05 53 95 98 62 (F) ☎ 01763-261584; fax 01763-263359 (UK); www.french-news.com.

Eausparke: La Bidonne, St Rémy-sur-Lidoire, 24700 Montpon; tel/fax 05 53 82 06 39; Mobile 06 07 50 37 16; e-mail alan@eausparke.com; www.eausparke.com. Contact Alan Sparke.

MAKING MONEY FROM YOUR PROPERTY

CHAPTER SUMMARY

○ **Bed and Breakfast.** The whys and wherefores of *gîtes* and *chambres d'hôtes*.
○ **Publicity.** Advertising your bed and breakfast can take up 15% of your income.
○ **Grants.** It pays to look for grants if you are starting a bed and breakfast.
○ **French Tax.** You are given a choice of how to be taxed on your income from bed and breakfast.
○ **UK Tax.** You are required to declare French rental income to the UK tax authorities, even if you pay tax in France, if you are UK tax-resident.
○ **Letting.** Drawing up the right kind of contract is vital to protect your interests.
○ **Rights of Owners.** It is important to be clear about your obligations and rights as a landlord.
○ **Starting a Business.** There are plenty of incentives to start a business in rural France, but you are required to go to a training course first.
○ **Selling On.** It is best to try to sell to other foreigners, who will give you a better price than the French.

BED AND BREAKFAST/GÎTES

For many Brits the best, or only, way to make a living in France is to rent out rooms in their property, either as *chambres d'hôte* (bed and breakfast) or as *gîtes* (basic self-catering accommodation). French rules state that if you have more than a certain number of rooms or *chambres d'hôte* in your property, then you are actually running a hotel and will therefore be liable for VAT and other paperwork. For the Dordogne the maximum number of rooms is five, but the number varies from region to region. The alternative to bed and breakfast are *gîtes:* the word originally meant a basic dwelling, but is now applied to any kind of self-catering lodgings. *Gîtes* are less lucrative than bed and breakfast, and it is reckoned that you need space for at least 15 people to make a living from them.

It is important to note that *chambres d'hôte* and *gîtes* come under a legal regime relating to farms: the original concept involved farmers letting people stay with them to make a bit of extra money. Before you can buy a farmhouse to make it into *chambres d'hôte* or *gîtes* the local farmers' co-operatives or SAFER have a right to make an offer on the property; although this practically never happens, it does make the buying process a little more uncertain. It is up to the notaire to contact anyone who has pre-emptive rights to make sure that they do not intend to exercise them.

Before you even consider buying property to let out furnished, you must be aware that it is not possible to rent out furnished property in *communes* with over 10,000 inhabitants if you are classed as a professional landlord, i.e. the majority of your income comes from rentals, or where rental income exceeds €23,000 a year. This restriction can be waived where a property is regularly let in a tourist area. You should make sure that you do not fall foul of this rule before you do anything else.

Before buying a property with a view to renting it to holiday-makers, you need to make a hard-headed analysis about the attractions of the place:

- Is the place easy to get to?
- Are there any cultural attractions nearby?
- How far is it from the sea/mountains/lakes?
- How will it look in a photograph?
- How much income do I need to make it viable?
- How many weeks of the year do I want to use it myself?
- Can I get a grant to renovate the place?
- How much will it cost to furnish?
- Can I install a swimming pool?
- Are there any shops nearby?

Making a success of *chambres d'hôte* requires a willingness to open your home to outsiders, and to be genuinely hospitable at all hours. There is no requirement to supply evening meals, although it is a plus point in country areas, where your guests may have to go a long way to find a restaurant. If cooking is not your forte, you might be best advised to have your *chambres d'hôte* near some restaurants. Not supplying dinners will cut down on your potential profit. Installing a swimming pool is the easiest way to maximise your takings, but not every property is big enough or suitable for one.

The *gîtes* business is rather different from *chambres d'hôte*. All that is needed is someone to handle the changeover between guests, and to see that they have everything that they require. There is also cleaning, of course. There are many agencies who will deal with the whole process but you will need to pay them 25% of your letting income. The organisation Gîtes de France is well-known in the UK, but it is not universally popular with foreign owners in France, who consider that it attracts too many undesirable customers. It is never that easy to accept complete strangers staying in your house and maybe doing damage to it.

Running *gîtes* is a very seasonal business: the core months are July and August. Often the rooms will be unsuitable for use in cold weather. It is a good idea to consider supplying some added services, such as sport facilities, rented bicycles or internet access. Giving your *gîtes* some kind of ecological theme can attract more customers.

Furniture and equipment for holiday rental property or *gîtes* needs to be adequate but not too expensive, since there will inevitably be breakages. It is best to buy plain local furniture that fits in with the surroundings. Older French houses tend to be dark and badly lit by British standards; holidaymakers prefer bright, light colours. It is sometimes suggested that you leave some food for the arriving guests. Any perishables, such as flour, rice, or porridge, will attract insects.

The English estate agency Jacwood Estates French Properties (2 Warwick New Road, Leamington Spa, CV32 2JF; ☎ 01926-883714; fax 01926-883714l; e-mail jacwood @compuserve.com) specialise in *gîtes* and holiday rental properties and also run a one-day course on 'How to Buy and Run a Gite Complex in France'.

Grants

Before you do any work on a property, or even buy it, look into the possibility of applying for grants for the building work. Grants for *gîtes* are distributed by the local Conseil Général – the departmental government – through Gîtes de France, which is organised on a regional basis. The amounts available vary considerably. If you are lucky Gîtes de France may match the amount you spend. One British owner in Normandy who had spent €3,600 on conversion work was told by Gîtes de France that the work couldn't possibly have cost that little and was given €4,500 in matching funds. In other areas, the *département* may have little money to hand out.

There are conditions attached: you have to agree to allow Gîtes de France to handle the letting and publicity for 10 years during the summer in return for a cut of your takings of some 15%. It has the final say in what kind of facilities your *gîtes* will have, and grades your premises in its catalogue with one to three *épis* or wheatears. If you sell the property within 10 years then the grant must be returned.

There are plenty of other organisations that can hand out grants, starting with the European Union. The most important person to talk to is the local mayor, who not only knows about possible grants, but also has the power to approve building permits. Some grants are handled by the local *Chambre de Commerce,* who will be very pleased to help you. Because of the very high unemployment in country areas, any kind of business initiative is viewed very favourably, but you should have the right people on your side first. You should also contact the local *Office du Tourisme* or the *Syndicat d'Initiative,* whose function is to promote all kinds of small businesses and investments as well as tourism. If you are buying a listed building or one with special historical associations, there will be more generous grants available, but any renovations will be subject to more stringent requirements. Whatever kind of renovation you plan to do, all the plans and estimates must be approved first before any work is started, otherwise you will not receive the grant.

Publicity

Some foreign owners find the demands of Gîtes de France intolerable and try to find other ways of publicising their *gîtes* or *chambres d'hôte.* There are other organisations that will handle your publicity, notably Chez Nous in the UK, but whoever you deal with you will have to pay a percentage of your takings. The alternative is to sign up with a website or advertise in UK magazines and newspapers, or even in local shops. If your *chambres d'hôte* are outstanding then you might be taken up by a specialised catalogue, such as Alastair Sawday's *Special Places to Stay in France,* but few qualify for this kind of honour.

Other organisations include:

www.abritel.fr. A French site.
www.chateauxandcountry.com. Specialises in châteaux.
www.cheznous.com
www.dordogne-vacances.com
www.holiday-rentals.co.uk
www.villarama.com.

Taxation and Bed and Breakfast

If running *chambres d'hôte/gîtes* is your full-time occupation, and your turnover is under €76,300 annually, then you will qualify as a *micro-entreprise.* Capital gains are not included in the above figure. You do not have to set up a business structure or pay TVA. The simple solution is to be taxed under the *Micro-BIC* regime. Your taxable income is your turnover minus 72%, so you are taxed on the remaining 28% (on 2002 income). This regime is not obligatory – you can choose to be taxed on your real income (*régime réel*) – and it is not necessarily favourable to the taxpayer. You will need to keep a record of all your expenses and income, in a standard daybook, but you do not have to present full accounts at the end of each year. On the tax return No.2042C you simply enter your total turnover, and the type of services supplied at different locations.

If the net income from rentals exceeds €23,000, or constitutes more than 50% of your household income, then you are considered a professional landlord; you will be required to register as a business and you will pay higher social security taxes on the income. If the property is sold the capital gains will be treated as business rather than private gains. Non-residents can be taxed under the *Micro-BIC* regime, and are then taxed at a flat rate 25% on the net rental income.

It is a moot point whether you will be liable for the *taxe professionnelle* if you rent out *gîtes* and *chambres d'hôtes*. There are three cases where exemption may be granted by the local administration, namely:

- ◐ The renting out of *gîtes* for six months or less per year in a principal or secondary dwelling.
- ◐ Premises classed as 'furnished premises for tourists' which form part of your principal dwelling.
- ◐ The renting out of any part of a dwelling, not covered by the former.

There is no certainty that you will receive this exemption; it depends on local practice.

If your household's net assets exceed €720,000 then you will be liable for wealth tax: ISF. It may be possible to have assets that you need to run *gîtes* or *chambres d'hôte* exempted from wealth tax.

If you rent out furnished property then you are considered a *loueur en meublés* by the taxman. Your guests are considered tenants, and you become liable for a tax that was once known as the *droit de bail* (letting tax), but is now called the *contribution sur les revenus locatifs* (CRL). The name has changed several times recently, and many still call it the *droit de bail*. If you come under the *Micro-BIC* regime, the basis of calculation is the net income exceeding €1,830 attributable to rentals. The tax is only levied on properties over 15 years old.

You should consider all the possibilities for tax deductions. If you have taken out a loan, the interest may be tax-deductible. The local tax office or an accountant will advise you. For further information on taxation of rentals, see *Letting French Property Successfully,* by Stephen Smith and Charles Parkinson, published by PKF Guernsey.

RENTING OUT

Short-Term Letting

Many Brits only rent out their second home occasionally to people they know, or privately through placing small ads in the UK. Short-term lets of holiday homes come under the *Location Libre* regime, which protects the owner as long as they observe certain conditions. If the right conditions are not observed, and the tenants refuse to leave the property, there will be major legal costs involved in evicting them. Amongst other things:

- The property should be fully furnished.
- The rental is for no more than three months.
- The tenants have a principal residence elsewhere.
- The property is only to be used for holidays.

It is advisable to draw up a written contract – *contrat de location* – which includes an inventory of the contents of the property, the *état des lieux*.

You may prefer to engage a local agent to handle the rental of your property. They will take about 25% for managing the rentals. The main consideration is to make sure that the agent is actually handing over the money to you from rentals. It is a good idea to install a telephone in the property that will only take incoming calls, so you can check up if there is someone actually staying there. There are other drawbacks in terms of undesirable tenants trashing your place or upsetting the neighbours. All these aspects have to be covered in letting contracts.

Eric Farlow tried renting out his property in the Cévennes with rather mixed results:

The whole thing has been a bit of a disaster. On the first occasion I rented out the property to a British couple, I got a phone call from a distraught wife. Apparently the local gangster/ladies man had taken a liking to her, and when she rebuffed his advances, had set fire to the couple's car. On another occasion the people I rented the place to left it in a terrible mess. These days I let friends use it, but I've gone off trying to rent it out.

The number of weeks you can expect to rent out a property depends on the climate, and the presence of a swimming pool. Except in the south of France or Paris, the letting season is not likely to cover more than 32 weeks. The core letting season is only July and August; most French take their holidays in August. This should be taken into account when you buy a property where the income is a significant factor in your decision.

Taxation

If you are not tax-resident in France, letting income from French property still has to be declared to the French tax authorities by April 30 of each year, on the usual income tax forms: No.2042, and No.2042C (specifically for rental income). These are sent to the Recette des Impôts des Non-Résidents, 9 rue d'Uzès, 75094 Paris Cedex 02. You can choose to be taxed under the *Micro-BIC* regime, explained above, in which case you will receive a flat-rate deduction of 72% from your gross letting income, which also includes an amount calculated on the basis of how much you have used the property yourself. The net letting income is taxed at a flat rate of 25%, unless the income is very small. You should declare your rental income to the UK taxman, and you will have to pay the difference between the 25% tax in France, and higher rate tax in the UK if it applies to you. You may be able to obtain tax relief on the mortgage interest from the UK taxman.

You can also opt to be taxed under the *'régime réel'* in which case you deduct your expenses, mortgage interest, and 4% annual depreciation from your gross income – *pro rata temporis* – to arrive at your taxable income. The *régime reel* requires you to present a lot more paperwork, but may be advantageous in the end.

There are considerable risks involved in not declaring letting income to the French authorities. If they discover that the property has been let, they can choose to tax you on 52 weeks' letting income, and you will lose the right to tax deductions. While you may get away with not declaring the odd week or two, it is not worth risking a much higher tax bill by not declaring.

Whether resident or non-resident, if you let your French property unfurnished, you become liable to the *taxe sur les revenus fonciers*. For this you fill in blue form No.2044. If your income is under €15,000 you can be taxed under the *Micro-foncier* regime; otherwise it is the *Foncier normal*. There are numerous deductions. The tax is charged on unbuilt land, lakes, factories, and everything that stands on land.

Long-Term Lets

Tenancy agreements (*bail* or *baux* in the plural) come under one of four possible legal regimes, only two of which are really relevant to foreigners. The most basic form of tenancy is the so-called *Location Libre* (free tenancy), which is subject only to the articles 1708 to 1762 of the *Code Civil,* the basic set of laws governing French residents. The rental agreement can be for a defined or indeterminate period of time, and can be verbal or written. Because the provisions of the *Code Civil* are in the lessor's favour, the state has imposed certain conditions to prevent abuses. In the first place, it is only applicable to fully furnished premises (fully furnished meaning that the tenant has everything they need to be able to live on the premises), or to second homes or holiday homes. Where the lessor rents out more than four properties of this type, the rental contract is always for one year, and is automatically renewed, unless one of the parties gives notice, which is three months from the side of the lessor, and one month from the side of the lessee.

Most long-term rental agreements now come under the law of 6 July 1989, which gives tenants considerable protection against eviction, but proprietors can still eject tenants who behave unreasonably, after obtaining an injunction from a civil magistrate (*juge d'instance*). Eviction is a long-winded process. If tenants cannot pay their rent then social services will be called in; tenants may appeal to a state hardship fund, the Fonds de Solidarité. It is particularly difficult to evict the socially vulnerable, and it can take years to get to the point of forcible eviction; the police are generally very reluctant to get involved.

Some of the grounds for eviction are:

- Failure to pay rent. Tenants are not allowed to withhold rent in order to put pressure on owners to make repairs. The intervention of a magistrate has to be sought first.
- Damage to the property. Unless there are clauses to the contrary in the rental agreement (*bail*), tenants have considerable freedom to install new equipment, even including double glazing, or shutters on windows, but knocking down walls or substantially altering the layout of the property are valid grounds for eviction.
- Causing a nuisance to neighbours. Tenants who infringe the rights of neighbours can be ejected.
- Failure to have adequate insurance. Tenants are required to have multi-risk insurance (*assurance multirisque habitation*). See under 'Insurance', in chapter 4, *Finance*.
- Nuisance from domestic animals. Tenants are legally allowed to have a dog or cat, but if their pet bothers the neighbours or damages the property, then the owner can end the rental agreement.

The only situation where a tenant can stop paying the rent is when the property has become uninhabitable. If the proprietor persistently refuses to make repairs, the tenant may first call in a bailiff (*huissier*) to make a report on the nature of the problem, and then obtain an injunction from a magistrate to carry out the repairs him or herself. The tenant can then legally withhold a part of the rent to pay the costs.

Tenants are generally given considerable leeway to make necessary improvements to a property, but any permanent additions become the property of the owner when they leave. They cannot, however, replace permanent appliances or equipment such as baths or heaters without the owner's permission. If they want to install a satellite dish or new aerial on the outside of the property, they are required to ask the owner's permission. If the owner doesn't respond within three months to a request, then it is assumed that permission has been given. Proprietors may be held liable for losses occasioned by theft if it can be shown that the construction of the house makes it easy for burglars to enter.

Uses of property not in the rental agreement: It is normal to carry on a profession in a rented property, such as working as an architect or doctor, while also living there. Tenants cannot, however, run a business from a rented property without prior agreement from the owner, particularly where this involves clients or employees coming and going from the premises.

Rental payment. Payment intervals can be set by agreement with the owner of the property, but the prospective tenant can legally insist that payment should occur monthly. The tenant can ask the owner to come to the property once a month to collect the rent in cash; owners cannot compel tenants to agree to pay by bank transfer, or other non-cash form of payment. In practice, payment will most likely be by standing order but this does not follow automatically.

As in the UK, rental payments may not be used in lieu of notice. The repayment of the rental deposit (*dépôt de garantie*) will only take place after the tenant has vacated the premises.

Increases in rent. The rental contract should spell out on what grounds rent can be increased. Improvements to the property can be used as a justification for an increase, but the general practice is to limit increases to rises in the index of building costs, or where the rent is manifestly too low. A cost-of-living index, or other indexes showing rises in average rents cannot be used to justify rent increases, on the principle that like must be compared with like. The proprietor will have to show that the rent is too low by giving examples of average rents in the area; in the Paris, Lyon and Marseille regions rents of six different properties comparable to the one in question will be listed, in the rest of the country only three. In the Paris area the rent can only be raised by half the difference between the average rent in the area and the rent in the contract. In the same region, where the owner has spent the equivalent of at least a year's rent on improvements, the rent can be raised by 15% per year.

Conciliation services. Where a dispute has arisen, one or both parties can apply for the mediation of a *conciliateur de justice*, a professional conciliator; the departmental prefecture will give you the name and address. The services of the conciliator are free of charge. Neither party is obliged to act on the conciliator's recommendations; these are deposited with the local civil magistrate, and will be taken into account if the case is heard in court.

Rights and Duties of Owners

The principal duties of owners are to supply the dwelling as agreed, to keep it in a good state of repair, and not to interfere with the tenant's use of the dwelling. As a bare minimum owners have to ensure that there is running water, although even this condition can be got around with the agreement of the tenant. Owners have to give warning if they plan to carry out major repairs. If the repairs go on for more than 40 days then the tenant is entitled to a reduction in rent.

Damage caused by defects in the construction of the house, e.g. water seeping through the walls, is the owner's liability. If a tenant is affected by 'hidden defects' (*vices cachés*) they can gain legal redress, similarly to when one buys a property. If the owner shows someone around a property and it subsequently comes to light that defects, such as damp patches or mould, were covered up, then tenants may ask for repairs to be carried out. If the defects in a property actually limit the tenant's ability to enjoy its use, then they may request a lower rent.

Who Pays for What?

The issue of who has to pay for what has been regulated by a decree no.87-713 passed in 1987, but this only covers a part of the possible items that could become a subject of dispute. In other cases, legal precedent will influence the judge to decide one way or the other. Rental agreements drawn up under the 1989 law do not allow owners to make tenants responsible for all repairs to the property. Under the *Location Libre* rules (see above), which derive from the *Code Civil*, tenants can in theory be made liable for all repairs, even including major ones, but the courts are likely to decide in the tenant's favour if the amount of money involved is excessive.

Certain general principles apply in disputes. Firstly, tenants are not expected to pay for repairs to any items that are not mentioned in the rental agreement, but the owner can always point to legal precedent to show that the law is on his or her side. Tenants are not required to pay for the maintenance of any item that they never actually use. If there is a swimming pool attached to your property and they never use it, then there is no way they can be made to pay for its maintenance.

As a guiding principle, tenants have to pay for 'running repairs' (*entretien courant*) which arise out of their use of the property, on the basis that the item should still be in working order when they leave the property. This does not mean, however, that they have to restore everything to its original condition. The owner is expected to pay for 'normal repairs' (*entretien normal*), which is interpreted as meaning major repairs to the premises, or replacement of the larger working parts of machinery. Tenants are not required to pay for the repair of equipment if it stops working because of old age. The tenant can obtain a statement from a repair person that the equipment is worn out. If the owner refuses to have the item repaired, they can go to a lower civil court – *tribunal d'instance* – and compel the owner to pay up.

As a rule of thumb, tenants pay for smaller repairs, and owners for the larger ones. The following gives some specific instances of who pays for what:

Tenant pays for:
- Broken tiles
- Cleaning of the property, including externally
- Emptying of cesspits and *fosses septiques*
- Garden maintenance, including replacing bushes and plants
- Internal redecoration
- Keeping guttering clear
- Maintenance of locks and replacement of keys
- Maintenance of the central heating system
- Running repairs to lifts/elevators

Owner pays for:
- Dampproofing of walls and cellars
- Dustbins, or wheelie bins
- Insulation and lagging of pipes
- Major repairs to lifts, central heating
- Repairs to walls, roof, ceilings
- Replacement of trees in all cases
- Rewiring

Holes in the walls must be made good by the tenants; the owner can send a bill for repairs. Tenants are supposed to clean limescale off sinks and baths, etc., but there is no duty to restore them to their original condition. Damage caused by tenants moving in or out of a property are their responsibility. The owner can withhold part of the tenant's deposit where there is actual damage. See chapter 7, *Renting* for further details on what happens with rental deposits.

Taxation and Rental Agreements

The taxation of rental income has been dealt with above. Certain taxes related to rented property are considered to be *charges récuperables* (charges to be paid for by the tenant). Owners are required to pay what is known as *la contribution sur les revenus locatifs* (CRL) or letting right tax to the central government. This works out at 2.5% of income from rental above €1,830 on properties older than 15 years.

Tenants are liable for a *taxe d'habitation* as from 1 January. The rental agreement can require them to pay from the time they move in. The land tax – *taxe foncière* – is the owner's responsibility (see Taxation). The tenant will be required to pay the local *taxe d'enlèvement des ordures menagères* – domestic rubbish collection tax – and the owner can send the bill through to you. Taxes for road cleaning or snow-clearing are also the responsibility of the tenant. Where the precise amount of the rubbish collection tax is not stated by the municipality in its tax demand, the tenant cannot be made to pay it.

RUNNING A BUSINESS FROM YOUR PROPERTY

Moving to France could provide the opportunity, or necessity, of starting up a business. There are all sorts of possibilities, such as starting up an art gallery, a dogs' beauty parlour, taking over a café, or running cultural holidays. A good deal of imagination may be needed to find an idea that will sell. One of the more original ones is the Camembert museum started up by Rosemary Rudland (see box). Before you can do anything, you will have to register with the local *Chambre de Commerce*, who will send you on a business management course to make sure that you are a fit person to run a business. You may not understand everything that you are being taught, but the bookkeeping advice will be useful.

> **English journalist Rosemary Rudland bought an old cottage in Camembert and decided to turn it into a cheese museum, the Relais Camembert. She then put up another building for a farm-produce shop.**
>
> *I planned to cook on site and sell take-away food, as well as having a space for people to sit outside and eat, so I needed permission from more than one agency. I went on a compulsory business course at the local Chambre de Commerce; you meet a notaire and an accountant. I also took the precaution of meeting the local heads of departments, such as the fire department, health department, Département de l'Équipement, in Alençon, so I knew exactly what I was doing when I filled in the forms. I wanted to sell local produce to visitors; as I didn't know which farmers to approach I talked to the oldest person in the village who took me around*

> *to everyone he knew. They were very supportive and provided me with personal bits and bobs for the museum. I also sell arts and crafts.*
> *Most of the locals were pleased with what I was doing, but there has been some jealousy as well. Some people were put out that an Englishwoman could set up a successful business right on the main square. As well as the shop we produce apples which we take the local pressoir to turn into cider for the shop. I've had a lot of fun with the business; as I own the buildings and don't employ anyone there are few overheads involved, but I'm quite prepared to move on if someone wants to take it on. My advice to those starting a business is not to be too idealistic, but be realistic about what's possible. The Chambre de Commerce will try to put you off. As they say, if your business doesn't crash within three years then it will survive.*
> *The Relais Camembert is on www.membres.lycos.fr/shopvente.*

As far as taxation goes, you can be considered a *Micro-Entreprise.* The ceiling on turnover is €76,300 if you are selling goods, or food; otherwise it is only €27,000. Above this, you have to register for TVA and keep full accounts. If you use premises that can be visited by the public you are liable for the *taxe professionnelle,* rather than the *taxe d'habitation.*

Further details can be found in the forthcoming *Starting a Business in France,* published by Vacation Work.

SELLING ON

When you buy your property, it is well worth thinking about how easy it will be to sell on. There are parts of France where prices of old property are not likely to increase in the future, namely Alsace-Lorraine and all of central France, especially Auvergne. On the other hand, Provence and the west coast are generally a very safe bet. More and more people are moving to western France, so Brittany and Normandy should see some price rises. Paris is more uncertain, as the population is going to get younger according to the projections of the French Institute of Statistics. If you are selling on to other Brits, then prices may depend on what happens to the UK property market. As we stated at the beginning of this book, buying property in France as an investment does not make much sense unless you know exactly what you are doing.

Selling Your Property

It is usual to place the property with an estate agent or a notaire, who will add their commission to the selling price. There are British estate agents in many areas who will do a better job of marketing your property than a French one would. The main thing is to have a good photograph of your property; this is not as easy as it sounds, and you may be best advised to use a professional photographer. Unless the photo is taken in the right way, the lines of the house tend to look distorted.

You can try to advertise it privately, or put your house on an English website featuring private sellers, such as www.frenchconnection.co.uk. Most British sellers try to sell to other foreigners, on the basis that they can expect to obtain a better price. In the current economic situation, the British are more likely to pay a little over the odds, while the poverty-stricken Germans will pay less. It is normal to emphasise the amount of attic space that could be converted, and to mention the proximity of railway stations and airports.

SHARP PRACTICES

At one time the Masheder family owned a house in a village near Uzès in the Gard. In 1992, when the property market was very sluggish, they let a local agent know that they wanted to sell the property. What happened next took them by surprise:

We received a phone call from a local Frenchman who was very excited about buying the property from us and asked us to come down to meet him as soon as we could. We got on the first plane and rushed down there, but were amazed to find that the supposed buyer had put up his own sign 'A Vendre' at a higher price than he was offering us. He was obviously hoping to find another buyer and pocket the difference. He used the excuse that he hadn't found a mortgage to get out of the contract. We never met the so-called buyer, and he removed the For Sale sign while our backs were turned. In the meantime, of course, we had lost a lot of time, and we couldn't sell the property until the following year. In the end we sold it to some Swiss.

The regulations governing French estate agents have been explained under *Buying a Home in France*. From the seller's point of view, you can choose to give the agent a *mandat simple* or a *mandat exclusif*. In the first case, you can place the property with as many estate agents as you like, or find a buyer yourself. The agent is paid a commission if they introduce a successful buyer to you. With a *mandat exclusif* only one estate agent will look for buyers. You have to specify whether you wish to retain the right to look for buyers yourself – a *mandat exclusif simple* – or whether you give up that right – the *mandat exclusif absolu*. In the first case, the agent's commission is reduced if you find a buyer yourself; in the second, you would have to pay the agent an indemnity if you found a buyer yourself.

A *mandat* is for a limited time period. The seller can withdraw from the *mandat,* subject to certain conditions. After three months, a *mandat exclusif* can, in all cases, be cancelled through a registered letter. It is normal these days for the buyer to pay the agent's commission.

Defects in the Property

As we have seen in chapter 6, under 'Inspections and Surveys', owners are required to have reports drawn up on the possible presence of termites and lead paint. A report on asbestos is only necessary where the property is in a pre-1997 *copropriété,* which should be dealt with by the *copropriété* as a whole.

As a general rule, the seller cannot be held liable for *vices apparents,* or visible defects in the property. The issue of *vices cachés* or hidden defects, is more complicated. You can take out insurance against the discovery of *vices cachés* by the buyer within a certain period of time.

Taxation on Property Sales

If you sell your French property within 22 years of having acquired it, then you will be liable to French Capital Gains Tax. There are potential ways around paying French CGT, which are explained in chapter 4, *Finance.* You are not subject to French taxes on proceeds if you sell a property outside France.

CASE HISTORIES

RICHARD AND CHRISTINA COMAN

Dr Richard & Christina Coman owned a property in the Vendée from 1982 to 2000 at St Étienne-du-Bois – a village south of Nantes – which they sold to a relative. They are now looking at property in the Aveyron.

How did you go about buying your first property in France?

We were over in the Vendée in August and we signed a *compromis de vente*; it took another four months for the final exchange of contracts. The property was a granite farmhouse with a barn, an oven house and a piggery and one hectare of land (10,000 sq.m.). The day we moved in I asked what we were going to do about the broken-down barn next to our house, until someone pointed out that it was my property as well. In the meantime the notary had to get the signature of everyone in the village that they had no right of way; there were terrible problems getting one 80-year-old lady to sign.

Any problems?

The farmer who was retiring kept the surrounding land for hay and maize. We were offered another 10 hectares adjoining at the very cheap price of £3,000, but we foolishly didn't take it. If we had taken it the farmer's two sons would have inherited the tenancy. The next year a much younger farmer who was only interested in raising beef cattle rented it. In the beginning we were on good terms and regularly bought wine from him. But then his cattle roamed over our land so we had to put up a *clôture* around our hectare at great expense. On top of that he put two huge mounds of silage covered with plastic on the land, so we got the smell; our notary told him to move it but he refused point-blank. Then he insisted on driving his tractor between our house and barn leaving huge ruts in the earth, and then drove into our boundary fence. He was generally disliked in the village and never spoke to us again.

Did you have a swimming pool?

There was quite an amusing situation with the swimming pool. After a lot of phoning around in London we got a plastic swimming pool with a metal frame from Harrods. It was so heavy we could barely get it over to France in my car. When we unpacked it we saw the label: Made in Nantes – just up the road. The pool was fine but the next time we got one locally.

Any other advice?

It isn't necessarily a good idea to have too much land attached to your property, otherwise you may find yourself spending your holidays cutting back grass and brambles. There is not much point bringing over British-made showers and piping: you won't be able to fix them later if they're in imperial measurements. For us having this property was marvellous because we have nine sons and we had 18 years of free holidays. But you do need to accept that there are always going to be some difficulties when you buy a property in France: it's just part of the deal.

RICHARD BURTON

Richard is 57 and was Professor of French at the University of Sussex. He is now living about 100 miles southeast of Paris, and is currently writing *Discovering Rural France*, to be published in 2005.

What made you decide to move to your area?

The main reason is that it hasn't been taken over by other Britons. Also it's one-and-a-half hours from Paris. For this reason quite a few Parisians have second homes here. Generally, the countryside is quite nondescript and it's fairly cold in winter, but it suits me fine.

How was the buying process for you?

Everything went very smoothly. Fortunately, I had the assistance of two French friends, but I could understand the documents myself in any case. I admit that the buying process could be a lot more complicated if you don't speak fluent French, but on the other hand, I haven't come across any Brits who have had serious problems with buying a property. After signing the *compromis de vente* it took just 11 weeks before I took possession of the house.

How are the neighbours?

I was careful to look out for any possible problems with neighbours, such as loud dogs and other noise nuisances, but I hadn't reckoned on two parrots living next door. I asked the owners to get rid of them, and they agreed; they were fed up with them too. Generally, the French practise a 'live and let live' ethos. The French are noisy people, and they don't respond sympathetically to complaints about barking dogs and the like. On the whole, I didn't check nearly enough on the neighbours and the locality; it is not as quiet as I expected. I didn't realise that there is a private airfield 20 miles from here – they are common in France – so that came as a nasty surprise. At least look on a map to see if there is one in the vicinity.

How about the heating and utilities?

I'm waiting to see what it's like in winter. I have lots of wood. I'm only going to heat half of the house with central heating. This is *gaz de ville* which is a great advantage. In addition I plan to use paraffin heaters, which are a lot better than in England and don't smell. Heating is crucial in a cold area; at least check that your central heating is working and get in plenty of fuel.

As for electricity, there are never enough power points, and a lot of French wiring is dangerous, so check up on everything, especially the earthing (*raccordement à la terre*). A lot of these old systems would never pass a safety test, so you must have it all checked by a professional. Finally, contrary to what some might say, British electrical equipment works fine here, apart from TVs. If you want to watch UK videos, bring a UK video and TV which will work OK, but you won't be able to watch French TV.

What is your opinion of French tradesmen?

Generally, extraordinarily slow and unreliable. You have to put continuous pressure on them to do something. I would advise getting estimates (*devis*) from three or four people, because some of them won't deliver. I was frequently let down because I didn't get enough estimates. The *professionnels,* especially builders, here have a huge backlog of work, so think six months ahead. You must follow them up at weekly intervals. And use local tradesmen.

What advice would you give to prospective British buyers?

Firstly, take your time. The more time you can spend looking around the better. If you go to an *agent immobilier* make sure that they have their professional certificate displayed on the wall, or ask them to show it. I would also advise on learning French as soon as possible, otherwise your social life is going to be limited to other foreigners. Certain areas of Normandy and the Dordogne are now so over-populated with Britons that you can walk into a bar and not find a single French person. This is not really a problem as far as the French are concerned, but it rather defeats the object of going to live abroad.

JAMES FERGUSON

James Ferguson, 47, married with two children, owns a semi-detached Cévenol-style house in a village in the Gard (Provence), which he inherited from his father.

How did you come to buy this property?

My father owned it, and I inherited it along with my brother. My father bought it back in 1971 from another Englishman. When he died we declared the value to the UK taxman and paid inheritance tax on it at UK rates. As my father had always been domiciled in the UK and never lived in France, the French tax authorities did not have to be involved, but we did get a notary to draw up a declaration that the property was legally ours. It was a lot simpler to deal with the UK tax authorities, rather than having to go through the French legal system, and there was in any case no obligation to pay French inheritance tax.

How do you find the locals?

We go down there during the summer with our children, and occasion-ally at other times. We have many friends in the area, but they tend to be other incomers, especially French-speaking Swiss and Belgians. Many of the older people in the village know me and address me as *tu* but I have to address them as *vous* back. There are others of my age that I can *tutoie*. As we don't live full-time in the village it is natural that we don't get to hear all the local gossip. The local society is fairly closed.

The fact that our house adjoins the post office has been helpful in preventing burglaries. On the other hand the neighbours won't allow the water from our roof to run onto their property. On one occasion a tennis ball got lodged in a down pipe and caused a catastrophic leak;

water cascaded into the house and the whole place had to be redecorated and replastered. The insurance didn't pay the full cost of the work as the original plastering wasn't in such good condition.

Have you tried to renovate the house?
This is a traditional house in the village square, made of local rough-hewn stone and mortar; we had the original thick layer of roughcast rendering or *crépi* removed which greatly improved the appearance of the property. Originally it was three small shops side by side, but with the decline in the rural population all the shops have closed down, so there is now only one entrance where once there were three. My parents had the roof redone in 1972, and we plan to do the same soon. The roof beams and laths are very primitive; they tend to rot here because of the rain that is driven horizontally by the wind through the tiles. The roof is of Provençal curled tiles and you can see daylight in between the gaps, so we will have a membrane put in to make it waterproof. Local houses tend to be several storeys high with small rooms, which helps to keep warm; we have knocked one wall through and put in a joist to make a larger living room.

How are the local craftsmen?
They are unfailingly late, but their work is always good. Our neighbour had the misfortune of hiring a plumber who was an alcoholic to put in a new toilet. He forgot to make sure the outlet was sloping so they ended up having to put their toilet onto a tall platform; the effect is amusing to say the least.

What do you use for heating?
We have a combination of paraffin, calor-gas and wood-burning stoves. The cast-iron free-standing stove generates a lot of heat. We have thought of getting a *citerne* to have a gas supply, but we decided against it. There is no *gaz de ville* here.

INDEX

Vacation Work Publications

	Paperback	Hardback
Summer Jobs Abroad	£9.99	£15.95
Summer Jobs in Britain	£9.99	£15.95
Supplement to Summer Jobs Britain and Abroad *published in May*	£6.00	-
Work Your Way Around the World	£12.95	-
Taking a Gap Year	£11.95	-
Taking a Career Break	£11.95	-
Working in Tourism – The UK, Europe & Beyond	£11.95	-
Kibbutz Volunteer	£10.99	-
Working on Yachts and Superyachts	£10.99	-
Working on Cruise Ships	£10.99	-
Teaching English Abroad	£12.95	-
The Au Pair & Nanny's Guide to Working Abroad	£12.95	-
The Good Cook's Guide to Working Worldwide	£11.95	-
Working in Ski Resorts – Europe & North America	£11.95	-
Working with Animals – The UK, Europe & Worldwide	£11.95	-
Live & Work Abroad – A Guide for Modern Nomads	£11.95	-
Working with the Environment	£11.95	-
The Directory of Jobs & Careers Abroad	£12.95	-
The International Directory of Voluntary Work	£11.95	-
Buying a House in France	£11.95	-
Buying a House in Spain	£11.95	-
Buying a House in Italy	£11.95	-
Live & Work in Australia & New Zealand	£10.99	-
Live & Work in Belgium, The Netherlands & Luxembourg	£10.99	-
Live & Work in France	£10.99	-
Live & Work in Germany	£10.99	-
Live & Work in Italy	£10.99	-
Live & Work in Japan	£10.99	-
Live & Work in Russia & Eastern Europe	£10.99	-
Live & Work in Saudi & the Gulf	£10.99	-
Live & Work in Scandinavia	£10.99	-
Live & Work in Scotland	£10.99	-
Live &Work in Spain & Portugal	£10.99	-
Live & Work in the USA & Canada	£10.99	-
Drive USA	£10.99	-
Hand Made in Britain – The Visitors Guide	£10.99	-
Scottish Islands – The Western Isles	£12.95	-
Scottish Islands – Orkney & Shetland	£11.95	-
The Panamericana: On the Road through Mexico and Central America	£12.95	-
Travellers Survival Kit Australia & New Zealand	£11.95	-
Travellers Survival Kit Cuba	£10.99	-
Travellers Survival Kit Lebanon	£10.99	-
Travellers Survival Kit Madagascar, Mayotte & Comoros	£10.99	-
Travellers Survival Kit Mauritius, Seychelles & Réunion	£10.99	-
Travellers Survival Kit Mozambique	£10.99	-
Travellers Survival Kit Oman & The Arabian Gulf	£11.95	-
Travellers Survival Kit South America	£15.95	-
Travellers Survival Kit Sri Lanka	£10.99	-

Distributors of:

Summer Jobs in the USA	£10.99	-
Internships	£19.99	-
World Volunteers	£10.99	-
Green Volunteers	£10.99	-
Archaeo-Volunteers	£10.99	-

**Vacation Work Publications, 9 Park End Street, Oxford OX1 1HJ
Tel 01865-241978   Fax 01865-790885**

**Visit us online for more information on our unrivalled range of titles for work,
travel and gap years, readers' feedback and regular updates:**

www.vacationwork.co.uk